P9-BIK-907

TRAVEL
&LEISURE

San Francisco

and the Wine Country

by Leslie Plummer Clagett

Macmillan • USA

MACMILLAN TRAVEL
A Simon & Schuster Macmillan Company
1633 Broadway
New York, NY 10019

Find us online at **http://www.mgr.com/travel** or on America Online at Keyword: **Frommer's**

ISBN: 0-02-860693-0
ISSN: 1088-4823

Editor and Map Editor: Douglas Stallings
Design by Amy Peppler Adams—designLab, Seattle
Illustrations on pages 10, 14, 39, 41, 55, 69, 76, 78, 83, 87, 90, 98, 141, 146, 213, 225, 231, and 232 by Ray Skibinski

SPECIAL SALES
Bulk purchases (10+ copies) of Frommer's and selected Macmillan travel guides are available to corporations, organizations, institutions, and charities at special discounts, and can be customized to suit individual needs. For more information write to Special Sales, Macmillan General Reference, 1633 Broadway, New York, NY 10019.

Manufactured in Singapore

CONTENTS

List of Maps

About the Author

The culture of America's great cities has proved an inexhaustible subject of fulfilling investigation for Leslie Plummer Clagett. She has written on the arts of New York, the architecture of Los Angeles, and the less cerebral but no less aesthetic domain of fine wine and food. As a well-traveled resident of Oakland, she enjoys a 3-bridge panorama of the City by the Bay, as well as a perspicacious view of it.

An Additional Note

Please be advised that travel information is subject to change at any time—and this is especially true of prices. We therefore suggest that you write or call ahead for confirmation when making your travel plans. The author, editor, and publisher cannot be held responsible for the experiences of readers while traveling. Your safety is important to us, however, so we encourage you to stay alert and be aware of your surroundings. Keep a close eye on cameras, purses, and wallets, all favorite targets of thieves and pickpockets.

Foreword

This book is for travelers who are possessed by a spirited curiosity about the world. If you can appreciate the merits of a simple cottage as well as those of a five-star hostelry, are equally intrigued by minimalist artworks and grand-scale opera, find happiness in both an empty stretch of coastline and the hubbub of the city, and recognize the culinary credentials shared by a humble hamburger and steak tartare, I think you'll find that this guide to *San Francisco and the Wine Country* is very well attuned—tailored, even—to your interests.

We'll escort you off the touristic treadmill and introduce you to the nuances of northern California's most energetic metropolis and its bucolic counterpart, the wine country. From boutiques offering sophisticated one-of-a-kind apparel to casual neighborhood cafes with bay views to mountain-top hand-crafted brandy distilleries, we're pleased to bring you the best experiences a confirmed or aspiring bon vivant will enjoy.

Have a great trip.

—Leslie Plummer Clagett

SAN FRANCISCO . . . CITY BY THE BAY

It is an odd thing, but anyone who disappears is said to be seen in San Francisco.

Oscar Wilde

SAN FRANCISCO HAS MASTERED THE ART OF THE FLIRT. From the formative Gold Rush days, when glittering nuggets lured legions to its streets and shoreline to more recent times, with the promise of expanding personal freedom, the city has played siren to adventurous persons from around the globe.

A large part of the city's appeal comes naturally, generated by the coquettish duet between the weather and the terrain: Its famous fogs drift like a veil across the hills, alternately concealing and revealing views of the distinctive architecture and landscapes. In turn, those same hills define a collection of singular neighborhoods, each with its own character; exotic, picturesque, hard-working, or avant garde, their cachets combine to amplify San Francisco's capricious persona.

Residents, unapologetically infatuated with their city as they are, regularly are labeled insular, much as Parisians are regarded as snooty, New Yorkers pushy, Los Angelenos chronically laid-back. Visitors as well, once they succumb to San Francisco's charms, are liable to acquire some of the tell-tale signs of the citizenry: a placid skepticism about anything that originates beyond a radius of 50 miles, an escalating enthusiasm for walking, and an irrepressible desire for low-fat lattés with extra foam.

San Francisco Today

Memories of the most recent earthquake—and the prospect of another—make for great community spirit. In 1906, earthquake and fire killed thousands of people and destroyed 80% of the city, leaving 200,000 citizens homeless. Rebuilding began while the ruins were still smoking. A short 9 years later, the splendidly reconstructed town hosted a glittering International Exposition. In 1989 the Loma Prieta earthquake wreaked $2 billion worth of damage in the Bay Area. But, as befits a city whose flag features a phoenix, San Francisco once again preened its feathers and rose from the ashes. The result of this shared adversity is an uncommon civic solidarity.

The ancestors of many living here today often labored long and hard to reach the California shores. Even those who arrived in comfort came to change their lives. And they are proud of what has been built out of opportunity and, in the early days at least, hardship.

As Hollywood of the 1930s framed the self-image of Los Angeles, so the gold rush of 1849 set the tone for its northern neighbor. The era is burned into San Francisco's collective psyche. The city is 49 square miles; the local football team is the 49ers; the "scenic drive" is mapped around a route of 49 miles. And the original '49ers made up the core population around which San Francisco first began to grow.

Inevitably, the city attracted dreamers, most of them young, who were fired by ambition, opportunity, or greed. Many came equipped with the energy and enterprise to turn their visions into reality. As the biggest port on the West Coast and a toehold on the golden land that was California, "The Barbary Coast" lured adventurers and explorers, ruffians and runaways, throughout the 19thC. The city today continues to be an irresistible magnet to those in search of personal freedoms, prosperity, or lifestyles alternative to those in Kansas City, Canton, or County Cork.

Of course, San Francisco's reality is less than an idyll of racial harmony, economic prosperity, and uninhibited behavior. The newcomers were not always welcomed by the straight-laced burghers of San Francisco, the solid blue-collar working class who built its industrial base, or the nouveau riche anxious for respectability. In the not-too-distant past, artists have been censored, minorities persecuted, political leaders assassinated. The number of homeless has grown to rival that of a Third World city. The AIDS epidemic has exacted—and continues to exact—a shocking toll.

The recession of recent years has taken some of the gloss off the Golden State overall, and the Bay Area hasn't been immune; defense industry cutbacks and local military base closures have had a significant ripple effect on the city and its surrounding communities. International trade relations with the Far East are undergoing close scrutiny, the effects of which clearly resound in the banks and harbors of Oakland and San Francisco. The region is beginning to wake up from its often narcissistic daydream and to face a future that has shifted resolutely westward. San Francisco, along with the rest of California, has become an integral player on the Pacific Rim. As we approach what pundits have labeled the "Pacific Century," the city's economy, combined with those of its geographical brethren from Tokyo to Vancouver, Singapore to San Diego, is likely to explode.

Writer and environmentalist Wallace Stegner has observed that San Francisco is "America, only more so." Movie producer and San Francisco resident Francis Ford Coppola puts it more laconically: "I kinda like this place." So do a great many other people. Perhaps this is because the California State Constitution provides for the right to "pursue and obtain happiness." Elsewhere in America, only the right of pursuit is enshrined in legislation. It's a distinction that makes all the difference.

The City and Its People

The city of San Francisco sits like a thimble on the thumb of its peninsula. It has a population of just 723,959, making it only the 4th largest of California's cities. However, this figure is misleading; the population of the 9 Bay Area counties approaches 6 million, and many people commute into the city proper to work and play. And what diversity they encounter within its intimate scale!

Distances between cultural, linguistic, and culinary traditions that elsewhere are worlds apart are measured in San Francisco in city blocks. The journey from Chinatown to Little Italy is simply a matter of crossing Columbus Avenue.

It's said that a hundred different languages are spoken here. That could be an exaggeration, but only slightly. Official figures show that 1 in 3 San Franciscans comes from a home where a language other than English is spoken. The largest communities counted by ethnic origin are Chinese, Italian, African, Hispanic, British, Irish, and German. There are many more. Basques, Filipinos, Russians, Iranians, Japanese, Vietnamese, Khmers, Ethiopians—the list of ethnic groups reads like the roll call of the United Nations General Assembly. For the most part, the people of San Francisco enjoy a more relaxed coexistence than do the diplomatic delegates. But there can be a certain degree of linguistic and cultural isolation, especially among the elderly and recent arrivals.

The lives of these people, unlike those of their neighbors in a certain southern California megalopolis, are not ruled totally by the internal combustion engine. Certainly, San Franciscans like the convenience of the automobile and rush hours are severely congested. But they also take buses, cable cars, trains, and bicycles. They even walk—the greatest incentive being the city's intimacy and human scale.

With the exception of the downtown Financial District, San Francisco has few deep canyons of soulless concrete, nor the featureless suburban sprawl of larger, younger, or less vibrant cities. There is no mistaking the busy, narrow alleys of Chinatown, the ritzy, moneyed solidity of Pacific Heights, the Neapolitan ease of North Beach, or the gay atmosphere of the Castro; people walk here because it's a pleasure.

Even for the first-time visitor, the distances and the directions of the city are easily comprehended and managed. Some of the steeper of San Francisco's 42 hills admittedly require a well-developed set of calf and thigh muscles as well as a strong heart and lungs. But the stunning vistas and ebullient street life go a long way to offset any minor pains. When Rudyard Kipling lamented, "San Francisco has only one drawback . . . 'tis hard to leave," he wasn't talking about the traffic jams.

Neighborhoods in Brief

To borrow from the vernacular of nearby Silicon Valley, San Francisco is user-friendly. Its distinct neighborhoods—and, more to the point, their multiplicity of inhabitants—give the city a most human face, as opposed to the anonymity so typical of other modern metropolises. To really get the flavor of San Francisco, it is necessary to explore at least a few of these varied locales; here's a primer on what you can expect to discover.

The Avenues

As a whole, the west side of the city is broadly referred to as the Avenues, after the numbered north-south thoroughfares that run across the mostly flat terrain. Golden Gate Park marks the division between the area's 2 residential expanses: the **Sunset,** which lies south of the park, and the **Richmond,** to its north.

In the Richmond, Clement Street reflects the tremendous ethnic diversity of its residents with its mix of Chinese, Vietnamese, Thai, and Laotian restaurants and businesses. There's a Russian enclave around the midpoint of Geary Boulevard, and a large community of Japanese citizens. To a lesser degree, this vibrant heterogeneity is evident in the Sunset, too.

The Castro

Much of the San Francisco gay community's social and cultural life centers around Polk Street between Geary and Pacific, and Castro Street south of Market to about 19th Street. Merchants in restored Victorian storefronts offer both the necessities and the niceties of life; bars, clubs, and restaurants are very much in tune with their clientele. It's a safe and lively part of town.

Chinatown

Among San Francisco's earliest residents, the Chinese lived for many years in a veritable city-within-a-city, first of their own choosing and later as victims of ethnic discrimination. To the north of downtown, the main

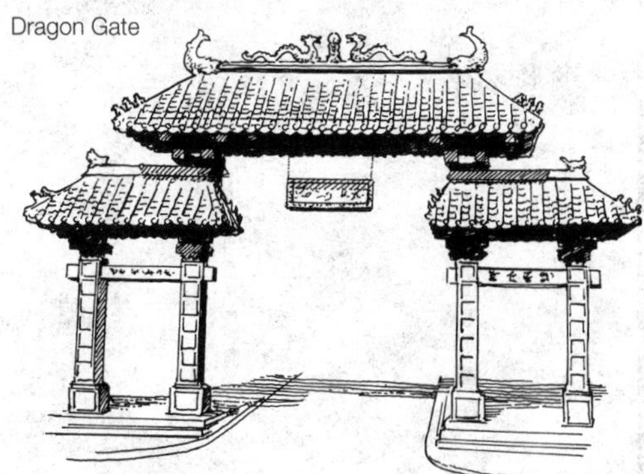
Dragon Gate

San Francisco Orientation

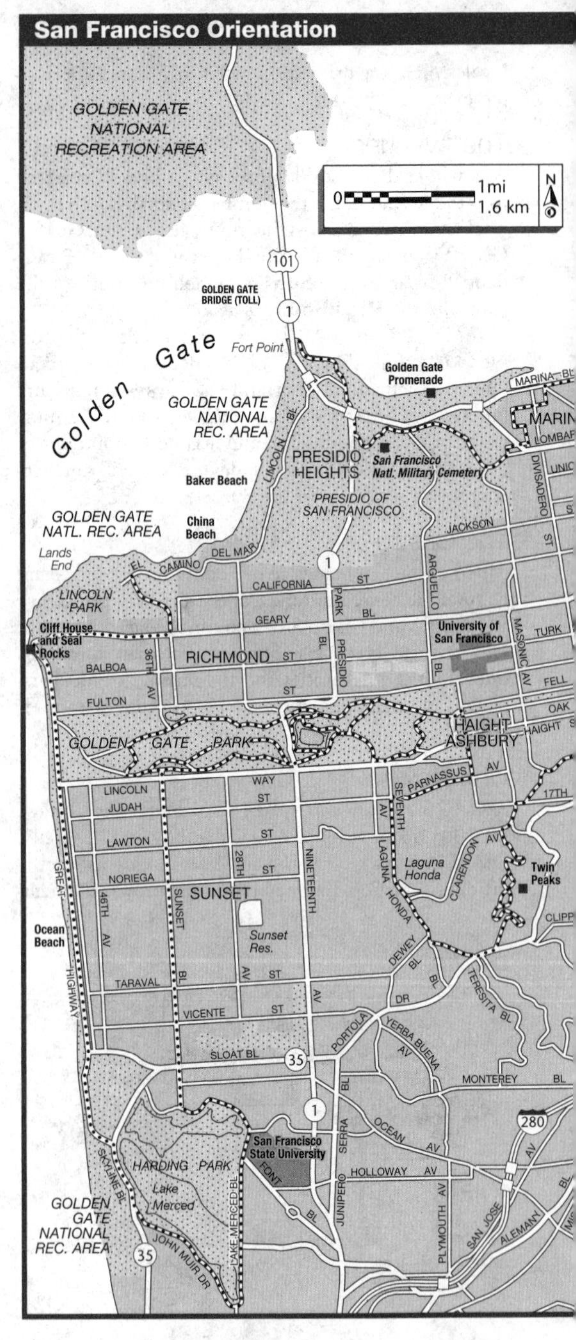

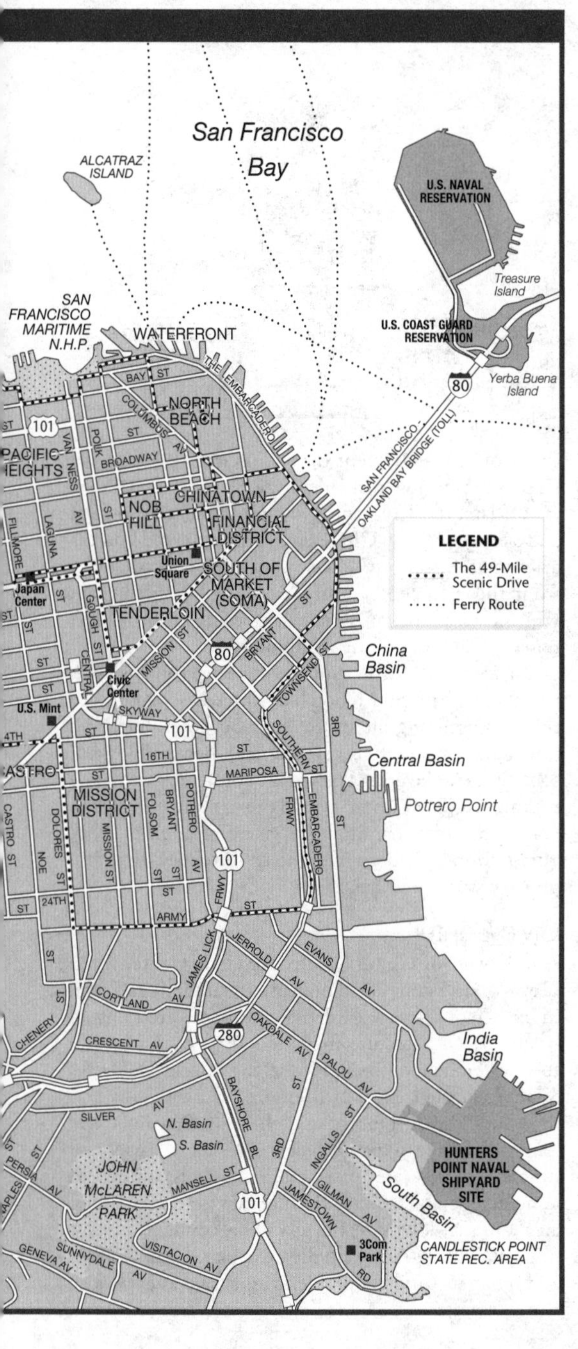

San Francisco Bay
ALCATRAZ ISLAND
U.S. NAVAL RESERVATION
Treasure Island
U.S. COAST GUARD RESERVATION
Yerba Buena Island
SAN FRANCISCO MARITIME N.H.P.
WATERFRONT
NORTH BEACH
PACIFIC HEIGHTS
NOB HILL
CHINATOWN
FINANCIAL DISTRICT
Union Square
SOUTH OF MARKET (SOMA)
Japan Center
TENDERLOIN
Civic Center
U.S. Mint
CASTRO
MISSION DISTRICT
SAN FRANCISCO-OAKLAND BAY BRIDGE (TOLL)
LEGEND
The 49-Mile Scenic Drive
Ferry Route
China Basin
Central Basin
Potrero Point
India Basin
HUNTERS POINT NAVAL SHIPYARD SITE
South Basin
CANDLESTICK POINT STATE REC. AREA
3Com Park
JOHN McLAREN PARK
N. Basin
S. Basin

City Hall

artery of their settlement was and is Grant Avenue from Bush Street to just past Broadway.

Of late, the large and growing population of first and later generation Chinese have burst the old boundaries in all directions, as the more affluent move away from the city center. But some 75,000 still live in Chinatown, and Grant, with its imposing Dragon Gate, remains the heart of the community.

In truth, the dedication to amusing tourists with restaurants, bars, and tchotchke stores is secondary to the self-sustaining life of the neighborhood. Stockton Street and its side streets are more authentically Asian, sometimes to the point that a smile combined with some rudimentary sign language will prove more effective in communicating than inquiries made in English. Here, curio shops yield to workaday butchers, fish and grocery stores, and bakeries.

Civic Center

A mile west of Union Square, the Civic Center is the heart of San Francisco's political and cultural life. Here, in an 8-block area regarded as the finest grouping of beaux arts architecture in the country, are City Hall, the San Francisco Opera House, the Louise M. Davies Symphony Hall, the War Memorial Building, the San Francisco Public Library, and the Bill Graham Civic Auditorium, an expansive hall used for a variety of functions. There are many fine restaurants attuned to concert-goers' schedules throughout the surrounding area. On the downside, the city's burgeoning homeless population congregates in the civic plazas. Panhandlers and muggers can be a problem, especially after dark.

A subset of the Civic Center area, **Hayes Valley** sits to the west of the government complex. It's recently emerged as a hipster haven, with plenty of idiosyncratic shops and eateries along its main drag (which happens to be Hayes Street).

Financial District

Montgomery Street, sometimes called the "Wall Street of the West," is convenient shorthand for the city's long-established Financial District, which is to the east of Union Square and is concentrated on but not limited to Montgomery between Market and California streets. On what had been mud flats, the city's commerce center grew, like so much else, from the gold rush. The hulks of ghost ships, abandoned by crews infected with gold fever, were used as foundations for hastily constructed assayer's offices, telegraph stations, and other buildings germane to the mining industry. It was here that A. P. Gianninni founded the Bank of Italy, which later became the Bank of America.

As with similar districts worldwide, this isn't the liveliest place for evening entertainment, except for a few after-work watering holes. The stolid architecture of the banks and other financial institutions, and the public art in and around them, are the main attractions. Tucked away in office buildings in the area are 2 worthy, if small, museums of history, the Bank of California Old Coin and Gold Exhibit and the Wells Fargo History Room.

Haight-Ashbury

Adjoining the southern side of Golden Gate Park's panhandle, the area centered around its eponymous intersection remains a draw for the counterculturally inclined, who rely upon its extensive book and record shops, unorthodox fashion boutiques, and eclectic dining places for diversion. The street scene, save for a number of remarkable examples of Edwardian and Victorian architecture, can lean a little towards the motley side, but most simply accept it as part and parcel to the milieu that is the Haight.

Japantown

Since the 19thC, members of San Francisco's sizable Japanese population have resided, for the most part, in a compact area stretching 3 blocks north from Geary Boulevard, between Franklin and Fillmore streets.

While today many Japanese-Americans opt to go beyond these borders, the infrastructure and ambiance of Japantown are still a magnet for the community, and the area remains its cultural (and to some extent, spiritual) nexus.

The district has a number of distinctly Japanese hotels, shops, nightclubs, restaurants, Buddhist temples, festivals, movie theaters, traditional massage parlors, and even hardware stores, in and near a 3-block long commercial and cultural center on the southern edge of the neighborhood. The admittedly bland architecture is enlivened somewhat by the 5-story Peace Pagoda monument.

Japantown is spick, span, and bustling by day. However, a note of caution should be sounded: Gangs from the adjacent Western Addition have been known to prowl by night, so vigilance is recommended for after-dark pedestrians.

The Marina

The district of pleasant Mediterraneanish apartment dwellings unwittingly achieved national recognition in 1989, as a number of its buildings collapsed into the shifting soils (the blocks, many of them the former site of the 1915 Panama-Pacific International Exposition, are mostly unstable landfill) and burned in the Loma Prieta earthquake. The young, upwardly mobile professional is alive and well in these parts, as the bounty of lively bars, restaurants, and trendy stores along Chestnut Street attests. But the Marina isn't completely culturally devoid; the Palace of Fine Arts stands on

Peace Pagoda

its western perimeter, home to the Exploratorium science museum. Harborside, the Marina Green is a popular spot for strollers, kite-flyers, joggers, and sunbathers.

The Mission

Radiating out from the intersection of 24th and Mission streets, the Mission is essentially a residential community with a strong sense of Hispanic identity. Mexicans and Mexican-Americans predominate, with substantial numbers of Salvadorans, Chileans, and other Latin Americans sharing the space. The neighborhood's relatively affordable rents cut across ethnic boundaries to attract the young and adventurous, who have generated a cafe culture of their own. The resultant blend of commerce—Hispanic markets next to funky thrift stores shouldered by bargain taquerias and coffeehouses—is invigoratingly, emphatically urban.

The city's oldest building, Mission Dolores, which marks the beginning of European civilization in San Francisco, is here. A more contemporary sight is the district's 200 murals, which brighten the environs.

Nob Hill

Characterized by Robert Louis Stevenson as "the Hill of Palaces," the origin of this pinnacle's name is subject to contention. Some insist it derives from nabob *née* nawab, a term for a wealthy Mogul governor; others argue it is simply a variant on the geophysical descriptive *knob,* meaning a hillock. Its slopes, girded by

Washington, Leavenworth, Bush, and Stockton streets, are the once and future home of the elite of San Francisco gentry.

North Beach

The wedge bordered by Broadway, Columbus Avenue, and Telegraph Hill is not a beach at all, but it is a rewarding place to go for its cafes, saloons, bakeries, and budget-friendly restaurants. The centerpiece of this traditionally Italian district is Washington Square, which, with the Romanesque church of Saints Peter and Paul as its backdrop, is a prime spot to observe the North Beach brio.

The area has always enjoyed a slightly alternative flavor. Here, the infamous Barbary Coast of red-light districts, gambling parlors, and shanghaied sailors raged. Jack London and Mark Twain knew the neighborhood well, and the bohemian Beat generation of the 1950s was birthed in its coffeehouses.

North Beach is one of the city's liveliest quarters for nightclubs—including the sleazy variety whose lurid signs and pushy barkers tend to dominate along the stretch of Broadway west of Columbus. Happily, these appear to be headed for extinction, as more worthwhile establishments take root in their midst.

Pacific Heights

Grand mansions of all styles (a number of them discreetly converted into condominiums and apartments) line the shady streets of this posh residential area, which stretches from the Marina on the north to California Street on the south, between Van Ness and Lyon streets. A smattering of consulates and prep schools accent the quietly exclusive atmosphere.

Presidio Heights

San Francisco began life as a Spanish military settlement under the name Yerba Buena in 1776. The Presidio, the longest continuously occupied army base in the country, occupying much of the northwest corner of the San Francisco peninsula, was decommissioned in 1994, its jurisdiction turned over to the National Park Service. The development of this prime 2-square-mile parcel is being fiercely debated, as moneyed private and corporate interests jockey with the cash-strapped local and federal agencies for control of the facilities. The Presidio Museum is within its confines, as are historic Fort Point and sandy Baker Beach, both of which are part of the Golden Gate National Recreation Area.

Russian Hill

This hill—roughly in the middle of the quadrant formed by Chestnut, Jones, Vallejo, and Van Ness streets—is so called owing to the Russian fur traders and sailors who were long ago buried beneath its slopes. Nowadays it is an alluring mixture of bohemian charm and patrician elegance, its contours laced by secluded stairways and byways—none of them as renowned as the area's twisting Lombard Street, but easily a match for its visual appeal. Architecture buffs enjoy strolling its streets, admiring the abodes big and small.

South of Market

This once residential area has been redefined by the Moscone Convention Center, built in 1981 and named after the city's assassinated mayor, and Yerba Buena Gardens, the block-square contemporary arts development. In the manner of New York's SoHo district, its warehouses are upgrading into restaurants and nightclubs, many of them centered around Folsom and 11th streets. To the southeast, the neighborhood has become a center for factory outlet shopping opportunities as well.

The Tenderloin

Ironically sandwiched between Union Square and the Civic Center, the streets of the Tenderloin in recent decades have been the territory of the drug addled and destitute. Its apartment buildings and mom-and-pop businesses are the domain of immigrants from southeast Asia, who are working hard to improve the neighborhood.

Union Square

Named for the pro-Union rallies held on the site on the eve of the Civil War, the Square is the retail vortex of the city, with department stores and upscale shops thick throughout its 10-block area, bounded on the south by O'Farrell Street, on the north by Sutter, on the west by Jones, and on the east by Kearny. The Square itself, centered around a 90-foot Corinthian column that commemorates the 1898 victory of naval commander George Dewey over the Spanish armada at Manila, is a neat island of trim greenery and flower beds amid all the conspicuous consumption, a pleasant spot to take in the air, feed the pigeons, and watch the street parade. Hotels and theaters abound in the neighborhood, which is also home to a handful of civic and society fraternities, among them the Bohemian Club and the Olympic Club.

The Waterfront

Although vestiges of the working port remain, the northerly stretch of bayside is now almost entirely tourist country, containing the commercial seaside entertainments of Fisherman's Wharf and Pier 39, along with 2 landlocked complexes, The Cannery and Ghirardelli Square. There's ample opportunity to overdose on shopping for souvenirs, with stores offering every conceivable trinket interspersed with fresh seafood stalls purveying chowder in sourdough bowls and walkaway crab cocktails. The Powell Street cable car lines conveniently terminate near the San Francisco Maritime National Historical Park and docks, Aquatic Park, and the Municipal Pier.

Beyond the City Limits

What of areas outside the city? First of all, don't call them suburbs. The locals will hold it against you. Contrary to what more chauvinistic San Franciscans believe, there's life beyond their city's limits.

Lotta's Fountain at Kearny, Geary, and Market streets

Anchoring the southernmost point of the bay, in Santa Clara County, sits **San Jose,** the unofficial capital of Silicon Valley. It has the heaviest concentration of high-tech industries on earth and perhaps the densest population of whiz-kid boffins, who keep it buzzing with innovation.

Midpoint on the San Francisco peninsula is **Palo Alto,** home to Stanford University, whose groomed campus—snidely called "The Farm" by arch-rival proletarian UC students—shelters its own share of intellectual movers and shakers; more than 10 Nobel Prize winners are counted among its faculty.

Eight and a half miles due east across the Bay Bridge is the proud port of **Oakland,** which handles more than 90% of the cargo that passes under the Golden Gate. On its northern flank is the university town of **Berkeley,** a stronghold of liberal, highly informed opinions, and the self-anointed social laboratory of California.

Cross the Golden Gate Bridge into affluent **Marin County,** which craftily dodges the limelight by doing little to dispel its persistent but outmoded image as a hotbed (or hot tub) of hedonism. Its residents are hardly the empty-headed band of truth-and-beauty seekers popularized 2 or 3 decades ago. Hang out in the coffeehouses of **Mill Valley** or **Tiburon** and you're more likely to make idle chitchat with telecommuting CEOs than itinerant troubadours.

The wine country, only an hour's drive north of the city, encompasses portions of **Napa** and **Sonoma** counties. Its vineyards are punctuated by small towns that have managed to grow from rural backwaters to tourist attractions with an inspiring amount of grace, if not ease.

DINING

WITH THE OCEAN'S BOUNTY TO THE WEST AND THE cornucopia of California's vast central valley to the east, dining in the Bay Area—whether it's sturdy Mediterranean, delicate Asian, or mainstream American—is characterized by market-fresh ingredients. Factor in the harvests of the Napa and Sonoma wine country to the north, and the table is well set indeed. Such abundance frees chefs to toy with the boundaries of traditional cooking schools. Some, however, choose to let the provender speak for itself in classic recipes.

Food trends in the Bay Area don't seem to ever go away—they just become assimilated into the ever-expanding local culinary canon. Take Mediterranean and American cooking, for example: No one does a double take at the prospect of going to a tapas bar or has to be coaxed into admitting a fondness for fried chicken (free range, natch) any longer. French bistro fare is on the cusp of complete acceptance, having enjoyed a few steady years in the spotlight. As of this writing, there's a growing interest in Asian small plates; dishes more complex than dim sum, more adventurous than standard Far Eastern fare.

Price Chart

$ = Under $15

$$ = $15–$25

$$$ = $25–$35

$$$$ = $35 plus

In the listings that follow, price categories cover the average cost for a first course, entree, and dessert (not including tip or tax). Of course, your meal may cost more or less, depending on what you choose to order. Tax in San Francisco is 8.25%; the same is true for East Bay destinations Berkeley and Oakland.

Establishments assigned 1 or 2 stars are especially recommended.

Restaurants by Neighborhood

Civic Center
California Culinary Academy. **$$**
★ Geva's. **$$**
★ Hayes Street Grill. **$$$**
★ Millennium. **$$**
Miss Pearl's Jam House. **$$**
★★ Stars. **$$$$**
Suppenküche. **$$**
Zuñi Café. **$$$**

Downtown/Financial District/Theater District
Bix. **$$$**
California Pizza Kitchen. **$**
Cypress Club. **$$$**
Dottie's True Blue Cafe. **$**
German Cook. **$$**
★ Grand Cafe. **$$$**
John's Grill. **$$$**
La Quiche. **$$**
Le Central. **$$**
Lefty O'Doul's. **$**
Palio d'Asti. **$$**
★★ Postrio. **$$$$**
Rubicon. **$$$**
★ Savoy Brasserie. **$$**
Sol y Luna. **$$**
★ Tadich Grill. **$$**
★ Tommy Toy's Cuisine Chinoise. **$$$**
★ Vertigo. **$$$**
Yank Sing. **$**

Haight-Ashbury
Dish. **$**

The Mission
★★ Flying Saucer. **$$$**
La Rondalla. **$**
Ti Couz. **$**

Nob Hill/Russian Hill
Crustacean. **$$**
Le Petit Cafe. **$$**

North Beach
Brandy Ho's. **$$**
Cafe Jacqueline. **$$**
Caffe Macaroni. **$$**
Campo Santo. **$**
Gold Spike. **$**
★ Moose's. **$$**
★ Rose Pistola. **$$**
The Stinking Rose. **$$**

Pacific Heights/Marina
Barney's Gourmet Hamburgers. **$**
★ Cafe Marimba. **$$**
The Elite Cafe. **$$**
★★ The Heights. **$$$$**
Noah's Bagels. **$**
★ PlumpJack Cafe. **$$$**

South of Market (SoMa)
Bistro M. **$$$**
★ Bizou. **$$**
BRAIN/wash. **$**
The Fly Trap. **$$**
★ Fringale. **$$**
The Half Shell Restaurant and Oyster Bar. **$$**
Hamburger Mary's. **$**
★ Hawthorne Lane. **$$$$**
Julie's Supper Club. **$$**
★ LuLu. **$$**
★ One Market Restaurant. **$$**
Ristorante Ecco. **$$**
Rôti. **$$**
South Park Cafe. **$$**

Telegraph Hill
★ Fog City Diner. **$$**
Hunan. **$**
Il Fornaio. **$$**

Union Square
★★ Fleur de Lys. **$$$$**

Waterfront
★ Boulevard. **$$$**
The Buena Vista. **$**
★ Chez Michel. **$$$**
★ 42 Degrees. **$$**
Greens. **$$$**
Harry Denton's. **$$$**
McCormick & Kuleto's. **$$**
The Ramp. **$**

Elsewhere in San Francisco
★★ Alain Rondelli. **$$**
Firefly. **$$**
Russian Renaissance. **$$$$**

East Bay (Oakland, Berkeley)

★ Bay Wolf (Oakland). **$$$**
★★ Chez Panisse (Berkeley). **$$$$**
★ Ginger Island (Berkeley). **$$**

Marin County

★ Manka's Inverness Lodge. **$$$**

Restaurants by Cuisine

American

Barney's Gourmet Hamburgers. **$**
Bix. **$$$**
★ Boulevard. **$$$**
The Buena Vista. **$**
Cypress Club. **$$$**
Dish. **$**
Dottie's True Blue Cafe. **$**
The Elite Cafe. **$$**
The Fly Trap. **$$**
★ Fog City Diner. **$$**
★ Ginger Island. **$$**
Hamburger Mary's. **$**
Harry Denton's. **$$$**
John's Grill. **$$$**
Lefty O'Doul's. **$**
★ Manka's Inverness Lodge. **$$$**
Noah's Bagels. **$**
★ One Market Restaurant. **$$**
The Ramp. **$**
Tadich Grill. **$$**

Californian

★ Bay Wolf. **$$$**
★★ Chez Panisse. **$$$$**
★ Hawthorne Lane. **$$$$**
★★ The Heights. **$$$$**
★ Moose's. **$$**
★★ Postrio. **$$$$**
Rubicon. **$$$**
★★ Stars. **$$$$**
★ Vertigo. **$$$**
Zuñi Café. **$$$**

Caribbean

★ Geva's. **$$**
Miss Pearl's Jam House. **$$**

Chinese

Brandy Ho's. **$$**
Hunan. **$**
★ Tommy Toy's Cuisine Chinoise. **$$$**
Yank Sing. **$**

Eclectic

BRAIN/wash. **$**
California Culinary Academy. **$$**
Firefly. **$$**
★★ Flying Saucer. **$$$**
★ Grand Cafe. **$$$**
Julie's Supper Club. **$$**
Ti Couz. **$**

French

★★ Alain Rondelli. **$$**
Bistro M. **$$$**
★ Bizou. **$$**
Cafe Jacqueline. **$$**
★ Chez Michel. **$$$**
★★ Fleur de Lys. **$$$$**
★ Fringale. **$$**
La Quiche. **$$**
Le Central. **$$**
Le Petit Cafe. **$$**
Rôti. **$$**
★ Savoy Brasserie. **$$**
South Park Cafe. **$$**

German

German Cook. **$$**
Suppenküche. **$$**

Italian

Caffe Macaroni. **$$**
Gold Spike. **$**
Il Fornaio. **$$**
Palio d'Asti. **$$**
Ristorante Ecco. **$$**
★ Rose Pistola. **$$**
The Stinking Rose. **$$**

Mediterranean

★ 42 Degrees. **$$**
★ LuLu. **$$**
★ PlumpJack Cafe. **$$$**
Sol y Luna. **$$**

Mexican

★ Cafe Marimba. **$$**
Campo Santo. **$**
La Rondalla. **$**

Pizza

California Pizza Kitchen. **$**

Russian

Russian Renaissance. **$$$$**

Seafood

Crustacean. **$$**

The Half Shell Restaurant and Oyster Bar. **$$**

★ Hayes Street Grill. **$$$**

McCormick & Kuleto's. **$$**

Vegetarian

Greens. **$$$**

★ Millennium. **$$**

Restaurants A to Z

★★ Alain Rondelli

126 Clement. ☎ 415/387-0408. MC, V. Reservations recommended. Wheelchair accessible. Closed Mon and Tues. FRENCH. **$$**.

With a year as chef to the former French President Valéry Giscard d'Estaing and 6 years under the tutelage of Marc Meneau at a Michelin 3-star restaurant to his credit, Alain Rondelli has at last come into his own as an ingenious interpreter of classic French cooking. In a simple but inviting room with the wood-beamed ceiling a casual counterpoint to Old Master–school oil paintings on the honey-colored walls, his passion is evident: tender scallops napped with plum-lime marmalade, lamb *pot-au-feu* in an oregano-scented broth, rosemary brioche scattered with caramelized onions—the edible arts of a man in the embrace of a culinary muse. For those who seek a deeper understanding of French food and wine, Rondelli offers the *menu ambroisie:* a 20-course affair designed to be savored over an entire evening.

Barney's Gourmet Hamburgers

3344 Steiner St. ☎ 415/563-0307. No Credit Cards. Wheelchair accessible. AMERICAN. **$**.

Yes, you can cringe over the much-abused "gourmet" appellation, but Barney's doesn't overstate their case. They've raised the lowly burger to an art form with fresh ingredients and mad scientist topping combinations. (The environs aren't so lofty; tidy, sunny, and generic with glass-topped tables and bud vases.) Turkey burgers are available, as are salads and other sandwiches. If the colorful clientele at Hamburger Mary's isn't your cup of tea, here's your best burger bet.

★ Bay Wolf

3853 Piedmont, Oakland. ☎ 510/655-6004. MC, V. Reservations recommended. Wheelchair accessible. Closed for lunch on Sat and Sun. CALIFORNIAN. **$$$**.

The capricious menu is derived from executive chef Michael Wild's trustworthy intuitions and is thematically attuned to the seasons of harvest: April in Paris, August in America, October in Tuscany, and so on. At any time of year, duck in its many guises is the *chef-d'oeuvre:* Glazed with ginger and basil, smoked with gamay sabayon, all of Wild's preparations are outstanding. The wine list is original and well priced. Of the 3 dining areas, each studded with original paintings and ceramic works (most are gifts to Wild by the artists), the angular Craftsman-esque room may be the best choice; it's more spacious than the other indoor space and more

Critic's Choice

San Franciscans are often quick to embrace extremes—to the point of peripeteia. And what arena of urban life is more subject to fancy and whim than that of restaurants, where chefs come and go and food fads run hot and cold in the twinkling of an eye? Mindful of this, we offer an of-the-moment guide to the Bay Area's most memorable dining experiences, in which culinary and ambient excellence together are the principal standard of measure.

Social touchstone for the cotillion set include **The Heights, PlumpJack Cafe,** and **Postrio.** The same category, but for iconoclasts, includes **Flying Saucer, 42 Degrees,** and **Millennium.**

Restaurants most conducive to romance (with universal appeal) include **Bix, Cafe Jacqueline,** and **Manka's Inverness Lodge.**

For a celebration, your best bets are **Grand Cafe, Moose's,** and **Stars.** Several choices have intergenerational appeal: **Cafe Marimba, California Pizza Kitchen,** and **Gold Spike.** For those who believe breakfast really *is* the most important meal of the day, go to **South Park Cafe** or **Zuñi Café.** Our votes for most extreme interiors go to **Cypress Club, La Rondalla,** and **Sol y Luna.** For connoisseurs of classic fare, we would suggest **Alain Rondelli, Fleur de Lys,** or **Hayes Street Grill;** for cutting-edge gadflies: **Boulevard, Hawthorne Lane,** or **Vertigo.**

---

accommodating than the sheltered street-side deck.

Bistro M

55 5th St. ☎ 415/543-5554. AE, D, MC, V. Reservations recommended. Wheelchair accessible. FRENCH. **$$$**.

Michel Richard's first Bay Area effort has been a bit slow to take off—a change in chefs and culinary style should repair the situation. He's bid au revoir to the rich bistro fare in favor of a more Citrus-style menu, bringing north more of the lighter California tastes popularized by his L.A. restaurant. The premises are a visual delight; housed in the remodeled 1913 building that's now Hotel Milano, the 2-story arched windows flood the place with light, revealing every dishy detail in Wayne Olds's 125-foot fresco *San Franciscobilis.*

Bix

56 Gold St. ☎ 415/433-6300. MC, V. Reservations recommended. Closed for lunch on Sun. AMERICAN. **$$$**.

Just finding Bix can be an exercise in urban trailblazing—halfway down a midblock alley, its discreet neon sign portends little indication of the luxe within. Modeled after a suave 1930s' supper club, complete with grand piano, the mezzanine that runs around the dove-grey room affords some diners a lofty view of the bon vivants below (doubtless some of them portrayed in the *mise en scène* mural above the bar). The menu concentrates on contemporary interpretations of American favorites, such as rack of lamb and smoked chicken hash. The bartenders are pros, with a shared specialty in hand-shaken martinis.

★ Bizou

598 4th St. ☎ 415/543-2222. AE, MC, V. Reservations recommended. Wheelchair accessible. Closed Sun. FRENCH. **$$**.

If your server tries to talk you into an order of Bizou's signature Italian flatbread, don't resist—wafer-thin and sprinkled with bits of caramelized onions and rosemary, it's a perfect palate-teaser for the rustic fare tocome. Bouillabaisse with salt cod and fennel pleases, as does the grilled lamb chop that's paired with seasonal accompaniments. The room, with butterscotch-glazed walls and white tablecloths, is flanked by a small oak bar that's *trés français*. On our last visit, none other than Stars chef Jeremiah Tower seemed to be enjoying the *bagna cauda* crock of summer vegetables immensely.

★ Boulevard

1 Mission St. ☎ 415/543-6084. AE, D, MC, V. Reservations recommended. Wheelchair accessible. Closed for lunch on Sun. AMERICAN. **$$$**.

The interior, another creation by prolific designer Pat Kuleto, is typically overwrought in it nouveau mannerisms, but when you're assigned to complement Nancy Oakes's inventive fare, you'd best pull out all (or at least most) of the stops. When she was named by *Food & Wine* magazine as one of the country's most promising chefs, it only confirmed what lucky locals already knew; a taste of her boneless rabbit stuffed with portobello mushrooms or a corn skillet cake–crab salad Napoleon leaves no doubt.

BRAIN/wash

1122 Folsom St. ☎ 415/861-3663. MC, V. No reservations. Wheelchair accessible. ECLECTIC. **$**.

Ever wish you could do three things at once? Live out this modernist fantasy at BRAIN/wash, where you can simultaneously: (1) Do your laundry, (2) Gorge on yummy sandwiches and salads in the cafe, and (3) Listen to live experimental music. The rest rooms—one designated for readers, the other for writers—are participatory experiences.

Brandy Ho's

450–452 Broadway. ☎ 415/362-6268. AE, D, MC, V. Reservations accepted. Wheelchair accessible. CHINESE. **$$**.

The fanciful, fire engine red lacquer and gilt interior of this well-liked Hunan restaurant may be a metaphor for the intestinal inferno propagated by dishes such as smoked ham with garlic and lamb with crispy rice noodles. Tables by the rear windows look out onto the schist of Telegraph Hill.

The Buena Vista

2765 Hyde St. ☎ 415/474-5044. No reservations.

Meals until 9:30pm, bar service to 2am. AMERICAN. **$**.

Even sangfroid San Franciscans can't resist the BV: On a blustery morning (or for that matter, a sunny one) there's no more mellow way to start the day than with a fog-clearing Irish coffee and an order of sourdough toast in this spot overlooking Aquatic Park and the bay. More robust appetites can opt for corned beef hash or steak and eggs. For late risers, lunch and dinner are served in the classic tavern setting. Shared tables add to the camaraderie; heart-of-gold waitresses contribute their own brand of character.

Cafe Jacqueline

1454 Grant Ave. ☎ 415/981-5565. MC, V. Reservations recommended. Wheelchair accessible. Closed Mon and Tues. FRENCH. **$$**.

The rose-washed walls and low lighting at this 1-dish restaurant are subdued and seductive. The soufflés are abundant, designed to be shared by two. Cap off a romantic stroll through North Beach with one of the sinful (or is it saintly?) dessert versions.

★ Cafe Marimba

2317 Chestnut St. ☎ 415/776-1506. MC, V. Reservations accepted. Wheelchair accessible. MEXICAN. **$$**.

Better bring your sunglasses to this rainbow-hued, folk-arty eatery, where the flavors of Oaxaca, the Yucatan, and Veracruz virtually jump off the plate. Don't expect the rote taco-burrito-enchilada routine—executive chef Reed Hearon excels in regional specialties such as snapper grilled on banana leaves with achiote, authentic mole negro and mole rojo, and calamari with jalapeños and garlic.

Caffe Macaroni

59 Columbus Ave. ☎ 415/956-9737. MC, V. No dinner reservations. Wheelchair accessible. Closed Sun and for lunch on Sat. ITALIAN. **$$**.

Barely bigger than your grandmother's kitchen, this recent addition to the neighborhood draws *cognoscenti* of good Italian cooking by virtue of its market-fresh menu, which changes daily. Classic pasta dishes are a staple, of course.

California Culinary Academy

625 Polk St. ☎ 415/771-3500. AE, MC, V. Reservations recommended. Wheelchair accessible. Closed Sat and Sun. ECLECTIC. **$$**.

Odds are even that you'll preview the next Jeremiah Tower in training at the auditorium-like dining room of this prestigious culinary school. Contrary to the coldness of the setting, the food is first-rate, the prices reasonable, and the service friendly; for the students, each meal is tantamount to a final exam. The huge teaching kitchen is like an open laboratory; set at the head of the room, it's entertainment without a cover charge.

California Pizza Kitchen

438 Geary St. ☎ 415/563-8911. AE, MC, V. No reservations. Wheelchair accessible. PIZZA. **$**.

A flashy black-and-yellow palette sets the tone for the repertoire of rambunctious pizzas that pop from the wood-burning oven. Tandoori chicken, Jamaican shrimp, and BLT are but a few of the fun combos from which to choose. Cholesterol counters can

Dining Near Union Square

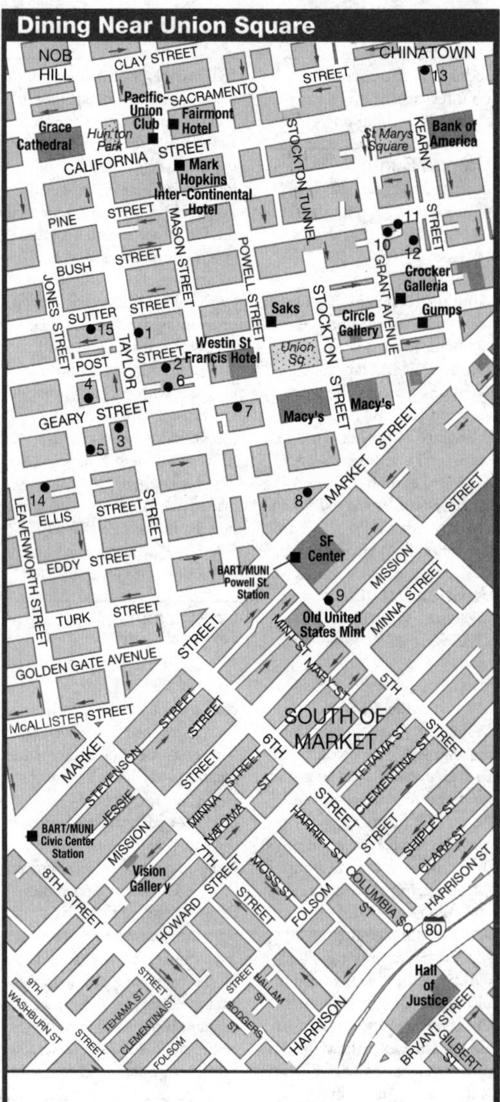

Bistro M **9**
Cafe Claude **12**
Cafe de la Presse **10**
California Pizza Kitchen **6**
Dottie's True Blue Cafe **5**
Fleur de Lys **15**
German Cook **14**
Grand Cafe **3**
John's Grill **8**
La Quiche **1**
Le Central **11**
Lefty O'Doul's **7**
Palio d'Asti **13**
Postrio **2**
Savoy Brasserie **4**

indulge in the cheeseless counterparts or be extra good and stick to the filling salads.

Campo Santo

240 Columbus Ave. ☎ 415/ 433-9623. MC, V. No reservations. Wheelchair accessible. Closed Mon. MEXICAN. **$**.

Another Technicolor Mexican joint, this one an uptown exuberant diorama of tombstones and tap-dancing skeletons—*campo santo,* you see, translates as "country of the saints": in other words, the cemetery. The burritos and fajitas do exhibit an other-worldly flair, especially when chased with a cool Dos Equis or Bohemia Negro.

★ Chez Michel

804 North Point. ☎ 415/ 775-7036. MC, V. Reservations recommended. Wheelchair accessible. Dinner only; closed Mon. FRENCH. **$$$**.

When the "lusty peasant fare" craze fails to move you, head to this jewel of a restaurant for a refined restorative in the French tradition. Chef Denis Soriano's stylish preparations of duck confit, sautéed scallops in whole grain mustard sauce, and other classic dishes reaffirm the pleasures of sophisticated cooking. The clean-lined interior is clad in blond ash and chrome, with shuttered windows adding an air of casual exclusivity to the room. Owner Michel Elkaim is the consummate host, cordially monitoring the dozen or so tables.

★★ Chez Panisse

1517 Shattuck Ave., between Cedar and Pine streets, Berkeley. ☎ 510/548-5525. AE, MC, V. Reservations required. Wheelchair accessible. Dinner only; closed Sun. CALIFORNIAN. **$$$$**.

If the whole is the sum of its parts, a meal at Chez Panisse is an unquantifiable experience. Individually, the ingredients are the finest; when combined in food-guru Alice Waters's inimitable and unerring kitchen, the results are sublime. Should you be fortunate enough to secure a reservation, keep your eyes peeled for the vine-draped, unassuming Craftsman house—it's easy to drive right past it. Sometimes there's an attitude problem with the personnel, a confusing contretemps in this veritable temple to the simple goodness of nature. The atmosphere (and the prices) are more down-to-earth upstairs in the cafe (☎ 510/ 548-5049) where lighter lunch and dinner fare is served.

Crustacean

1475 Polk St. ☎ 415/ 776-CRAB. AE, MC, V. Reservations accepted. Wheelchair accessible. Dinner only; open daily. SEAFOOD. **$$**.

The 2nd-floor shopping center location may be a deterrent to some, but for those who overcome such superficialities, the payoff comes on a platter: garlic-roasted crabs straight from heaven. Don't be distracted by anything else on the Asian-oriented menu; you're on a mission here. The neon squiggles on the walls are a rudimentary attempt at art—ignore them, too, and order some more crab before the folks at the next table get the last one.

Cypress Club

500 Jackson St. ☎ 415/ 296-8555. AE, MC, V. Reservations recommended. Wheelchair accessible. Dinner only; open daily. AMERICAN. **$$$**.

Bulbous copper walls and bodacious lighting fixtures (some see them as anatomically suggestive; the eye of the beholder, I guess) give this big room an exaggerated, exotic aura. The kitchen does its best to keep pace with the architectural fantasy (you won't find chicken pot pie in these environs), and it does a commendable job with the creative American menu. Desserts can be the literal pinnacle of a meal here.

Dish

1398 Haight St. ☎ 415/431-3534. MC, V. No reservations. Wheelchair accessible. AMERICAN. **$**.

Sunday morning, before you make the rounds of Golden Gate Park, feast on any of the outstanding brunch preparations here; the macadamia-nut waffles are delectable. By the way, you're eating in an anti-establishment artifact: This is the site of the infamous Drogstore, where the counterculture of the 1960s once flouted authority by cultivating marijuana in the window boxes.

Dottie's True Blue Cafe

522 Jones St. ☎ 415/885-2767. MC, V. No reservations. Wheelchair accessible. Open only 7:30am–2pm. AMERICAN. **$**.

If you're in the mood for a hearty helping of America and apple pie, here's your quintessential mid-century coffee shop: Formica counters, leatherette seating, stainless steel kitchen. Those in the know claim the pancakes are the best in town.

The Elite Cafe

2049 Fillmore St. ☎ 415/346-8668. D, MC, V. No reservations. Wheelchair accessible. Dinner only; Sun brunch. AMERICAN. **$$**.

A Big Easy ambiance is conjured by the ceiling fans, high-backed wooden booths, and tile floors that grace this light-filled space; on summer nights, you could swear there are cicadas droning in the distance. The effect is underscored by the Creole/Cajun menu, which stars blackened red snapper, rock shrimp étouffée, and a hefty house-smoked pork chop topped with peach-jalapeño chutney—all of which taste better when preceded by a potent Sazerac.

Firefly

4288 24th St. ☎ 415/821-7652. AE, MC, V. Reservations recommended. Wheelchair accessible. Dinner only. ECLECTIC. **$$**.

The culinary credo of this neighborhood place (that has just happened to garner some national attention) is "home cooking with no ethnic boundaries." What this means for the diner is a gustatory grand tour, encompassing elements of American, Chinese, Mexican, and Vietnamese cooking. Start with the signature appetizer of shrimp and scallop potstickers, then move on to the honey-roasted Cornish hen with cornbread-wild rice stuffing. Sometimes ingredients are a bit too ambitiously combined, but the spirited service overcomes this as well as the work-in-progress ambiance, which leans to a quasi-domestic side—the odd sconce, the occasional knick-knack.

★★ Fleur de Lys

777 Sutter St. ☎ 415/673-7779. AE, D, MC, V. Reservations recommended. Coat and tie preferred. Wheelchair accessible.

Dinner only; closed Sunday. FRENCH. **$$$$**.

Swathed in miles of red paisley, the beguiling, tentlike interior here (designed by the late Michael Taylor) invokes an encampment of gypsies with exquisite taste. Such standards are also upheld by Hubert Keller's kitchen, which consistently creates innovative, yet thoroughly French dishes, such as medallions of lamb wrapped in zucchini in a piquant merlot sauce. The waitstaff is positively clairvoyant.

The Fly Trap

606 Folsom St. ☎ 415/243-0580. AE, DC, MC, V. Reservations not required. Wheelchair accessible. Closed Sun and for lunch on Sat. AMERICAN. **$$**.

This nostalgic menu focuses on ample, well-prepared portions of San Francisco staples such as hangtown fry and chicken sauté sec. The dining room is an eye-catcher in a conservative vein; walls are papered with a collage of architectural and botanical engravings limned in gold leaf. Lunch is lively yet efficient, when the Trap attracts many attorneys from the neighborhood. After hours, the bar does a brisk business.

★★ Flying Saucer

1000 Guerrero St. ☎ 415/641-9955. MC, V. Reservations recommended. Wheelchair accessible. Closed Mon. ECLECTIC. **$$$**.

This tiny place achieved cult status early on, and it wasn't for its funky storefront premises. Uncannily eclectic dishes such as mango-topped artichoke-lobster salad and pistachio chicken sausage both confound and elate with their sense of unbridled adventure; desserts are preternaturally unpredictable.

★ Fog City Diner

1300 Battery St. ☎ 415/982-2000. D, MC, V. Reservations recommended. Wheelchair accessible. Closed Mon. AMERICAN. **$$**.

All chrome, beveled glass, and shining oak trim, in a highly stylized take on a 1930s' roadside diner, Fog City is home to the reinvented blue plate special. A plethora of "small plates" like crab cakes, quesadillas, sesame chicken, and sirloin chili make meals a series of delicious decisions. With the development of the Embarcadero, the patio has been enclosed—no more exhaust fumes in your french fries. These "back room" seats offer a refuge from the bustle of the main dining area, should you desire—but the friendly frenzy of Fog City is an integral part of its appeal.

★ 42 Degrees

235 16th St. ☎ 415/777-5558. AE, D, DC, MC, V. No reservations. Wheelchair accessible. Closed for lunch on weekends and for dinner Sun–Tues. MEDITERRANEAN. **$$**.

The name refers to the latitude of Provence, a significant influence on the menu of this out-of-the-way spot—and one that's worth the detour, as much for the animated atmosphere as for the food. If the weather's willing, sit outdoors and nibble at a Niçoise salad or portobello pizzetta; when it's cool, move inside the hanger-scaled building—an airy amalgam of swankiness and technology—and order something more substantial, like the baked shrimp empañada or spinach

Dining Near North Beach

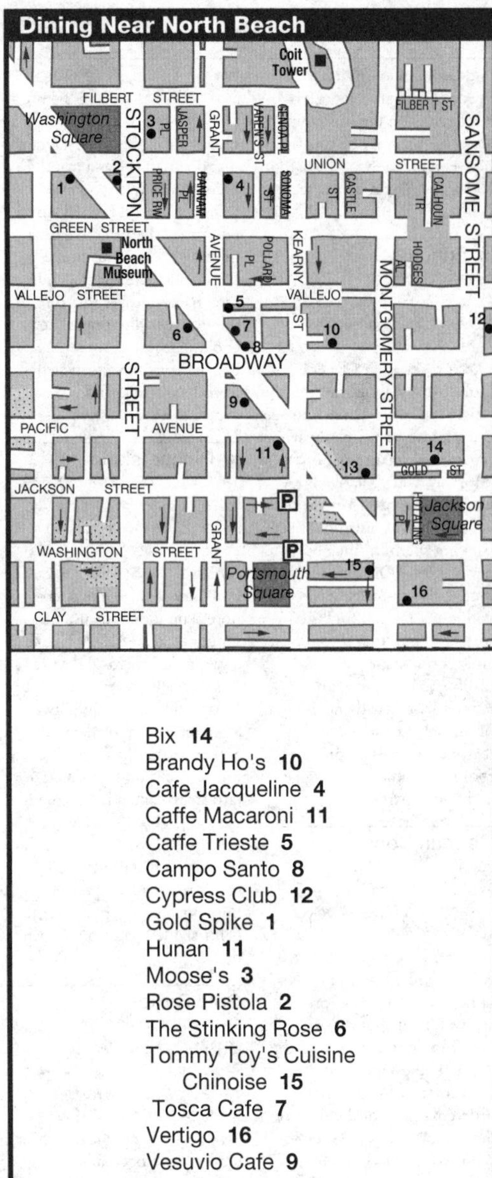

Bix **14**
Brandy Ho's **10**
Cafe Jacqueline **4**
Caffe Macaroni **11**
Caffe Trieste **5**
Campo Santo **8**
Cypress Club **12**
Gold Spike **1**
Hunan **11**
Moose's **3**
Rose Pistola **2**
The Stinking Rose **6**
Tommy Toy's Cuisine Chinoise **15**
Tosca Cafe **7**
Vertigo **16**
Vesuvio Cafe **9**

and lamb ravioli in garlic brodo. There are a few cloistered tables on the mezzanine, although you may be torn between the view of the harbor and spying down on the scene below.

★ Fringale

570 4th St. ☎ 415/543-0573. AE, MC, V. Reservations recommended. Wheelchair accessible. Closed Sun and for lunch on Sat. FRENCH. **$$**.

Don't worry about finding this SoMa stalwart—when you see the beehive of people swarming around an anonymous doorway, you've arrived. Gerald Hirigoyen's unassuming yet purposeful bistro has been packing them in since opening day in 1991. Once inside, diners give in to fringale—colloquial French for "the urge to eat"—and tuck into robust and refined plates of California-Basque food. After a frisee salad and a bowl of mussels steamed and seasoned to perfection, save room for the iced Armagnac and coffee parfait.

German Cook

612 O'Farrell St. ☎ 415/776-9022. AE, MC, V. Reservations accepted. Wheelchair accessible. Closed for lunch Sun–Tues. GERMAN. **$$**.

A blue-collar bonhomie—or rather *Gemütlichkeit*—presides at this quaint spot that's comfortably worn around the edges. The potato pancakes are awesome; we would have ordered a plate of them for dessert, but the single server who works the diminutive room disappeared into the après-entrée twilight zone.

★ Geva's

482A Hayes St. ☎ 415/863-1220. AE, MC, V. Reservations accepted. Wheelchair accessible. Closed Mon and for lunch on Sat and Sun. CARIBBEAN. **$$**.

Finally, a Caribbean restaurant that doesn't pose as a tropical theme park. With its coral wainscoting and framed family photos on the walls, Geva's is more like a gracious home in the islands (save for the sculptural banana leaves that shroud the overhead lighting). The cooking is just as authentic: pepper pot soup, fish poached in coconut milk, and eye-watering jerked dishes.

★ Ginger Island

1820 4th St., Berkeley. ☎ 510/644-0444. AE, DC, MC, V. Reservations recommended. Wheelchair accessible. AMERICAN. **$$**.

Culinary thrill-seekers, take note: The judicious use of ginger by chef Alison Negrin awakens a farrago of flavors in this basically American menu. Roast salmon is piqued by a ginger beurre blanc; with a plate of the house fries (a mixture of potato, yam, and taro strips) and a baby greens salad tossed with ginger vinaigrette, you've got it made. Ambiance is sophisticated south-seas nautical; nurse a homemade ginger ale on the palm-shaded patio on a hot day.

Gold Spike

527 Columbus Ave. ☎ 415/421-4591. AE, D, MC, V. Reservations accepted. Wheelchair accessible. Closed Wed. ITALIAN. **$**.

Travelers with teenagers, your prayers have been answered. Here's a place where the brood can ingest massive quantities of Italian food served family-style, and parents won't be bankrupted. Nor will there be any rolling eyes or withering stares cast because of a quasi-juvenile environment; this North Beach eatery is crammed with dusty San Francisco memorabilia.

★ Grand Cafe

501 Geary St. ☎ 415/292-0101. AE, D, MC, V. Reservations recommended. Wheelchair accessible. ECLECTIC. **$$$**.

The descriptive "grand" is actually a somnambulistic evaluation of the fin de siècle spectacle of this former ballroom. An outrageous art nouveau interior—with serpentine terrazzo patterns on the floor, elaborate chandeliers dangling from 30-foot ceilings, and decadent chocolate brown leather and velvet booths—provides an ironic setting for what management describes as "European comfort food." Duck confit on a bed of star anise risotto, seared foie gras with fire-roasted peaches on toasted brioche, and a grilled eggplant Napoleon give form to this concept.

Greens

Building A, Fort Mason Center. ☎ 415/771-6222. D, MC, V. Reservations recommended. Wheelchair accessible. Closed for lunch on Mon and dinner on Sun. VEGETARIAN. **$$$**.

The rising tide of opinion posits that the glory days of this vegetarian pioneer are a thing of the past, but in actuality Greens hasn't faltered—rather, the new competition has raised the standard of veggie cuisine. The quality of the home-grown ingredients is as high as ever, the Golden Gate vista still unmatched, and the timbered dining room and its floor-to-ceiling windows continue to be a serene retreat for health-conscious consumers.

The Half Shell Restaurant and Oyster Bar

64 Rausch St. ☎ 415/552-7677. AE, MC, V. Wheelchair accessible. Closed Sun. SEAFOOD. **$$**.

Off the beaten path it may be (a side street in SoMa), but the Half Shell is familiar territory to those with a fanatical fondness for seafood. Almost every night there's a bar special being served in the redwood-sided room: "Shrimp and an Elephant" Thursdays bring a pound of spicy peel-and-eat shrimp with a pint of Elephant Red Ale.

Hamburger Mary's

1582 Folsom St. ☎ 415/626-1985. AE, D, MC, V. No reservations. Closed Mon. AMERICAN. **$**.

A cross-section of San Francisco's kaleidoscopic citizenry bellies up to this fun and funky tavern. On any given day or night you'll rub shoulders with journalists, bikers, lawyers, and bouncers. And they've all gathered to enjoy the mythical Mary's *raison d'être:* her legendary burger.

Harry Denton's

161 Steuart St. ☎ 415/882-1333. AE, DC, MC, V. Reservations recommended. Wheelchair accessible. AMERICAN. **$$$**.

People here talk too loud and laugh too hard—and that's the way the affable Mr. Denton likes it. Some of us have a different opinion. This is a criminally popular scene for the radical fringe element of the Junior League—you know who we mean. The shrug-worthy menu obediently takes a backseat to the over-the-top saloon decor, heavy on the brass, polished woods, and velvet drapery. Score a table that overlooks the bay, order simple, and you've got a chance at some peace. A better idea: Head over to Harry's latest and more civilized creation, Harry Denton's Starlight Room, at the St. Francis Hotel.

★ Hawthorne Lane

22 Hawthorne St. ☎ 415/ 777-9779. D, MC, V. Reservations recommended. Wheelchair accessible. Closed for lunch on Sat and Sun. CALIFORNIAN. **$$$$**.

The fanfare surrounding the opening of this expansive, airy space is just beginning to die down, and the kitchen, under the direction of Anne and David Gingrass (late of Postrio, and previously Spago) has gotten down to business, as well. Boldly flavored dishes that blend Asian and European influences—horseradish-crusted scallops with cabernet sauce and cucumber salad, roasted duck with green onion buns and apricot mustard—match the modern environment in inventiveness. An elliptical bar of cherry wood gives shape to the cafe section, where the best tables are the elevated booths nearest the main dining room. Marble-topped waiters' stations are the focus of the latter, embellished with baroque floral arrangements, a still-life of baked goods, and polished silver and crystal.

★ Hayes Street Grill

324 Hayes St. ☎ 415/ 863-5545. MC, V. Reservations recommended. Wheelchair accessible. Closed for lunch on Sat and Sun. SEAFOOD. **$$$**.

Pick your favorite of the grilled fish (yellowfin tuna, Pacific snapper, northern halibut, and many others), then pair it with one of the flawless sauces (lemon caper butter, béarnaise, pasilla beurre blanc, plus half-a-dozen more) for a memorable meal in this aesthetically spare but old-fashioned interior. The Grill is co-owned by Patricia Unterman, a respected restaurant critic and author.

★★ The Heights

3235 Sacramento St. ☎ 415/ 474-8890. AE, D, MC, V. Reservations recommended. Wheelchair accessible. Closed Mon. CALIFORNIAN. **$$$$**.

There's an understated but appealingly quirky personality to the 3 little dining rooms here: Massive baskets of apples mark the entry; chairs are skirted in a subdued palette of solid colors, with an occasional graphic vegetable print thrown in for visual spice; arches and ogees frame doorways and windows. Charles Solomon's cooking, on the other hand, is single-minded and straightforward. With credentials from Bouley, the Quilted Giraffe, and Charlie Trotter's, his recipes don't trade on shocking seasonings or presentations; rather, he strikes an elusive equilibrium of ingredients in dishes such as roasted lavender-glazed duck au jus, accompanied by braised endive and slices of caramelized pear.

Hunan

924 Sansome St. ☎ 415/ 956-7727. AE, MC, V. Reservations accepted. Wheelchair accessible. Closed Sat and Sun. CHINESE. **$**.

A cavern of a place that has been likened to a decorated gymnasium, constantly filled with diners who feel up to the test of what is widely considered the city's most fiery food. As a consequence of its popularity, service (particularly at noontime) can occasionally be frustrating, but the merits of the kitchen outweigh these rare slips. The full menu is served in the bar area, where the din is diminished.

Il Fornaio

1265 Battery St. ☎ 415/986-0100. AE, D, MC, V. Reservations recommended. Wheelchair accessible. Closed for dinner on Sun. ITALIAN. **$$**.

An elegantly casual composition in chrome, grey marble, and mahogany, Il Fornaio offers a taste of la dolce vita in 3 distinct environments: the bar, where you can sip an espresso in the morning or a Campari after dark; the dining rooms, airy and relaxed, with huge majolica vases for flowers; and the patio, set by the fountains of Levi Plaza and sheltered by an awning. Wood-fired pizzas are a specialty, and the fresh pastas can't be faulted. There's a bakery that turns out breads and cookies that are not of this earth (soft olive loaves, baguettes rolled in anise, sesame, and poppy seeds, and much more) and a take-out department on site, too, if you want to sit in the park and munch a panini.

John's Grill

63 Ellis St. ☎ 415/986-0069. AE, D, MC, V. Reservations recommended. Wheelchair accessible. Closed for lunch on Sun. AMERICAN. **$$$**.

Another of San Francisco's restaurants with a past, this one with a literary bent: If these wood paneled walls could talk, they'd tell tales of Dashiell Hammett's Sam Spade passing time on these premises in *The Maltese Falcon*. Founded in 1908, the grill serves manly portions of steaks and chops to a mixed-bag clientele of natives and out-of-towners.

Julie's Supper Club

1123 Folsom St. ☎ 415/861-0707. AE, MC, V. Reservations recommended. Wheelchair accessible. Dinner only; closed Sun. ECLECTIC. **$$**.

Alice and Ralph Cramden might choose this place—a 1950s-flavored spot that's fine for a high-spirited quasi-camp night out—to paint the town red on pay day. While the entrees are competent, it's more fun to order a cocktail or two and graze through a parade of appetizers.

La Quiche

550 Taylor St. ☎ 415/441-2711. AE, D, MC, V. Reservations recommended. Wheelchair accessible. FRENCH. **$$**.

Convenient for pre- or post-theater dining, this elderly French eatery offers a warm setting—invariably, you're treated like family—and a well-priced, well-prepared *campagne* menu that goes well beyond its namesake. In Paris, this modest establishment with no design pretense would be a real neighborhood restaurant, as it is here.

La Rondalla

901 Valencia St. ☎ 415/647-7474. MC, V. No reservations. Wheelchair accessible. Closed Mon. MEXICAN. **$**.

It's Christmas 'round the clock at this Mission District cantina, where strolling mariachis wail away in a veritable jungle of colored lights and tinsel. Margaritas by the pitcher pleasantly intensify the experience, and have the added effect of mitigating the filling, but nothing-special food.

Le Central

453 Bush St. ☎ 415/391-2233. AE, MC, V. Reservations

Dining Around Town

- Alain Rondelli **10**
- Anchor Brewing **36**
- Barney's Gourmet Hamburgers **2**
- Bizou **57**
- Boulevard **46**
- BRAIN/wash **38**
- The Buena Vista **7**
- Cafe Flore **29**
- Cafe Marimba **1**
- California Culinary Academy **17**
- Cava 555 **55**
- Chez Michel **7A**
- Crustacean **13**
- Dish **25**
- The Elite Cafe **11**
- Firefly **28**
- The Fly Trap **52**
- Flying Saucer **33**
- Fog City Diner **40**
- 42 Degrees **59**
- Fringale **56**
- Geva's **21**
- Gordon Biersch Brewery **49**
- Greens **3**
- The Half Shell Restaurant and Oyster Bar **37**
- Hamburger Mary's **34**
- Harry Denton's **48**
- Hawthorne Lane **51**
- Hayes & Vine Wine Bar **22**
- Hayes Street Grill **23**
- The Heights **9**

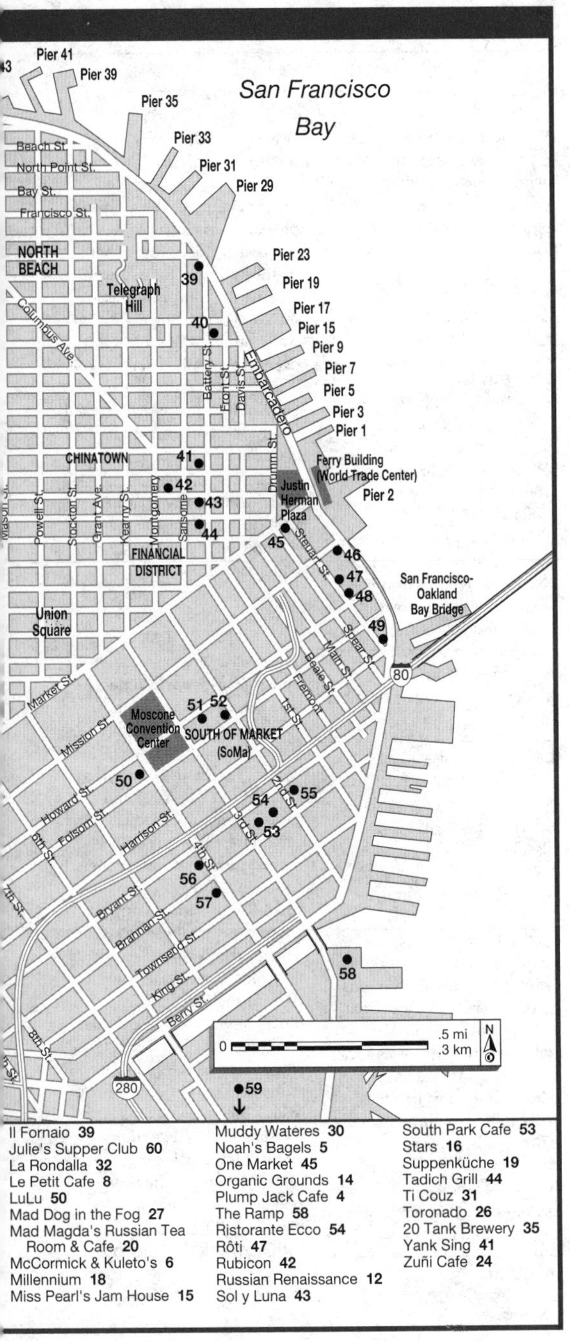

San Francisco Bay
Pier 41
Pier 39
Pier 35
Pier 33
Pier 31
Pier 29
Pier 23
Pier 19
Pier 17
Pier 15
Pier 9
Pier 7
Pier 5
Pier 3
Pier 1
Pier 2
Beach St.
North Point St.
Bay St.
Francisco St.
NORTH BEACH
Telegraph Hill
Columbus Ave.
Battery St.
Front St.
Davis St.
Embarcadero
Drumm St.
Ferry Building (World Trade Center)
Justin Herman Plaza
CHINATOWN
Powell St.
Stockton St.
Grant Ave.
Kearny St.
Montgomery
Sansome
FINANCIAL DISTRICT
Steuart St.
San Francisco-Oakland Bay Bridge
Union Square
Spear St.
Main St.
Beale St.
Fremont
1st St.
80
Market St.
Mission St.
Moscone Convention Center
SOUTH OF MARKET (SoMa)
Howard St.
Folsom St.
Harrison St.
2nd St.
3rd St.
4th St.
Bryant St.
Brannan St.
Townsend St.
King St.
Berry St.
7th St.
8th St.
280
0 .5 mi .3 km
N
39
40
41
42
43
44
45
46
47
48
49
50
51
52
53
54
55
56
57
58
59
Il Fornaio 39
Julie's Supper Club 60
La Rondalla 32
Le Petit Cafe 8
LuLu 50
Mad Dog in the Fog 27
Mad Magda's Russian Tea Room & Cafe 20
McCormick & Kuleto's 6
Millennium 18
Miss Pearl's Jam House 15
Muddy Wateres 30
Noah's Bagels 5
One Market 45
Organic Grounds 14
Plump Jack Cafe 4
The Ramp 58
Ristorante Ecco 54
Rôti 47
Rubicon 42
Russian Renaissance 12
Sol y Luna 43
South Park Cafe 53
Stars 16
Suppenküche 19
Tadich Grill 44
Ti Couz 31
Toronado 26
20 Tank Brewery 35
Yank Sing 41
Zuñi Cafe 24

recommended. Wheelchair accessible. Closed Sun. FRENCH. **$$**.

With justification, Le Central is probably better known for being *Chronicle* columnist Herb Caen's hangout away from home than for the merits of its food, although they do serve a mean cassoulet. There's always a quiet buzz at the brasserie's copper-topped bar, and the tables are seldom empty.

Le Petit Cafe

2164 Larkin St. ☎ 415/776-5356. AE, D, MC, V. Reservations accepted. Wheelchair accessible. Closed for dinner on Sun and Mon. FRENCH. **$$**.

This corner hideaway is a paean to *la vie Parisian:* lacy cafe curtains and Thornet chairs, a steaming bowl of café au lait, and any of the buttery pastries make a soothing start to any day. Come back for dinner, when candles light the room.

Lefty O'Doul's

333 Geary St. ☎ 415/982-8900. No credit cards. Wheelchair accessible. AMERICAN. **$**.

"Bring the Children," the sign invites, lest passersby labor under the impression that O'Doul's is exclusively a tavern. In truth, it's an institution. Monster turkeys, hams, and roasts are the stars of the steam table, and what buffet would be complete without little cups of tapioca for dessert? After dark, the piano bar (and its habitués) starts rolling, with septuagenarians, cops in uniform, and Bermuda-shorted tourists warbling "Goody, Goody" and the requisite "Danny Boy" into the wee hours.

★ LuLu

816 Folsom St. ☎ 415/495-5775. AE, MC, V. Reservations recommended. Wheelchair accessible. MEDITERRANEAN. **$$**.

A meal at LuLu's may stir up memories of a family reunion—if, that is, the kindred count is 180 people plus one terrific cook, who in this case happens to be chef-of-the-moment Reed Hearon. The rustic-industrial interior—the former warehouse features a brick oven and a vaulted ceiling—is supportive of the peasanty French/Italian fare that's served family-style on oversized glazed Italian platters.

★ Manka's Inverness Lodge

40 Callander, Inverness. ☎ 415/669-1034. AE, MC, V. Reservations recommended. Dinner only; closed Tues and Wed. AMERICAN. **$$$**.

The proliferation of pseudo–hunting lodge environments only serves to make us more appreciative of the genuine article. Well out of town, and well worth the drive through some of the Bay Area's most pastoral environs, Manka's is a rural retreat that serves spit-roasted game and fowl in an authentic setting that would make Ralph Lauren hang his salt-and-pepper head in shame. The gravlax is house-cured; the wild boar sausage is grilled right in the fireplace. (First-timers might want to consider booking a room or cabin at the lodge to avoid the after-dark return trip on unfamiliar back-roads.) Inverness was once a stronghold of Czech immigrants, and their hearty culinary roots are still in evidence here; *dobré chutnání!*

McCormick & Kuleto's

900 North Point St. ☎ 415/929-1730. AE, D, MC, V. Reservations accepted.

Wheelchair accessible. SEAFOOD. **$$**.

In this venture, restaurateur extraordinaire Pat Kuleto set out to create an eatery that would appeal not only to out-of-towners, but also to residents—a picky lot who would normally rather be caught dead than be seen treading the touristic turf of Fisherman's Wharf. He's succeeded with this stunner of a room, a huge, split-level affair where every table has a view of the bay. The kitchen can do no wrong when it comes to piscatorial preparations, whether they're seafood pizzas or grilled ahi. There's a fresh crab and oyster bar, too.

★ Millennium

246 McAllister St. ☎ 415/487-9800. MC, V. Reservations recommended. Wheelchair accessible. Closed Mon. VEGETARIAN. **$$**.

More than a few enlightened eaters believe that this newcomer is the heir to Greens' reign as vegetarian nirvana. And it's hard to disagree. Eric Tucker's kitchen turns out not so much healthy, delicious food than examples of culinary legerdemain. Shiitake and cilantro spring rolls dressed in an Asian cherry vinaigrette, the grilled portobello mushroom topped with hummus and onion-ginger chutney, and a rosemary polenta torte typify (if such can be said) the dairy-free, mostly oil-free organic fare. Surely the staff must have fielded the question "Just what exactly is seitan?" a thousand times, yet they patiently and enthusiastically inform again. There's a small bar and cafe seating off the lobby of the Abagail Hotel; the main dining room is tucked into the courtyard level, and decorated with odd, arty sconces and banquettes that are more constructivist than cushy.

Miss Pearl's Jam House

601 Eddy St. ☎ 415/775-5276. MC, V. Reservations recommended. Wheelchair accessible. Closed Mon. CARIBBEAN. **$$**.

This mecca for the Jello Shot generation is permanently boisterous, and the cooking is on a par with the crowd: Spicy Caribbean concoctions like rasta pasta and oyster shooters are served to a reggae beat.

★ Moose's

1652 Stockton St. ☎ 415/989-7800. AE, MC, V. Reservations recommended. Wheelchair accessible. CALIFORNIAN. **$$**.

Party of two? Better get a table for three, as gregarious Ed Moose, affable proprietor of this eponymous establishment, may very well pull up a chair and chat like an old buddy. Cooking is creative and sure, and seasonally attuned: If the soft-shell crab tacos are on the menu when you stop by, don't, repeat don't, pass them up. The same goes for the individual lemon meringue pie for dessert. The wine list is intelligent and affordable. The bright, glass-fronted room nudges up on Washington Square, but more people peer into the restaurant than out to the park, in hopes of spotting a famous face or two—it's that kind of place.

Noah's Bagels

2075 Chestnut St. ☎ 415/775 2910. No credit cards. No reservations. Wheelchair accessible. AMERICAN. **$**.

To be blunt, these are the best bagels west of the East River. In response to cardiac-conscious noshers, Noah has devised a line of fat-free, flavored cream cheese schmears, of which the tomato-basil variety is *geschmekt*. Not to worry, if you're a purist: You can have your nova with the real thing as well. There is another Noah's at 3170 College Avenue in Berkeley (☎ 510/654-0944) and many more throughout the Bay Area. Premises are kosher.

★ One Market Restaurant

1 Market St. ☎ 415/777-5577. AE, MC, V. Reservations recommended. Closed for lunch on Sat. AMERICAN. **$$**.

From the man who turned mere pot roast into manna up at Marin County's Lark Creek Inn comes this urbane mega-restaurant, with seating for 250. Most times the deep-hued floral-patterned banquettes are filled to capacity at Bradley Ogden's airy place, which sits on Ferry Plaza. All-American farm-fresh provender is what keeps them coming. The kitchen routinely performs feats of transubstantiation; for instance, dressing humble pork chops with wine jam and potato fennel risotto. Dessert? The chocolate brioche custardbread pudding or rhubarb crisp.

Palio d'Asti

640 Sacramento St. ☎ 415/395-9800. AE, MC, V. Reservations recommended. Wheelchair accessible. Closed Sun. ITALIAN. **$$**.

Futurist antipasti carts, their revolving stainless steel trays laden with delectables, carom through the concrete aisles of this artsy eatery located in the core of the Financial District. It's amusing to watch fellow diners pick and choose from the peppers, olives, and other goodies. Piedmontese recipes comprise the main menu, with duck-filled agnolotti in wild mushroom sauce a hot order.

★ PlumpJack Cafe

3127 Fillmore St. ☎ 415/563-4755. AE, MC, V. Reservations recommended. Wheelchair accessible. Closed Sun and for lunch on Sat. MEDITERRANEAN. **$$$**.

A theatrical scrim of wire mesh unfurls at the window; cream-colored coats-of-arms do a Dali-like turn as sconces; and stylized stage curtains panel the walls. In this forward-Falstaffian setting, chef Maria Helm produces entertaining Mediterranean-influenced fare like saffron-scented risotto and pan roasted rabbit with chanterelles and polenta. Desserts step up for a curtain call: Try the bittersweet chocolate crème brûlée. The proprietors' interests include a retail wine shop further down the street that emphasizes unusual, affordable bottles; the cafe's terrific wine list is assembled along the same line.

★★ Postrio

545 Post St. ☎ 415/776-7825. AE, MC, V. Reservations required. Wheelchair accessible. Closed for breakfast and lunch on Sat and Sun. CALIFORNIAN. **$$$$**.

Flashy. It's the best characterization of both the cooking and the decor of Wolfgang Puck's San Francisco flagship. But it's an injustice to limit the description to one word for such inventiveness. Ribbons of red, black, and grey wend their way through the decor of the bar, mezzanine, and main dining room, a sinuous reference to the flowing staircase that grandly deposits diners in the thick of the action. The arrival of brothers

Mitchell and Steven Rosenthal in the kitchen brings dishes such as sautéed scallops with green curry sauce and gingered carrots to the visionary Californian menu. Don't worry about having to choose between the chocolate cake with blackberry sauce and the Gravenstein apple cheesecake for dessert—just order the sampler plate of sweets.

The Ramp

855 China Basin. ☎ 415/ 621-2378. AE, MC, V. No reservations. Does not serve dinner; brunch only on Sat and Sun; AMERICAN. **$**.

Pick a sunny morning to journey to this part of town and you'll be rewarded with a bayside seat on the large deck. The Ramp attracts a cut-offs and sandals bunch, with the fare equally casual. On summer Sundays, there's usually live music—and often a wait for a table as patrons tend to settle in for a lazy, Anchor Steam–cooled afternoon.

Ristorante Ecco

101 South Park. ☎ 415/ 495-3291. AE, MC, V. Reservations recommended. Wheelchair accessible. Closed for lunch on Sat and Sun. ITALIAN. **$$**.

Situated on the intimate oasis that is South Park, with a clever Italian menu and urbane interior, Ristorante Ecco attracts a steady stream of local movers and shakers. But the heavy customer traffic can tax the hard-working staff to a critical point: Table service can be slipshod, and the preparation and presentation of the food sometimes seems rushed as well. One night, our pasta appeared topsy-turvy, its luscious walnut cream sauce completely hidden underneath a tangle of linguini.

★ Rose Pistola

532 Columbus Ave. ☎ 415/ 399-0499. AE, DC, MC, V. Reservations recommended. Wheelchair accessible. ITALIAN. **$$**.

An Italian menu that is simultaneously original and authentic: mission impossible, you say? Not in the hands of Reed Hearon (Cafe Marimba, LuLu), who's mined the indigenous recipes of Genoa and the Ligurian coast and melded them with local ingredients. The upshot is an array of imaginative, satisfying antipasti and fresh fish and seafood (his cioppino sets the standard for the city). Every table in the warmly modernist restaurant is prime, from the heated sidewalk seating to the small counter fronting the open kitchen to the banquettes in the back of the house. Not long after opening, Rose Pistola was acclaimed "best Italian restaurant in San Francisco" in a *Chronicle* review, so go prepared for a crowd.

Rôti

155 Steuart St. ☎ 415/ 495-6500. AE, D, MC, V. Reservations recommended. Wheelchair accessible. Closed for lunch on Sat and Sun. FRENCH. **$$**.

Spit-roasted poultry and game hot from the brick rotisserie are principal players on the French-accented menu at this congenial brick-walled bistro. The sidewalk tables are great for an end-of-the-day cocktail; move inside for dinner and make an evening of it.

Rubicon

558 Sacramento St. ☎ 415/434-4100. AE, MC, V. Reservations recommended. Wheelchair accessible. Closed Sun. CALIFORNIAN. **$$$**.

Power-eating patrons sneak furtive glances at surrounding tables, hoping for a glimpse of any of the celebs (DeNiro, Williams, Coppola) backing this place. Given these glamorous connections, the restaurant is surprisingly conservative—bland, even—in appearance (not that we need another Planet Hollywood, thank you): white walls, teak chair rails, the obligatory jumbo floral arrangements. Chef Traci Des Jardins's food is the star of this show, and simple dishes, like a crisp-skinned chicken in its own thyme-tinged juices, are her strength. The wine list is noteworthy. Don't fret if you're led to an upstairs table; the service tends to be a bit less frazzled on the 2nd floor.

Russian Renaissance

5241 Geary St. ☎ 415/752-8558. AE, D, MC, V. Reservations accepted. Wheelchair accessible. Dinner only. RUSSIAN. **$$$$**.

You might think the prices on the menu are given in rubles; they're sadly inflated, indeed. Nonetheless, this establishment has been serving hearty cutlets, stroganoff, and piroshkis for 37 years. The moody, gold-flecked murals that ring the room took more than a decade to complete; executed in a 16thC style, they have a religious icon quality to them. Come for an icy vodka, and toast the empire of your choice in this dim and haunting place.

★ Savoy Brasserie

580 Geary St. ☎ 415/474-8686. AE, DC, MC, V. Reservations accepted. Wheelchair accessible. Dinner only. FRENCH. **$$**.

Originally constructed by the Gump family in 1915 as a grocery store, this pleasant restaurant stays true to its origins by serving market-fresh food. Among the most atmospheric casual French spots in town, the ample tables are surrounded by checkered wicker chairs; deep leather-seated booths and banquettes encourage dawdling. A simple house salad of wild greens, sassed up with balsamic vinegar and black currants, is a fine prelude to any of the grilled or roasted entrees. The Brasserie's prix fixe theater menu, prepared with the same care as the regular board, is quite a deal: 3 courses for $23.

Sol y Luna

475 Sacramento St. ☎ 415/296-8696. AE, MC, V. Reservations recommended. Wheelchair accessible. Closed Sun. MEDITERRANEAN. **$$**.

Theatrical sweeps of wood, concrete, and metal shoot through this multileveled space with a vigor that's reflected in the Spanish menu. Construct a meal from the many tapas plates, or work up an appetite and go for the paella. Flamenco performances are staged several times a week.

South Park Cafe

108 South Park. ☎ 415/495-7275. AE, MC, V. Reservations recommended. Wheelchair accessible. Closed Sun. FRENCH. **$$**.

This South Park pioneer has a timeless presence about it—and not simply because the clock is permanently, poetically stopped. The decor is understated, with framed black-and-white photographs constituting the only formal

Savoy Brasserie

ornament in the wainscoted room. Chicken preparations are simple and trustworthy, and the seasonal vegetable plate with couscous is very well done. If it's busy—and it usually is—the staff can set you up at the zinc-topped bar, but you can also press for one of the 2 or 3 sidewalk tables.

★★ Stars

150 Redwood Alley. ☎ 415/861-7827. AE, MC, V. Reservations recommended. Wheelchair accessible. Closed for lunch on Sat and Sun. CALIFORNIAN. **$$$$**.

The location initiates the allure: a narrow alley around the corner from the cultural and political heart of San Francisco. Inside, the excitement escalates, as a dull roar of clattering dishes and conversation envelops you; Stars, with its brass rails and brash scale, is a natural see-and-be-seen place. The food is high-profile, too. Rich, sometimes on the verge of extravagantly so, Jeremiah Tower's kitchen has hit its stride with a solid menu of fresh Californian fare. Right around the corner, **Stars Cafe** (500 Van Ness Ave.; ☎ 415/861-4344; **$$**; AE, MC, V; closed Mon) invites the hoi poloi (not to mention Stars' own overflow) to an only slightly less stellar party.

The Stinking Rose

325 Columbus Ave. ☎ 415/781-ROSE. AE, MC, V. Reservations recommended. Wheelchair accessible. ITALIAN. **$$**.

Nosferatu himself would be hard pressed to resist the aromas emanating from this temple to the stinking rose, i.e., garlic. If you're not up to an entree of 40-clove chicken, order a plate of baked bulbs (a dollar apiece) and construct an à la carte meal. Even die-hard fans of the pungent plant concede this single-subject eatery can get a little carried away— garlic ice cream is at best an acquired taste.

Suppenküche

601 Hayes St. ☎ 415/252-9289. MC, V. Reservations for parties of 6 or more. GERMAN. **$$**.

When it's crowded, you'll share the long pine tables with a patchwork clientele:

Members of the generation formerly known as X, assorted professionals, and normal people all cohabit this small, simple room. The bill of fare is soul-satisfying albeit style-conscious cooking; recipes give a nod to Teutonic tradition then boldly go where few would imagine Bavarian cuisine could go.

★ Tadich Grill

240 California St. ☎ 415/391-2373. No credit cards. No reservations. Wheelchair accessible. Closed on Sat and Sun. AMERICAN. **$$**.

Despite the spartan decor of bare wood booths and tables, the atmosphere of this old guard eatery is welcoming, owing to a near palpable air of satisfaction generated by the hungry hordes who congregate here. While there's a full American menu, seafood is the way to go; order a platter of sand dabs or a bowl of piping hot cioppino and you can't miss. If your schedule permits, beat the lunch and dinner crowds—and the almost inevitable wait for a table—by supping around three o'clock with other long-time Tadich fans.

Ti Couz

3108 16th St. ☎ 415/252-7373. MC, V. No reservations. Wheelchair accessible. ECLECTIC. **$**.

Hanker for a crepe? The once ubiquitous pancake (remember the Magic Pan?) is undergoing a resurgence in popularity, at least in this hip-but-homey Mission District spot.

★ Tommy Toy's Cuisine Chinoise

655 Montgomery St. ☎ 415/397-4888. AE, MC, V. Reservations recommended. Wheelchair accessible. Closed for lunch on Sat and Sun. CHINESE. **$$$.**

At the city's most upscale Asian restaurant, there's a delicious cross-cultural exchange ongoing between classic French and Chinese cuisines. Vanilla prawns with raisins and melon slices may sound like a culinary stretch, but the incongruous combination is sublime. And the service can't be faulted—if you're in a hurry, you're in and out with the same courtesy extended to diners who opt to linger in the opulent, tapestry-strewn interior, fashioned after the 19thC quarters of the Empress Dowager's sitting room.

★ Vertigo

600 Montgomery St. ☎ 415/433-7250. AE, MC, V. Reservations recommended. Wheelchair accessible. Closed Sun. CALIFORNIAN. **$$$**.

Triangles and tapering planes abound (after all, we're in the Transamerica Pyramid) in this Milanese-inspired interior, rich with dark woods and conical frosted-glass lights. The kitchen is capable of producing some dizzying fare: Cold crab and mango spring rolls are a light starter, perhaps followed by ginger-lemongrass roast poussin with tatsoi-shiitake salad. If there's a locus to all the action, it's the restaurant's lower level, edged on two sides by the kitchen; on the mezzanine, tables are above the buzz, and some are tucked into triangular alcoves that jut into the redwood grove that towers outside. Service is knowing and attentive—a necessity under such bustling conditions.

Yank Sing

427 Battery St. ☎ 415/781-1111. AE, D, MC, V. Reservations accepted. Wheelchair accessible. Lunch only. CHINESE. **$.**

Tadich Grill

Devotees of dim sum—savory Chinese snacks such as *ha gow* (shrimp dumplings), *cha siu bow* (steamed barbecued pork buns), *gee cheung fun* (steamed rice-noodle rolls) and *chun guen* (spring rolls)—make this Western-styled restaurant a regular refueling stop. There's no written menu; just select whatever delicacies you want from the parade of pushcarts that circulate through the room. The bill is tallied by counting the number of plates you've accumulated—and that can be quite a pile.

Zuñi Café

1658 Market St. ☎ 415/552-2522. AE, MC, V. Reservations recommended. Wheelchair accessible. Closed Mon. CALIFORNIAN. **$$$.** Ever-fashionable, this casual-chic restaurant has ridden the crest of several food fads since its inception in the early 1980s; certain immutable menu items remain among the choice picks. Half of San Francisco swears by the Caesar salad, and the remainder of the populace falls into a reverie over the hamburger on focaccia. Don't be afraid to balk if you're directed to a table in the back room on the upper level; the people-watching on the ground floor is worth waiting for.

Cafes and Coffee Bars

There's no reason to fall into the clutches of innocuous lunch counters for your morning (or afternoon or evening) java break. San Francisco is rife with coffeehouses of all characters: dingy espresso dives from the days of Kerouac to New Age holistic haunts.

So you think a latté is a latté is a latté? Better reconsider, dear reader. As the proprietors of **Organic Grounds** (1307 9th Ave.; ☎ 415/661-1255) point out, the hallowed bean is the world's 3rd largest pesticide-treated crop, following cotton and tobacco. Here you can rest assured your joe is pure.

Perhaps such P.C. trivia would interest the patrons of **Cafe Flore** (2298 Market St.; ☎ 415/621-8579), where it's virtually *de rigueur* to bring your Macintosh Powerbook, spread out the newspaper (*not* the Business section), and while away the afternoon revising your film script. Sounds like a poseur's paradise, you say? Well, maybe—go see for yourself.

(Should you have left your laptop at home, plug into the Internet at **Muddy Waters** (260 Church St.; ☎ 415/621-2233), where a quarter gets you 5 minutes of on-line time at their terminal.)

If you're inclined toward more old-fashioned media, check out **Cafe de la Presse** (352 Grant Ave.; ☎ 415/398-2680). Gitanes fill the air at this international newsstand cum cafe, a fine place to pick up a copy of *Der Stern* or *Paris Match* and observe less self-possessed visitors gawk at the gateway to Chinatown across the street.

From this spot it's only a few blocks to the storied coffeehouses of North Beach. But first, drop in at **Cafe Claude** (7 Claude Lane; ☎ 415/392-3505), a modernist cafe in the French way. Its umbrella-shaded bistro tables set in a cul-de-sac are usually filled by shopping bag–laden veterans of Union Square.

A trio of classic cafes awaits in the Italian quarter: At **Caffe Trieste** (609 Vallejo St.; ☎ 415/392-6739) they've been playing backgammon and drinking *doppios* here since way back when; next to City Lights Books, the bilevel **Vesuvio Cafe** (255 Columbus Ave.; ☎ 415/362-3370) has overlooked the bustle of Columbus Avenue since the 1940s. And just across the street, sink into the inviting coffee-colored dimness of **Tosca Cafe** (242 Columbus Ave.; ☎ 415/391-1244), order a trademark cappuccino with brandy, and let the operatic arias lilting from the jukebox take you where they will.

Conclude your caffeine-fueled excursion at **Mad Magda's Russian Tea Room & Cafe** (579 Hayes St.; ☎ 415/864-7654) where a half-dozen mismatched brass chandeliers droop overhead, tarot cards and mandalas are painted on the floor, and music that might be labeled "alternative harpsichord" wafts through the narrow space. Call ahead and you can have your fortune told over oat cakes and Russian tea.

Wine Bars

When the intimate champagne cellar **Cava 555** (555 2nd St.; ☎ 415/543-2282) opened a few years back, the chic clientele expressed collective high hopes that the food would quickly rise to the heights of the wine list. Well, they're still waiting, albeit as stylishly as ever. Grab a glass of bubbly while you wait for a cab to **Hayes and Vine Wine Bar** (377 Hayes St.; ☎ 415/626-5301) where the postmodern room's autumnal golds, greens, and purples recall a vineyard palette. A scant 45 patrons can sample and scrutinize the 350 still, sparkling, and dessert wines poured. Between 25 and 30 vintages are available by the glass, with 4-wine flight tastings offered to challenge the palates of expert and ingenue oenophiles alike.

Cozier still, the **Dare to be Different** wine bar at Stars (see the restaurant's entry, above) seats an elite 5 persons. Up to 20 wines are available in 2-ounce tastes or full glasses, with snacks or complete meals also offered.

Taverns/Beer Cellars

If you want to see where the city's most renowned beers are brewed, reserve a spot on a tour of the **Anchor Brewing Company** (1705 Mariposa St.; ☎ 415/863-8350), home to Anchor Steam and its seasonal guises (samples are given at the visit's end). **20 Tank Brewery** (316 11th St.; ☎ 415/255-9455) is at the forefront of the city's current crop of microbreweries; try a pint of the tongue-twisting Kinnikinick along with the above-average pub grub. The indigenous industrial quality of the building has been kept intact: a cast-iron catwalk acts as band stage. Because it's in the midst of many of the SoMa clubs (Boz Scaggs's **Slim's** is across the street), 20 Tank is a prime pre- and post-show watering hole for touring musicians.

The crowd at **Gordon Biersch** (2 Harrison St.; ☎ 415/243-8246) is more tony, and generally less interested in the house's German-style lagers than they are in impressing one other. The bayfront location in the former Hills Bros. coffee plant ensures a good view for diners on the 2nd floor.

A couple of notable watering holes in the Haight attract local suds devotees: **Toronado** (547 Haight St.; ☎ 415/863-2276) boasts more than 40 brews on tap from around the world; if you're looking for a game of darts with your Guinness, head for **Mad Dog in the Fog** (530 Haight St.; ☎ 415/626-7279).

ACCOMMODATIONS

BECAUSE IT'S SUCH A COMPACT CITY, NO MATTER WHICH part of town you stay in, you can still enjoy the diverse textures of San Francisco. If business brings you downtown, it's most convenient to room in one of that area's high-rise hotels—but the genteel lodgings of Nob Hill and Pacific Heights are only a 10-minute cable-car ride away. Leisure travelers, too, can take advantage of the city's small size: If you hang your hat near Golden Gate Park, the attractions of Yerba Buena Gardens or the Embarcadero are eminently reachable by car or public transportation.

Reservations

When making reservations (and in this most popular destination, they're a necessity at all times of year), there are some tricks of the trade that can help shave a few dollars off the asking price of a room. Inquire about weekend and corporate discounts. There are booking agents that secure lower rates at many hotels: Contact **California Reservations** (☎ 800/576-0003), **Hotel Reservations Network** (☎ 800/96-HOTEL), **Central Reservation Service** (☎ 800/548-3311), or **San Francisco Reservations** (☎ 415/227-1500 or 800/677-1550). A knowledgeable travel agent should be aware of these options, but it doesn't hurt to prompt him or her (since they typically work on a commission basis) to investigate them for you.

Price Chart
$ = Up to $120
$$ = $120–$150
$$$ = $150–$200
$$$$ = $200 plus

Keep in mind there is typically a range of accommodations offered by each establishment; rate categories have been assigned based on the cost of a standard double room, before the steep 14% San Francisco room tax is added. In Oakland, the surcharge is 11%.

Establishments assigned 1 and 2 stars are especially recommended.

Hotels by Neighborhood

Castro

★★ Anna's Three Bears. **$$$$**

Civic Center

★ The Archbishop's Mansion. **$$$$**
Inn at the Opera. **$$**
The Phoenix. **$**

Convention Center/ Yerba Buena Gardens

ANA Hotel San Francisco. **$$$**
Hotel Milano. **$$**
San Francisco Marriott. **$$$**

Downtown/Union Square

★ Campton Place. **$$$**
The Clift. **$$$$**
The Donatello. **$$$**
Hotel Diva. **$$**
★ Hotel Monaco. **$$**
Hotel Rex. **$$**
Hotel Triton. **$$**
The Palace. **$$$$**
Petite Auberge. **$$**
Prescott Hotel. **$$$**
Savoy Hotel. **$$**
White Swan Inn. **$$**

Embarcadero

Harbor Court Hotel. **$$**
★ Hotel Griffon. **$$**

Financial District

★ Mandarin Oriental. **$$$$**

The Haight/Golden Gate Park

The Red Victorian Bed & Breakfast Inn. **$**
Stanyan Park Hotel. **$**

Nob Hill

The Fairmont. **$$$$**
★★ The Huntington Hotel. **$$$**
★ Mark Hopkins Inter-Continental. **$$$$**
Nob Hill Lambourne. **$$**
★ The Ritz-Carlton San Francisco. **$$$**

North Beach

★ Hotel Bohème. **$**
San Remo Hotel. **$**
The Washington Square Inn. **$$**

Pacific Heights

El Drisco Hotel. **$**
★★ The Sherman House. **$$$$**

East Bay (Oakland)

★ Claremont Resort and Spa. **$$$**

Airports

Holiday Inn Oakland Airport. **$$**
Hyatt Regency San Francisco Airport. **$$**
Oakland Airport Hilton. **$$**
Radisson Hotel San Francisco Airport. **$$**

Accommodations A to Z

★★ Anna's Three Bears

114 Divisadero St., San Francisco, CA 94117. ☎ 415/255-3167; 800/428-8559; fax: 415/552-2959. 3 flats. AE, MC, V. **$$$$.**

Critic's Choice

If you're seeking to blend in with the citizenry, **Anna's Three Bears** is the choice for independent travelers; tucked away in a residential neighborhood, there is no sign to give away its identity, and you have an entire flat (and all its amenities) all to yourself. On the other hand, if you yearn to be treated like visiting royalty, the staff at the **Ritz-Carlton** specializes in spit-and-polish service. For those pursuing a more intimate form of pampering, the Carmen suite at the **Archbishop's Mansion** fits the bill with its romantic bath: an oversized claw-foot tub warmed by an antique marble fireplace. And if you want to get the ol' blood pumping in a more cardiovascular fashion, the superb health club facilities at the **Claremont** will have you glowing.

Even with no particular agenda, you have a choice of environments. Traditionalists favor the **Huntington,** the Nob Hill hostelry where linen towels and silk brocades set an elegant standard. With its flamboyant interiors, **Hotel Monaco** is the destination of the moment for modish travelers who want to check off another entry on the Been-There, Done-That itinerary. And capturing the title of "Lodging Most Pleasantly Lost in Time," **Hotel Bohème** charms with its Beat-era ambiance.

You don't so much check in to Anna's as come home to it. The 3 flats are on a quiet, tree-lined Buena Vista Heights block. Each has 2 or 3 bedrooms, kitchen, living room, and dining room, formally furnished with hand-picked Edwardian pieces. You can host your own intimate dinner using the crystal and antique place settings, then gather round the glowing fireplace for the evening or sit on your deck and watch the skyline. The fantasy will necessarily stop short if you wish to retire to the library with a good cigar—the premises are nonsmoking. For those who appreciate the rewards of immersing themselves in the unique patterns of local life (there's a manager on the premises, but for the most part, you're on your own), this is a fabulous find, particularly for extended stays where the constraints and impersonality of a hotel can be numbing. One drawback: Street parking can be hard to come by, so you can either confront the eccentricities of public transportation or rely on cab services.

★ The Archbishop's Mansion

1000 Fulton St., San Francisco, CA 94117. ☎ 415/563-7872; 800/543-5820; fax: 415/885-3193. 15 rooms. AE, MC, V. **$$$$**.

You might think you've intruded on a taping of

Masterpiece Theater—lustrous mahogany paneling, crystal chandeliers, classic artworks are everywhere—only this isn't a stage set, it's the real thing. Sumptuous is just a starting point when describing this 1904 structure, which faces redwood-studded Alamo Square park. A stained-glass dome crowns the grand stairway, collector's-quality Victorian and Belle Epoque furnishings grace the guest rooms, 10 of which have at least 1 working fireplace (the corner Carmen suite has 2, including 1 in the parlor-sized bathroom). While it's not suited to the needs of business travelers, couples looking for an amorous escape would be hard-pressed to find better accommodations. Breakfast, which is included in the room price, is served either in your room or in the banquet hall. *Amenities:* Conference facilities, in-room VCRs.

★ Campton Place

340 Stockton St., San Francisco, CA 94108. ☎ 415/781-5555; 800/235-4300; fax: 415/955-5536. 117 rooms. AE, D, DC, MC, V. **$$$**.

Of the lodgings that limn Union Square (a mix of mega- and mini-hotels), Campton Place pleases with its moderate size and superlative service, qualities that make it a repeat booking for business executives as well as leisure travelers. Typical of the pampering is the valet-assisted packing, in-house laundry, and room service from Campton Place Restaurant, which is under the delicious direction of Chef Todd Humphries. Last year's remodeling of the Chippendale- and Louis XVI–appointed rooms resulted in a notable upgrade of accommodations for guests with disabilities. *Amenities:* Restaurant, conference facilities, 12 rooms wheelchair accessible.

★ Claremont Resort and Spa

41 Tunnel Rd. Oakland, CA 94519. ☎ 510/843-3000; 800/551-7266; fax: 510/848-6208. 239 rooms. AE, D, DC, MC, V. **$$$**.

Toto, we're not in San Francisco anymore. Set among 22 idyllic hillside acres, the Claremont sprawls, a silver-white Victorian castle among the aromatic eucalyptus. A million-dollar view of the whole of San Francisco and the bay is at your feet, and the peerless facilities of the $6 million spa are at your beck and call, overshadowing any other Bay Area hotel's health club offerings. But it's not all play and no work at the Claremont; the hotel is adding 40 new rooms and suites to the north wing, designed with the needs of the business traveler in mind. This escape from San Francisco's concrete canyons is a quick 20-minute drive across the Bay Bridge—we've been stuck in Financial District traffic for much longer than that. *Amenities:* Large health club, spa, exercise room, 2 outdoor pools, 3 restaurants, conference facilities, 10 outdoor tennis courts (6 lighted), 8 rooms wheelchair accessible.

The Clift

495 Geary St., San Francisco, CA 94102. ☎ 415/775-4700; 800/HERITAGE; fax: 415/441-4621. 329 rooms. AE, D, DC, MC, V. **$$$$**.

Plan your assault on Union Square from this bastion of traditionalism, which celebrated its 80th anniversary in 1995. Elegant but not intimidating, the Clift's Georgian-accented rooms are washed in restful pastel hues; along with the Palace, it's one of downtown's two high-end holdovers against the wave of boutique lodgings that have sprung up throughout the area. Still, change is in the air. Long a choice of the blue-chip corporate set, the hotel, which is under new management, is now reaching out to families, evidenced by its enlightened attitude when it comes to children and—gasp!—pets. Under the aegis of the "Young Travelers Program," necessities from infant bathtubs to strollers are available through housekeeping; room service pitches in with Hershey's Kisses and other goodies on call. Books, games, and videos are also on hand. For 4-footed visitors, there's food, toys, and other creature comforts. Whether the Clift can successfully be all things to all guests without diluting its standards is a question to be answered over time. *Amenities:* Exercise room, 2 restaurants, conference facilities, 3 rooms wheelchair accessible.

The Donatello

501 Post St., San Francisco, CA 94102. ☎ 415/441-7100; 800/227-3184; fax: 415/885-8842. 94 rooms. AE, D, DC, MC, V. **$$$**.

No niche-marketing gimmickry here; this small, well-maintained hotel stands quite stylishly and steadily on its merits: unobtrusive service, unusually spacious guest quarters (request a room that opens onto the terrace) done in a contemporary mode, and a penthouse-level lobby that's an easeful place for an informal meeting or to unwind at day's end. Those whose tastes run to the wild consider the Donatello a bit bland, but if you're coming in on a quick trip and don't like surprises, you'll likely appreciate its restraint and central location. *Amenities:* Small health club, restaurant, conference facilities.

El Drisco Hotel

2901 Pacific St., San Francisco, CA 94115. ☎ 415/346-2880; 800/634-7277; fax: 415/567-5537. 30 rooms. AE, MC, V. **$**.

It's a fair bet that most San Franciscans wouldn't recognize the name of this intimate embassy-area hotel; discretion with distinction is the El Drisco's trademark. Constructed in 1903, it has played host to presidents Truman, Eisenhower, and Nixon. Yet the tariffs for the Federalist-style rooms and suites, most of which enjoy bay or city views, are a far cry from bloated government-scale budgets. While it could hardly be further from the business center of town, execs who value the psychological distance between the workplace and the home (or hotel room, as is the case) hold the El Drisco in esteem. Complimentary continental breakfasts are served in the dining room. *Amenities:* Conference facilities.

The Fairmont

950 Mason St., San Francisco, CA 94108-2098. ☎ 415/772-5000; 800/527-4727; fax: 415/789-3929. 596 rooms. AE, DC, MC, V. **$$$$**.

The Fairmont is the beloved dowager of San Francisco's upper-echelon hotels—but it's time someone told the old girl that hobble skirts are no longer fashionable. The premises adhere to a stiff, outmoded expression of luxury and could use a definite makeover. Reportedly, the recently realigned ownership is going to exercise some of their fiscal muscle and expedite the renovation, a move that will be of more note to the corporate and convention travelers who frequent the property rather than the polyester-clad tourists who stalk the lobby looking for the bearded guy who played Dr. Kiley (yes, this is that hotel). If you're Nob Hill–bound, you can do better. *Amenities:* Health club, 5 restaurants, conference facilities, 9 rooms wheelchair accessible.

Harbor Court Hotel

165 Steuart St., San Francisco, CA 94105. ☎ 415/882-1300; 800/346-0555; fax: 415/882-1313. 131 rooms. AE, D, DC, MC, V. **$$**.

By trying to appeal to both professional and recreational travelers, this hotel falls a little short at each end. The guest rooms are too residential in appearance for business standards and too cramped for the comfort of tourists, a fact that even the expansive wall mirrors, placed to optimize the striking bay and bridge views, can't disguise. And the perturbing dodge of supplying terry-cloth bathrobes only to the waterfront rooms is hardly hospitable. *Amenities:* Privileges at neighboring health club, restaurant, 5 rooms wheelchair accessible.

★ Hotel Bohème

444 Columbus Ave., San Francisco, CA 94133. ☎ 415/433-9111; fax: 415/362-6292. 15 rooms. AE, D, DC, MC, V. **$**.

You can almost hear the time-muted echo of bongos at this new North Beach lodge, where the Beats—as in Allen Ginsberg and Jack Kerouac—definitely still go on. The sunny rooms are tricked out in neo-Boho fashion, with lamp shades of jazz sheet music, wicker chairs, and black iron beds against walls painted in crazy shades of cantaloupe and sage. A hallway gallery of black-and-white photos by Jerry Stoll documents the North Beach scene of the 1950s and 1960s. Can you dig it? If you're free of spirit and don't mind climbing the hotel's stairs, chances are you will.

Hotel Diva

440 Geary St., San Francisco, CA 94102. ☎ 415/885-0200; 800/553-1900; fax: 415/346-6613. 108 rooms. AE, DC, MC, V. **$$**.

Formerly on the cutting edge of chic boutique hotels, the Diva has since dulled; the once-slick rooms are in need of a general spiffing up. Theater lovers may overlook any shortcomings, though, as the Curran and Geary venues are directly across the street. And the staff is as buoyant and accommodating as ever—although with so many superior choices in the immediate area, their efforts may be in vain. *Amenities:* Conference facilities, in-room VCRs, 6 rooms wheelchair accessible.

★ Hotel Griffon

155 Steuart St., San Francisco, CA 94105. ☎ 415/495-2100; 800/321-2201; fax: 415/495-3522. 62 rooms. AE, D, DC, MC, V. **$$**.

The loft-like feel of these quarters, with their exposed white-washed brick walls, soaring ceilings, and contemporary wooden furniture, is a stimulating switch from the overtly ornate decor that is found at many of the city's hotels. Add in bay views from some rooms, the ever-hot **Rôti** restaurant

Accommodations

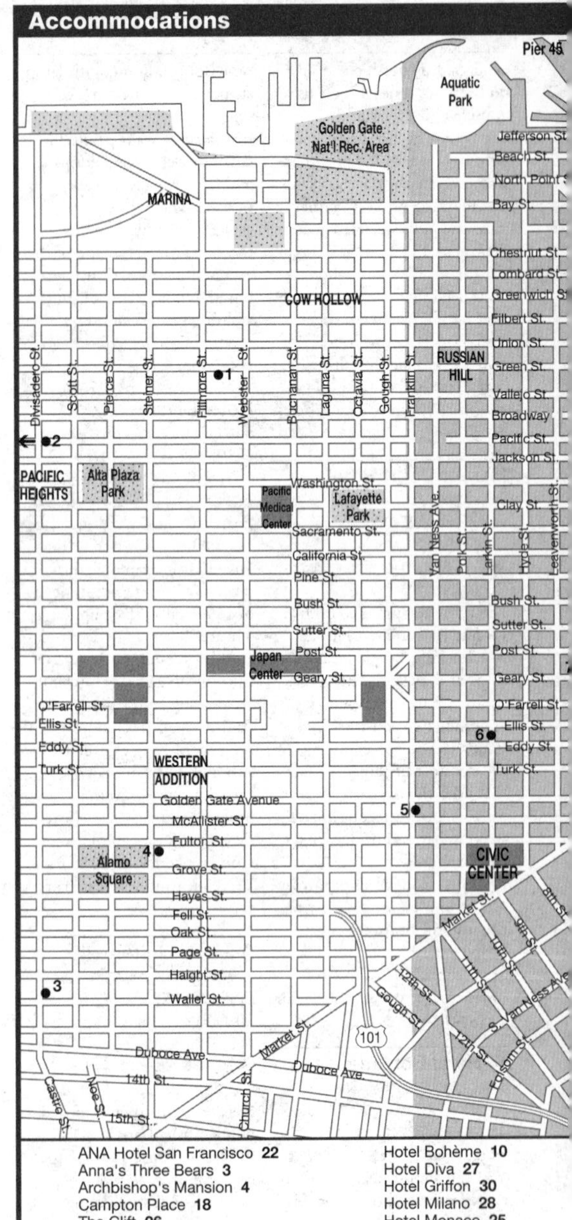

ANA Hotel San Francisco **22**
Anna's Three Bears **3**
Archbishop's Mansion **4**
Campton Place **18**
The Clift **26**
The Donatello **24**
El Drisco Hotel **2**
The Fairmont **13**
Harbor Court **31**
Hotel Bohème **10**
Hotel Diva **27**
Hotel Griffon **30**
Hotel Milano **28**
Hotel Monaco **25**
Hotel Rex **16A**
Hotel Triton **19**
Huntington Hotel **11**
Inn at the Opera **5**

Mandarin Oriental **20**
Mark Hopkins Inter-Continental **12**
Nob Hill Lambourne **17**
The Palace **21**
Petite Auberge **15**
The Phoenix **6**
Prescott Hotel **23**
The Red Victorian Bed & Breakfast Inn **33**
The Ritz-Carlton San Francisco **14**
San Francisco Mariott **29**
San Remo **8**
Savoy Hotel **7**
Sherman House **1**
Stanyan Park Hotel **32**
Washington Square Inn **9**
White Swan Inn **16**

downstairs (see review on page 37), and a comfortable proximity to the Financial District and Union Square, and you've got a winner. *Amenities:* Privileges at neighboring health club, restaurant, conference facilities, 3 rooms wheelchair accessible.

Hotel Milano

55 5th St., San Francisco, CA 94103. ☎ 415/543-8555; 800/398-7555; fax: 415/543-5843. 108 rooms. AE, D, DC, MC, V. **$$**.

Around the corner from the **Center for the Arts at Yerba Buena Gardens** (see listing on page 74), this SoMa newcomer is positioning itself to become the home-away-from-Hollywood for film crews on location shoots in the photogenic city; its conference room is wired for up to 80 direct-line telephones, and there's a professional screening room. But you don't have to be Quentin Tarantino to reap the benefits of the Milano; it's the smartest alternative for trade show visitors to the hulking hotel monoliths that pervade the convention center area. The interior takes its cues from Giorgio Armani's Milan digs, with light woods and sculptural forms throughout. It's worth the extra few dollars for a superior or deluxe room; otherwise, you could find yourself with an airshaft vista. *Amenities:* Small health club, exercise room, restaurant, conference facilities, 5 rooms wheelchair accessible.

★ Hotel Monaco

501 Geary St., San Francisco, CA 94102. ☎ 415/292-0100; 800/214-4220; fax: 415/292-0111. 201 rooms. AE, D, DC, MC, V. **$$**.

From the moment you set eyes on the front desk—an oversized faux Louis Vuitton steamer trunk—you know this isn't your average accommodation. Fresh from a $24-million makeover, the Monaco is filled with extravagant touches of the exotic that set it apart from the mainstream. Finished in lacquer, silk, and velour, the rooms boldly mix Asian, Mediterranean, and Middle Eastern motifs in uncompromising colors of persimmon, turquoise, and vermilion. In short, this place has attitude that wholly becomes its theater district location; Brooks Brothers types need not apply. Suites can be on the confining side, but number 720 has an especially enviable view of downtown. *Amenities:* Small health club, exercise room, restaurant, conference facilities, 12 rooms wheelchair accessible.

Hotel Rex

562 Sutter St., San Francisco, CA 94102. ☎ 415/433-4434; 800/433-4434; fax 415/433-3695. 94 rooms. AE, MC, V. **$$**.

Enthusiastically positioned by management as the "West Coast Algonquin for the 21st Century," this just-renovated hotel hopes to draw an arts and letters crowd. The atmospheric lobby, modeled after literary salons of the 1920s, is invitingly dim and furnished with period pieces and artworks. Rooms tend to be large and affect a chic-drab mode: dark woods, deep colors, somber patterns (an accessory oddly absent given the Algonquin aspirations: books in the guest quarters). Inquire about the discounted "arts rate," where a portion of the tariff is donated to your choice of local performance and exhibition groups. *Amenities:* Conference facilities, 4 rooms wheelchair accessible.

Hotel Triton

342 Grant Ave., San Francisco, CA 94108. ☎ 415/394-0500; 800/433-6611; fax: 415/394-0555. 140 rooms. AE, D, DC, MC, V. **$$**.

A spirited—no, make that an exuberant—hipness ferments here: Furnishings are the unbridled geometric creations of local designers, walls are hand-finished in graphic patterns with gold-leaf highlights. The Triton could be a prototype for Hotel MTV. In addition to the standard accommodations, there's a quartet of suites customized by the late Jerry Garcia, Nicholas Graham (aka Joe Boxer of undershorts fame), and Suzan Briganti, as well as 24 EcoRooms, where guests enjoy all-natural linens, energy-efficient lighting, biodegradable toiletries, and water and air filtration systems. Reflecting the creative clientele, weekday limo service runs to the South of Market area. If you're looking for a less frenzied but equally forward aesthetic experience, try the Hotel Monaco or Hotel Milano. *Amenities:* Exercise room, 2 restaurants, conference facilities, 7 rooms wheelchair accessible.

★★ The Huntington Hotel

1075 California St., San Francisco, CA 94108. ☎ 415/474-5400; 800/652-1539 (CA only); 800/227-4683 (U.S.); fax: 415/474-6227. 140 rooms. AE, DC, MC, V. **$$$**.

Comfort for the mind and body is the first concern of the staff at this Nob Hill retreat; the rich, famous, and otherwise privileged have appreciated these qualities since 1945, when the erstwhile apartment building on Huntington Park was converted into a hotel. More recently, its guest rooms have been completely redone by Los Angeles designer Charles Gruwell, with characters ranging from cushy cosmopolitan to elegant French Empire. The **Big Four Restaurant** (named for the quartet of 19thC railroad baron nabobs Leland Stanford, Collis Huntington, Charles Crocker, and Mark Hopkins) is an enclave of power eating. For our money, this is the best choice for Nob Hill lodgings if you're looking for a distinctive luxury experience. *Amenities:* Privileges at the **Club One Fitness Centers**, restaurant, conference facilities, 12 rooms wheelchair accessible.

Inn at the Opera

333 Fulton St., San Francisco, CA 94102. ☎ 415/863-8400; 800/325-2708; fax: 415/861-0821. 48 rooms. AE, D, DC, MC, V. **$$**.

The most personable of the Civic Center area's accommodations, this plush, intimate hotel at the confluence of the city's performing arts venues is popular with visiting artists (Luciano Pavarotti, Mikhail Baryshnikov, Twyla Tharp) and their well-heeled aficionados. Culture vultures will love the location; for more business-minded travelers, a complimentary limo runs crosstown to the Financial District. On weekends, when the bustle of the government center evaporates, this neighborhood can seem a little empty, so be prepared to strike out and explore to avoid ennui. Concierges from other hotels have been known to curry favor to obtain tickets that are put on hold for the Inn's guests. *Amenities:* Restaurant, conference facilities, 2 rooms wheelchair accessible.

★ Mandarin Oriental

222 Sansome St., San Francisco, CA 94104. ☎ 415/885-0999; 800/622-0404; fax: 415/433-0289. 158 rooms. AE, D, DC, MC, V. **$$$$**.

Occupying the top 11 floors of the city's 3rd-tallest tower, there isn't a bad sight in the house at the slick Mandarin. Amenities are comparably top-notch: The marble soaking bathtubs in the Mandarin rooms have picture windows. The level of personal service is literally singular, as the hotel maintains almost a one-to-one ratio between employees and guests. This is a significant effort for a chain establishment to make, and it pays off by eclipsing the cookie-cutter impressions made by the Mandarin's competitors throughout the city. Sophisticated business travelers will appreciate the state-of-the-art support center located off the street entrance. *Amenities:* Privileges at **Bay Club** health club, 2 restaurants, conference facilities, 11 rooms wheelchair accessible.

★ Mark Hopkins InterContinental

1 Nob Hill, San Francisco, CA 94108. ☎ 415/392-3434; 800/327-0200; fax: 415/421-3302. 391 rooms. AE, DC, MC, V. **$$$$**.

History is everywhere at this Nob Hill fixture, from the front door where uniformed doorman Mark "Smilin' Jack" O'Neil exchanged salutes with General Charles de Gaulle, to the 19th-floor **Top of the Mark** lounge, whose north-west nook earned the moniker "Weepers' Corner" when anxious wives and sweethearts of World War II servicemen clustered here, watching their loved ones' ships sail out from the Golden Gate. (Altitude enthusiasts—or acrophobes—take note: The Mark boasts the city's highest guests rooms.) Rising in 2 wings of the building, the accommodations are timeless; neoclassic furnishings were installed as part of a recently-concluded refurbishment. Sneak a peek at the 9 restored murals in the Room of the Dons, which depict the early days of California. *Amenities:* Exercise room; restaurants, conference facilities, executive floors, 12 rooms wheelchair accessible.

Nob Hill Lambourne

725 Pine St., San Francisco, CA 94108. ☎ 415/433-2287; fax: 415/433-0975. 20 rooms. AE, D, DC, MC, V. **$$**.

The service at the Lambourne is tailored to satisfy a very particular breed of guest: one who is equal parts workaholic and health enthusiast; the overall effect, while not unpleasant, bespeaks some sort of superbeing persona that can prove quietly disturbing to even first-generation New Agers. The PC, fax machine, and voice-mail phones found in its rooms are counterbalanced by their deep soaking tub and aromatherapeutic bath oils, stationary bike, and natural foods honor bar. Wellness videos from Joseph Campbell's "Power of Myth" to "Marty Liquori's Runner's Workout" are available at the front desk, which is adjacent to the 24-hour business center and its array of printers, photocopier, and modem. Rooms also feature fully stocked kitchenettes. *Amenities:* Privileges at **Nob Hill Health**

Mark Hopkins InterContinental

Club, massage room, conference facilities, in-room VCRs.

The Palace

2 New Montgomery St., San Francisco, CA 94105. ☎ 415/392-8600; 800/325-3535; fax: 415/543-0671. 550 rooms. AE, D, MC, V. **$$$$**.

The guest register reads like a history book: Ulysses Grant, Franklin Roosevelt, Enrico Caruso, Mark Twain, Cornelius Vanderbilt, Oscar Wilde . . . the list of luminaries who've hung their hats at this landmark goes on forever. The guest rooms are eminently comfortable but nothing special, the amenities first-class as expected, but it's the public areas that lend legitimacy to the hotel's name: the jaw-dropping Garden Court, its 80,000-pane leaded glass canopy floating 4 stories over the heads of tea-takers and diners; and the centerpiece of the **Pied Piper Bar,** a radiant, enormous 1909 Maxfield Parrish canvas. *Amenities:* Large health club, exercise room, indoor pool, 3 restaurants, conference facilities, executive floors, 20 rooms wheelchair accessible.

Petite Auberge

863 Bush St., San Francisco, CA 94108. ☎ 415/928-6000; 800/365-3004; fax: 415/775-5717. 26 rooms. AE, MC, V. **$$**.

We wonder why some folks come to the heart of the city only to stay in the country. Dyed-in-the-wool romantics may find it hard to tear themselves away from these French-country chambers, with frills and florals in full bloom. Eighteen snug rooms are kept toasty by fireplaces. Afternoon tea, accompanied by savories and sweets, is served in a cheery parlor (a tromp l'oeil farmer's market scene covers the walls) that opens onto a picturesque cottage garden. It's more likely you'll encounter Martha Stewart in these halls than Susan Powter.

The Phoenix

601 Eddy St., San Francisco, CA 94109. ☎ 415/776-1380; 800/CITY-INN; fax: 415/885-3109. 44 rooms. AE, DC, MC, V. **$**.

In spite of the surrounding sleaze, or perhaps because of it—it's located in one of the city's seediest neighborhoods—the Phoenix has attracted such notables as JFK Jr., Faye Dunaway, Pearl Jam, and k.d. lang to its para-tropical quarters. Much like the Chelsea in New York City, the low-key quality of this funky former motel appeals to those seeking to maintain a low profile. Rooms ring a swimming pool that's a work of art in its own right; the courtyard hums with piped-in recordings of crickets, waterfalls, and jungle birds; and Caribbean restaurant **Miss Pearl's Jam House** (see review on page 35) is right next door, completing the artistic escapist illusion. If you're looking for a tongue-in-cheek place to stay and are up for a literal walk on the wild side, bring your water wings—and earplugs wouldn't be remiss, either. *Amenities:* Outdoor pool, restaurant, 20 rooms wheelchair accessible.

Prescott Hotel

545 Post St., San Francisco, CA 94102. ☎ 415/563-0303; 800/283-7322; fax: 415/563-6831. 166 rooms. AE, D, DC, MC, V. **$$$**.

Sink into one of the sofas by the lobby hearth and the hustle of the city instantly slips away: You're in the insular embrace of the Prescott. Tones of taupe, hunter green, and gold are used to handsome effect throughout the neoclassical interiors. The elegance reaches an apogee in the 7-story Club Level. There guests can retreat to a private lounge where a personal concierge ministers to one's every whim. Sounds nice, but it's nothing new; what makes the Prescott unique among the city's burgeoning boutique hotel population? The hotel accords preferred seatings at **Postrio** (see review on page 36) to guests, and you can also enjoy Wolfgang Puck's culinary wizardry through room service—perhaps the ultimate indulgence. *Amenities:* Restaurant, conference facilities, executive floors, 1 room wheelchair accessible.

The Red Victorian Bed & Breakfast Inn

1665 Haight St., San Francisco, CA 94117. ☎ 415/864-1978; fax: 415/863-3293. 18 rooms, 4 with private bath. AE, MC, V. **$**.

If you're determined to recreate the Summer of Love while in San Francisco, put some flowers in your hair and check in at the Red Vic, the only credible lodgings in the Haight. Each of the clean chambers is decorated in a highly individual (air quotes would be appropriate here) fashion; in the Redwood Forest Room, you'll slumber under a willow-bough canopy, while in the Rainbow Room, the bed is swathed in tie-dyed netting. Suffice it to say the Red Vic certainly isn't for everyone—if you're a card-carrying member of the Woodstock Nation, you'll fit right in—but its friendly karma is contagious.

★ The Ritz-Carlton San Francisco

600 Stockton St., San Francisco, CA 94108. ☎ 415/296-7465; 800/241-3333;

fax: 415/296-8559. 336 rooms. AE, D, DC, MC, V. **$$$**.
When the Ritz-Carlton opened its doors in 1991, it redefined luxury to a city that already had a firm grasp of the concept. Housed in a 1909 neoclassical landmark building on the slopes of Nob Hill, the hotel is decorated with veddy tasteful 18th- and 19th-C artworks and furnishings that make the conservative clientele feel right at home. They form an elegant backdrop to a calendar of special events which range from black-tie cigar-smoker dinners to holiday teddy-bear teas for children. Everyday service, as well, is exemplary without being forced or fawning; we think it's the best in the city. *Amenities:* Large health club, exercise room, indoor pool, 2 restaurants, conference facilities, executive floors, 7 rooms wheelchair accessible.

San Remo Hotel

2237 Mason St., San Francisco, CA 94133. ☎ 415/776-8688; 800/352-REMO; fax: 415/776-2811. 62 rooms with shared bath; penthouse with private bath. AE, DC, MC, V. **$**.
This fully restored 3-story Italianate structure was originally built as emergency housing in the aftermath of the 1906 earthquake (an altruistic role it repeated in 1989). The small quarters outfitted in homespun antiques appeal to cost-conscious visitors who find the clone character of the Fisherman's Wharf neighborhood amid hotels and motels aesthetically stifling. If shared baths aren't your cup of cappuccino, reserve well in advance for the penthouse, which offers a 360° view—a rarity at any price.

Savoy Hotel

580 Geary St., San Francisco, CA 94102. ☎ 415/441-2700; 800/227-4223; fax: 415/441-2700. 83 rooms. AE, D, DC, MC, V. **$$.**
Feather beds, suites with sitting rooms, and afternoon sherry are some of the civilities offered at this tasteful Theater District–hotel, which borrows from the classic Parisian pied-à-terre in terms of decor. Breakfast is included in the room rate; it's served in the thoroughly pleasant **Savoy Brasserie** (see review on page 38). This spot merits high marks for value. *Amenities:* Restaurant, conference facilities, 1 room wheelchair accessible.

★★ The Sherman House

2160 Green St., San Francisco, CA 94123. ☎ 415/563-3600; 800/424-5777; fax: 415/563-1882. 14 rooms. AE, DC, MC, V. **$$$$**.
The adage "If you have to ask, you can't afford it" applies at the Sherman House, where the sure hand of interior designer William Gaylord has orchestrated an eclectic cache of furnishings—exquisite examples of Jacobean, chinoiserie, and Biedermeier styles among them—into a seductive Second-Empire ambiance at this 1876 French-Italianate mansion in Pacific Heights. Accommodations in the Carriage House, set in a restored Thomas Church garden, are more contemporary than their counterparts in the Main House; all are the stuff of dreams, with every detail in place. The Paderewski Suite, with its dark wood wainscoting, beamed ceiling, and brocade-wrapped four-poster, is warmed by 2 hearths—a most inviting lair

The Sherman House

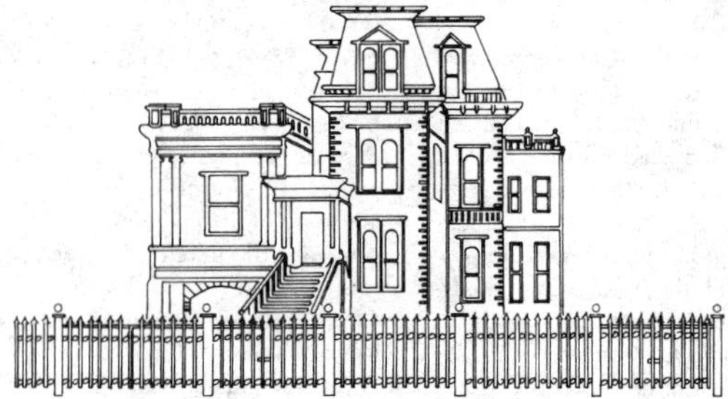

on a wet, windy day (although for the price of 1 night in the suite, you could jet off to balmier climes altogether). *Amenities:* Private dining room, conference facilities, 2 rooms wheelchair accessible.

Stanyan Park Hotel

750 Stanyan St., San Francisco, CA 94117. ☎ 415/751-1000; fax: 415/668-5454. 36 rooms. AE, MC, V. **$**.

Smack on the southeast corner of Golden Gate Park, this fully restored 1905 structure is scaled and sited just right for families and children who look to take advantage of all the park's attractions: the Asian Art Museum, the M. H. de Young Memorial Museum, the Natural History Museum, and its many and diverse horticultural highlights. Reproductions of American and English period pieces give the rooms—particularly the ones with fireplaces—a very cozy character. Once you've exhausted the possibilities of San Francisco's backyard, you might want to sample city life in a more central location; while tops as a base for park excursions, the Stanyan—set in a residential area—is a bit removed from the urban action. A continental breakfast, included in the cost of the room, is served in the guests-only dining room.

The Washington Square Inn

1660 Stockton St., San Francisco, CA 94133. ☎ 415/981-4220; 800/388-0220; fax: 415/397-7242. 15 rooms, 10 with private bath. AE, D, DC, MC, V. **$$**.

Midway between Fisherman's Wharf and the Financial District, this homey inn can serve as a comfortable base for both vacationers and business travelers. Filled with European antiques of a serviceable rather than museum quality, the rooms with bay window seats are fine vantage points to observe the happenings on historic Washington Square. If it were transplanted to Boston or Philadelphia, the Inn would be right at home—and in context-conscious San Francisco, that's quite the rub. We'd like to see it dusted off and respond to the potential of its location.

White Swan Inn

845 Bush St., San Francisco, CA 94108; ☎ 415/775-1755; 800/

999-9570; fax: 415/775-5717; 26 rooms; AE, MC, V. **$$**. The quiet sophistication of this English-flavored inn suits travelers looking for a genteel getaway. Indeed, it's the choice of many Bay Area suburbanites for weekend-in-the-city getaways. Spacious guest rooms are warm and welcoming, with mahogany four-posters and fireplaces. The library, outfitted with tufted wing-back chairs, tartan-covered couch, and well-stocked bookshelves, has an air of relaxed exclusivity—again, reassuring trappings of domesticity for those who are neither amused or intrigued by flash. In conjunction with other Four Sisters properties in the wine country, Monterey, and southern California, visitors can accumulate "frequent guest" benefits.

Hotels near the Airports and Convention Center

As is the norm, national chain lodgings predominate in airport locations. Modern and well-maintained, there are no surprises here: serviceable rooms at moderate prices.

Convenient to San Francisco International Airport

Hyatt Regency San Francisco Airport
1333 Bayshore Blvd., Burlingame, CA 94010. ☎ 415/347-1234; 800/233-1234; fax: 415/347-5948. 793 rooms. AE, D, DC, MC, V. **$$**.
Amenities: Health club, outdoor pool, 3 restaurants, conference facilities, complimentary airport van, 40 rooms wheelchair accessible.

Radisson Hotel San Francisco Airport
1177 Airport Blvd., Burlingame, CA 94010. ☎ 415/342-9200; 800/333-3333; fax: 415/342-1655. 301 rooms. AE, DC, MC, V. **$$**.
Amenities: Indoor and outdoor pool, restaurant, complimentary airport van, 4 rooms wheelchair accessible.

Convenient to Oakland Airport

Holiday Inn Oakland Airport
500 Hegenberger Rd., Oakland, CA 94621. ☎ 510/562-5311; 800/HOLIDAY; fax: 510/636-1539. 290 rooms. AE, D, DC, MC, V. **$$**.
Amenities: Exercise room, outdoor pool, 2 restaurants, conference facilities, complimentary airport van, 15 rooms wheelchair accessible.

Oakland Airport Hilton
1 Hegenberger Rd., Oakland, CA 94621. ☎ 510/635-5000; 800/445-8667. 365 rooms. AE, D, DC, MC, V. **$$**.
Amenities: Exercise room, outdoor pool, 2 restaurants, conference facilities, complimentary airport van, 5 rooms wheelchair accessible.

Convenient to the Moscone Convention Center, San Francisco

At the ready to provide business travelers with the basics, these 2 hotels strike a professional balance between atmosphere and efficiency.

ANA Hotel San Francisco

50 3rd St., San Francisco, CA 94103. ☎ 415/974-6400; 800/ANA-HOTELS; fax: 415/543-8268. 667 rooms. AE, DC, MC, V. **$$$**.

Amenities: Restaurant, conference facilities, executive floors, 14 rooms wheelchair accessible.

San Francisco Marriott

55 4th St., San Francisco, CA 94103. ☎ 415/896-1600; 800/228-9290; fax: 415/896-6176. 1,500 rooms. AE, D, DC, MC, V. **$$$**.

Amenities: Large health club, exercise room, indoor pool, 5 restaurants, conference facilities, executive floors, 42 rooms wheelchair accessible.

Sights and Attractions

"THE GAYEST, LIGHTEST-HEARTED, MOST PLEASURE-loving city of the Western Continent," was Will Irwin's assessment of San Francisco. Vitality and a sense of fun are key aspects of the city's personality, but beneath this froth, there's a bedrock of substantive culture and history: San Francisco is home to one of the West Coast's most important collections of modern art, one of the country's finest museums of natural history, and a wealth of eclectic architecture.

Lots of the city's sights are inexpensive to visit, and many more are totally free. At least 1 day a month, the major museums waive their regular admission fees, and schemes designed to facilitate attendance proliferate. For example, a Muni 1-, 3-, or 7-day **Passport** secures discounted admission to 24 attractions. **The Golden Gate Culture Pass** slices 30% off entry fees to the Asian Art Museum and the de Young Memorial Museum (☎ 415/391-2000 for details). And dollars-off coupons are widely available in visitor publications, making San Francisco a most affordable place in which to soak up the sights.

General Tours

Agentours (126 West Portal, ☎ 415/661-5200). Guided half-day tours in German, French, Italian, Spanish, Portuguese.

Gray Line of San Francisco (Union Square at Powell and Geary streets, ☎ 415/558-9400). Double-decker bus and 4-wheel "cable car" excursions through the city, day and night.

Quality Tours (5003 Palmetta, Suite 83, Pacifica, ☎ 415/994-5054). Their 7-passenger Chevy Suburbans

For First-Time Visitors

An itinerary of must-sees:

- Cable Cars
- Chinatown
- Fine Arts Museums of San Francisco: California Palace of the Legion of Honor and M. H. de Young Memorial Museum
- Golden Gate Bridge
- Golden Gate National Recreation Area
- Golden Gate Park
- North Beach
- Union Square
- Wine Country
- Yerba Buena Gardens

offer sedan comfort and mobility—Lombard Street curves–approved.

Special-Interest Tours

There's a lot more to San Francisco and the Bay Area than the postcard sights known to all.

Articulate Art: SF 1930s (☎ 415/285-0495). Famed muralist Diego Rivera had both immediate and extended artistic influence on San Francisco in the 1930s with his socially conscious work. Masha Zakheim provides insightful explanations of his frescoes (and those of his protégés) at Coit Tower, Rincon Annex, the San Francisco Art Institute, and other locations.

City Guides (☎ 415/557-4266). Free summertime strolls through specific San Francisco neighborhoods given by Main Library volunteers who are . . . well, walking encyclopedias of authority. "Art Deco in the Marina," "City Scapes and Roof Gardens," and "Brothels, Boardinghouses, and Bawds" are but a few of the fascinating topics covered.

Cruisin' the Castro (☎ 415/550-8110). Few tourists—or locals, for that matter—are as aware of the historical and sociological forces that shaped the Castro District into the crossroads of gay culture as Trevor Hailey, who brings the story to life in her three-hour walking tour of the area.

Dashiell Hammett Tour (☎ 707/939-1214). Slip into your gumshoes as you stalk the streets that San

Francisco's most celebrated fictional detective, Sam Spade, made famous.

A Day in Nature (☎ 415/673-0548). You're picked up at your door and whisked via comfy four-wheel-drive vehicle to the Marin Headlands where knowledgeable naturalist Colin Sloan shows and tells all about the flora and fauna of this spectacular coastal region.

East Bay Tours (☎ 510/465-5791). Former party members trace the 13-year history of the Black Panther Party, visiting its birthplace at Merritt College in Oakland and attending a re-enacted rally on the steps of the Alameda Court House led by an actor portraying Huey P. Newton.

San Francisco on Film (☎ 510/536-4731 or 415/469-2088). Flashback to where Steve McQueen careened through the streets in *Bullitt,* where Alfred Hitchcock directed James Stewart and Kim Novak in *Vertigo,* and many other sites of cinematic significance in "the city with no bad angles."

Flower Power Haight-Ashbury Walking Tour (☎ 415/221-8442). The long, strange trip of the 1960s revealed in detail: the site of the first Human Be-In, the Grateful Dead's communal crash pad, and more.

Friends of Recreation and Parks (McLaren Lodge in Golden Gate Park, Stanyan at Fell ☎ 415/221-1311). Guided walks through Golden Gate Park.

Javawalk (☎ 415/673-WALK). Coffeehouse culture past and present is explored on this 2-hour jaunt through North Beach and environs.

The Mexican Bus (☎ 415/546-3747). Board El Volado—a 1965 GMC school bus in a former incarnation, now a mobile museum of Mexican folk art replete with hundreds of colored lights and paintings—for either a look at the Mission District murals or a nighttime spin to a trio of salsa clubs.

Milieu (☎ 415/552-0470 or 415/673-7617). Personalized limousine tours of private artists' studios, with a 4-star restaurant lunch break.

One Dollah Statuewalks (☎ 510/523-1988). Convene at the Civic Center fountain on the Polk Street side of City Hall for an all-day annotated trip around the city's monuments.

Precita Mural Walk Tours (☎ 415/285-2287). The Mission District is brightened by more than 200 contemporary murals, many of them hidden indoors, in cul-de-sacs, and backstreets. Discover them (including

Vendanta Temple on Union Street

the astounding visuals of Balmy Alley) and learn their history on this escorted walk.

San Francisco Jewish Landmark Tours (☎ 415/ 921-0461). A stimulating look at the accomplishments of the Jewish community in San Francisco, a legacy which stretches back to the gold rush days.

San Francisco Heritage (☎ 415/441-3000). Specialized period-architecture sojourns: Victorian residences, beaux arts civic structures, and more.

Stairway Walks in San Francisco (☎ 415/ 398-2907). An expert in all routes vertical, the indefatigable Adah Bakalinsky offers lots of different expeditions through the city's network of 350 stairways.

Three Babes and a Bus (☎ 415/552-2582). No cover charge hassles, no disdainful bouncers, no designated driver, no prayers to the parking god: This high-energy escorted club crawl hits various hot spots after dark.

Wok Whiz Chinatown Walking Tours (☎ 415/ 981-5588). A tasty blend of cuisine and culture led by cookbook author Shirley Fong-Torres, you'll visit Chinese markets, herb shops, and bakeries. A dim sum lunch caps off the experience.

Best Bets for Kids

If you are traveling with children, you'll be pleased to know that there are plenty of ways to keep them occupied in San Francisco. The next chapter, "Frisco for Kids," discusses those options in some detail, including tips on shopping and restaurants.

Special Moments

Truck drivers, interior designers, and insomniacs gather for an early morning breakfast at San Francisco's wholesale **Flower Market** (5th St. between Brannan and Bryant, ☎ 415/495-7162). Most of the merchants' stands are open strictly to the trade until 9am, when a number of them allow the general public in to buy.

Continuing the floral theme (but without the bustle), time spent at the **Ikenobo Ikebana Society** (1737 Post St., ☎ 415/567-1011) can be a serene experience indeed; appreciate the austerity of the arrangements and the total concentration of their creators.

They're dwindling in number, but there are still **survivors of the 1906 earthquake and fire** living in the city. They gather every April 18 at Lotta's Fountain (the intersection of Geary, Kearny, and Market streets) to observe the anniversary of the disaster. It's alternately moving and illuminating as the old-timers reminisce about their lost friends and family and tell first-hand anecdotes of the event. Another commemoration is made at Church and 20th streets, where a **fire hydrant**—allegedly the only one in the city that continued to function during the ensuing inferno—is painted gold.

For a psychic tune-up, head to **Karma Moffett's Tibetan Bell Ceremony** (3895 18th St., ☎ 415/621-8135 for times). It's sheer spiritual theater, centered around a carillon of chiming, tinkling, tolling, Asian bells of all shapes and sizes; conch-shell horns; drums; and flutes. The performance takes place by candlelight.

A visit to the **Names Project Visitor Center** (2362-A Market St., ☎ 415/863-1966; open daily noon–5pm, Wed until 10pm) can be simultaneously uplifting and sorrowful. An exhibit traces the history of the **Names Project Quilt,** started as a symbolic memorial to those who have died of AIDS. Sewing machines, workspace, and advice are available to panel makers.

A tradition that continues to thrive despite grumblings from City Hall (the Sanitation Department, to be specific) and a few overly-sensitive environmental groups is the **New Year's Eve calendar toss** in the Financial District (Pacific Coast Stock Exchange, 301 Pine St.). No matter if it's been a bullish or bearish annum, buyers, brokers, and sellers open their windows and throw away the past.

The "songs" of the **Wave Organ,** a construction of submerged pipes and air chambers that produce abstract sounds as water rushes through them, can be mesmerizing—especially at sunset, when the skies beyond the Golden Gate Bridge turn shades of pink and orange. Find it at the end of the jetty at the foot of Baker Street.

For an alternative to the commerciality of the Cliff House, trek through the overgrown, faded grandeur of the **Sutro Heights Garden** and the nearby **ruins of the Sutro Baths** (Point Lobos Ave. at 48th Ave.). Once manicured by 17 gardeners, philanthropist Adolf Sutro's 1880 sanctuary is now being reclaimed by nature; between June and September, the property is brightened by the golden-yellow blossoms of the dune tansy.

Sights and Attractions by Category

Architecture

★★ Civic Center
★ Haas-Lilienthal House
★★ Palace of Fine Arts
Transamerica Pyramid
★ Victorian Homes

Art Museums

★ Ansel Adams Center for Photography
★★ California Palace of the Legion of Honor
★ Cartoon Art Museum
★★ Center for the Arts at Yerba Buena Gardens
★★ M. H. de Young Memorial Museum
★ Murals of the Mission
★★ Oakland Museum of California Art, Ecology, and History
★ San Francisco Art Institute Galleries
★★ San Francisco Museum of Modern Art

Children's Attractions

Fisherman's Wharf
Pier 39

Churches

Grace Cathedral
★★ Mission San Francisco de Asis (Mission Dolores)
★ St. Mary's Cathedral of the Assumption
Temple Emanu-El
★ Tien Hou Temple

Historical Sites, Landmarks, and Monuments

★ Alcatraz
★★ Chinatown
★ Coit Tower
Crookedest Street (Lombard Street)
★ Ferry Building and Farmers Market
★ Fort Point
★★ Golden Gate Bridge
Jackson Square

History and Cultural Museums

Bank of California Old Coin and Gold Exhibit
Cable Car Museum, Powerhouse, and Car Barn
★ California Historical Society
Chinese Culture Center
★ Chinese Historical Society of America
★ Fort Mason
Jewish Museum San Francisco
★ Museum of the City of San Francisco
★ San Francisco Fire Department Museum
★ San Francisco Maritime National Historical Park
★ Wells Fargo History Room

Outdoor Attractions

★★ Filbert Steps
★★ Golden Gate National Recreation Area

★ Sigmund Stern Memorial Grove

Parks

★★ Angel Island State Park
★★ Golden Gate Park
★ Washington Square
★★ Yerba Buena Gardens

Science Museums

★★ California Academy of Sciences
★★ Exploratorium

Other

Anchor Steam Brewery
★★ Cable Cars
Japan Center
Moscone Convention Center
★★ San Francisco Public Library
★★ San Francisco Zoological Gardens
★ Vintage Streetcars of Market Street

Sights and Attractions by Neighborhood

Chinatown

Chinese Culture Center
★ Chinese Historical Society of America
★ Tien Hou Temple

Civic Center

★★ San Francisco Public Library
★ Victorian Homes

Downtown/Financial District/Theatre District

Bank of California Old Coin and Gold Exhibit
Jackson Square
Transamerica Pyramid
★ Vintage Streetcars of Market Street
★ Wells Fargo History Room

Golden Gate Park

★★ California Academy of Sciences
★★ M. H. de Young Memorial Museum

The Haight/Japantown

Japan Center
★ San Francisco Fire Department Museum
★ Victorian Homes

The Mission

★★ Mission San Francisco de Asis (Mission Dolores)
★ Murals of the Mission

Nob Hill/Russian Hill

Cable Car Museum, Powerhouse, and Car Barn
Crookedest Street (Lombard Street)
Grace Cathedral
★ St. Mary's Cathedral of the Assumption
★ San Francisco Art Institute Galleries
★ Victorian Homes

North Beach

★ Coit Tower
★★ Filbert Steps
★ Washington Square

Pacific Heights/Marina

★★ Exploratorium
★ Haas-Lilienthal House
★★ Palace of Fine Arts
Temple Emanu-El
★ Victorian Homes

SoMa

Anchor Steam Brewery
★ Ansel Adams Center for Photography
★ California Historical Society
★ Cartoon Art Museum
★★ Center for the Arts at Yerba Buena Gardens
Moscone Convention Center
★★ San Francisco Museum of Modern Art
★★ Yerba Buena Gardens

Waterfront

★ Ferry Building and Farmers Market
Fisherman's Wharf
★ Fort Mason
★ Fort Point

★★ Golden Gate Bridge
★★ Golden Gate National Recreation Area
Jewish Museum San Francisco
★ Museum of the City of San Francisco
Pier 39
★ San Francisco Maritime National Historical Park

Other

★ Alcatraz
★★ Angel Island State Park
★★ Cable Cars
★★ California Palace of the Legion of Honor
★★ Oakland Museum of Art, Ecology, and History
★★ San Francisco Zoological Gardens
★ Sigmund Stern Memorial Grove

San Francisco A to Z

Alamo Square (See Victorian Homes)

★ Alcatraz

Reservations advised for boats in all seasons, but especially in summer when they may be reserved 2–6 weeks in advance. For information or reservations, call or write the **Red and White Fleet,** Pier 41, San Francisco, CA 94133. ☎ 415/546-2833. Arrive at least 20 minutes early, even if you have purchased your tickets in advance. Ferries leave from Pier 41, and crossings take about 20 minutes. Daily 9am–4:30pm. Admission charged.

Alcatraz rises a craggy and commanding 135 feet out of the forbidding tides of San Francisco Bay. One of the city's most dominating sights, from certain angles the infamous prison has a decidedly Mediterranean air. The outcrop on which it was built is oddly lush; wild flowers grow there in riotous profusion. The views of the San Francisco skyline and the Golden Gate Bridge are magnificent.

But for a century, Alcatraz (a variant on the Spanish word *álcatraces,* which means "pelicans") was a byword for grim incarceration. Since 1859 it has been a fortification, a military prison, an army disciplinary barracks, and a federal penitentiary run under an administrative code of total control. In this last role, "The Rock" acquired its legendary reputation as a place of no escape. No more than 250 captives at a time occupied its 450 cells, patrolled by as many as 100 staff.

In spite of this, in 1962, 3 inmates, Frank Lee Morris and John and Clarence Anglin, managed to dig their way out with sharpened spoons. Their apparently successful feat (none of them was ever found) was the subject of *Escape from Alcatraz,* the 1979 movie with Clint Eastwood, in which the prison played one of its several starring Hollywood parts. *The Birdman of Alcatraz,* the story of Robert Stroud (who, by the way, wasn't allowed to keep any birds while passing his 17 years on

Alcatraz

The Rock), with Burt Lancaster in the title role, was another.

After the prison closed in 1963, the 12-acre island was claimed by a group of Native Americans as their birthright; they occupied it from 1969 to 1971. Since 1973 it has been open to the public under the custodianship of the National Park Service as a part of **the Golden Gate National Recreation Area.** Those with a taste for self-imposed claustrophobia will find the main prison block–with its 9-by-5-foot cells and "dark holes," where uncooperative inmates cooled their heels in solitary blackness—still intact.

In addition to ranger-accompanied walks (topics change daily), visitors can don headphones for a self-guided tour of the island (commentaries in English, German, Japanese, Mandarin, Spanish, and French are available). Including ferry-travel time, allow about 3 hours for this excursion.

Anchor Steam Brewery

1705 Mariposa St. ☎ 415/863-8350. Tours Mon–Fri at 2pm; advance reservations required. Admission free.

At this home of San Francisco's signature brew, you can take a 1-hour tour culminating in a sampling of the products.

★★ Angel Island State Park

☎ 415/435-1915 for information. Hours 8am–sunset. Admission free.

This largest island in San Francisco Bay offers a 740-acre haven for hikers, cyclists, and picnickers. There are three hiking trails, in addition to camping, barbecue and picnic facilities. For outdoor types, a day spent trekking its forested slopes and sandy inlets can be exhilarating.

Once known as the "Ellis Island of the West"—until 1940 it housed immigration and quarantine stations—Angel Island has also been the site of military installations dating back to the Civil War.

Ferries depart for Ayala Cove from both San Francisco (☎ 415/452-2628, or 415/546-2805 for schedules and information) and the town of Tiburon in Marin

San Francisco Sights

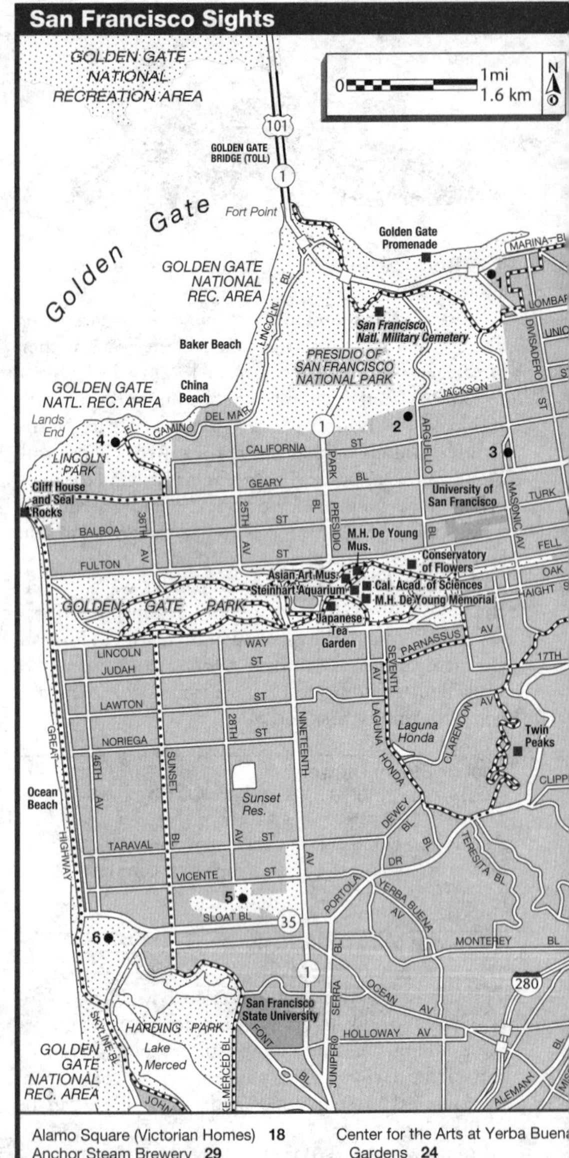

Alamo Square (Victorian Homes) **18**
Anchor Steam Brewery **29**
Ansel Adams Center for Photography **23**
Bank of California Exhibit **17**
Cable Car Barn & Museum **13**
California Historical Society **27**
California Palace of the Legion of Honor **4**
Cartoon Art Museum **22**
Center for the Arts at Yerba Buena Gardens **24**
Coit Tower **10**
Exploratorium **1**
Ferry Building **16**
Fisherman's Wharf **8**
Fort Mason **7**
Grace Cathedral **12**
Haas-Lilienthal House **11**

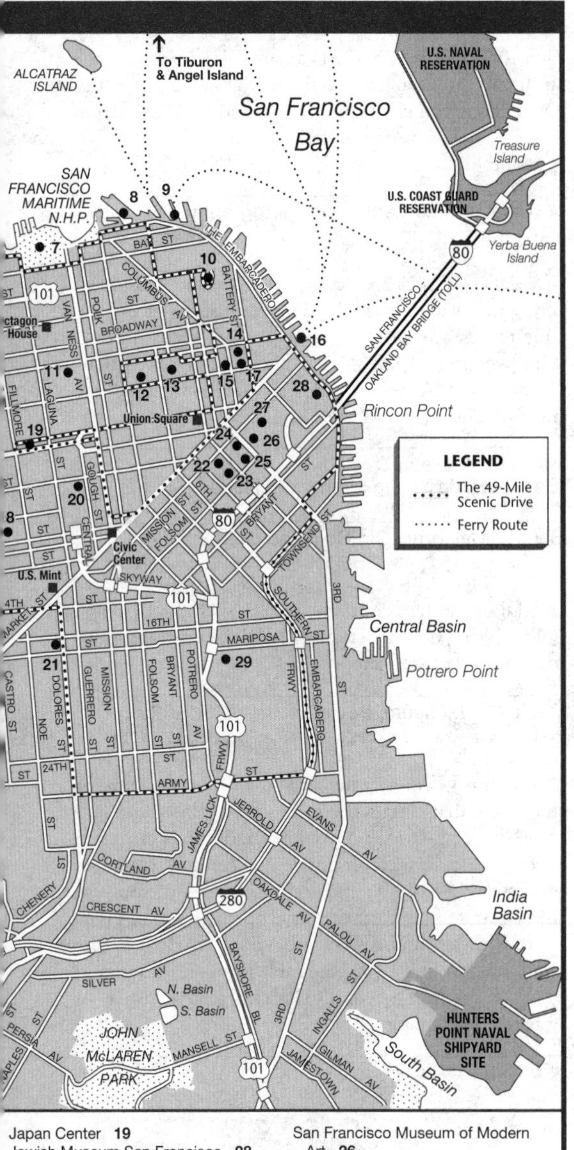

Japan Center **19**
Jewish Museum San Francisco **28**
Mission Dolores **21**
Moscone Convention Center **25**
Palace of Fine Arts **1**
Pier 39 **9**
St. Mary's Cathedral **20**
San Francisco Fire Department Museum **3**
San Francisco Museum of Modern Art **26**
San Francisco Zoological Gardens **6**
Sigmund Stern Grove **5**
Temple Emanuel-El **2**
Transamerica Pyramid **14**
Victorian Homes (Alamo Square) **18**
Wells Fargo History Museum **15**
Yerba Buena Gardens **24**

County (☎ 415/435-2131); boats sail daily during the summer, and weekends only in the winter months. Once there, you can explore the island on your own or hop on a motorized tram for a tour of its historic buildings and beaches.

★ Ansel Adams Center for Photography

250 4th St. ☎ 415/495-7000. Tues–Sat 11am–6pm. Admission charged.

Five galleries in all are dedicated to creative photography, with changing exhibits on the history of the art. One room is devoted to the legacy of Adams himself, who lived from 1902–84. His photographs, in particular those of the Yosemite Valley, are noted as some of the most potent images of the California landscape.

Asian Art Museum (See M. H. de Young Memorial Museum)

Bank of California Old Coin and Gold Exhibit

400 California St. ☎ 415/765-0400. Mon–Thurs 10am–3pm, Fri 10am–5pm. Closed Sat, Sun, and bank holidays. Admission free.

In addition to rare coins, the display includes pieces of gold-bearing quartz that show how the precious metal looks in its natural state.

Cable Car Museum, Powerhouse, and Car Barn

Washington at Mason Street. ☎ 415/474-1887. Daily 10am–5pm. Admission free.

The control center, where the 11 miles of wrapped steel cable that carries the cable cars is played out and reeled in, is a 3-story red brick barn. Exhibits include 3 vintage models, including inventor Andrew Hallidie's prototype Car No. 8, and scale examples of some of the 57 types of cable car that have operated in San Francisco. A mezzanine gallery provides a window to the giant winders that thread the cable through sheaves and onto the streets. There is also an informative display of historic photographs.

★★ Cable Cars

Powell-Mason and Powell-Hyde lines run from Powell and Market streets to the northern waterfront. The California Street line runs from California St. at Market St. to Van Ness Ave. Fare charged.

A cherished part of the city's public transportation system and a national landmark, San Francisco's cable cars offer an exhilarating and inexpensive way (tickets cost $2, $1 for children and seniors) to see the soaring hills and swooping dales of the city. They were invented in San Francisco before the turn of the century to haul passengers up and down hills too steep for horse-drawn carriages. A lurching joyride to the tourist, and a lifeline to the city's commuters, the preservation of these moving museum-pieces has not been without cost.

Mothballed in 1982, when engineers found that 109 years of service had taken an irreparable toll on the cable cars' mechanical systems, the network was rebuilt after sympathizers from all over the world sent contributions. Most of the $60 million for the restoration came from a combined effort of public and private funding. Residents and commuters were then subjected to 2 years of appalling traffic disruption as the life-saving surgery was performed; 69 blocks of streets were torn up before the cars made a glorious, bell-clanging comeback in 1984.

★★ California Academy of Sciences

Golden Gate Park, via entrance road from 8th Ave. and Fulton St. ☎ 415/221-5100, or 415/750-7145 for recorded schedule of events. Daily 10am–5pm. Admission charged; free 1st Wed of each month.

One of the finest natural history museums in the United States, the Academy has 8 departments, some of which function on separate schedules, and a changing program of special exhibits. It is set amid the 1,017 acres of Golden Gate Park.

The **Morrison Planetarium** has a 65-foot domed ceiling that is used for star and Laserium light shows, which are presented in the Planetarium on selected evenings (☎ 415/750-7138 for information).

The **Discovery Room** (behind Morrison Planetarium; Tues–Fri 1–4pm, Sat–Sun 11am–3:30pm, closed Mon) is a hands-on environment designed to introduce youngsters to everything from spices to seashells and animal skulls.

The most dramatic element of the **Steinhart Aquarium** is the Fish Roundabout, a kind of reverse theater-in-the-round where observers are completely immersed in a huge school of all the great Pacific-coast sport fish (yes, there are sharks) swimming against an induced current in a 100,000-gallon cylindrical tank. In all, the aquarium shelters more than 14,000 finny species. Feeding frenzies take place every 2 hours starting at 10:30am; the penguins receive their chow twice daily. Other aquatic attractions include a simulated swamp (yes, with alligators), a touch tidepool, and coral reef tank.

★ California Historical Society

678 Mission St. ☎ 415/357-1848. Call for hours. Admission free.

Pioneer diaries, paintings of virgin landscapes, and an intriguing aggregation of maps tracing the geographical evolution of California make up just a tiny portion of the Society's collection. The collection includes more than 500,000 photographs, 150,000 manuscripts, and near-countless pieces of ephemera documenting life in the Golden State from the 16thC to the present day. Its newly renovated facilities allow for expanded gallery exhibits.

★★ California Palace of the Legion of Honor

Lincoln Park, 34th Ave., Clement St. entrance. ☎ 415/750-3600 or 415/863-3330 for recorded message. Tues–Sun 10am–4:45pm; 1st Sat to 8:45pm. Closed Mon. Admission charged.

Fresh from a $3^1/_2$-year renovation that included seismic strengthening, restoration of historic architectural elements, and an underground expansion of gallery space, conservation facilities, and public amenities, the Legion reopened its beaux arts doors to the public on November 11, 1995—71 years to the day of its initial opening in 1924.

Architect Edward Larrabee Barnes has placed a glass pyramidal skylight (à la Louvre) in the colonnaded courtyard of George Applegarth's structure, illuminating 6 new subterranean galleries. The art and culture of ancient civilizations and Europe from 2500 B.C. through the 20thC are the focus of the permanent collection. A new restaurant takes in extra-ordinary views of the Pacific Ocean and the museum's gardens.

★ Cartoon Art Museum

814 Mission St. ☎ 415/227-8666. Wed–Fri 11am–5pm, Sat 10am–5pm, Sun 1pm–5pm. Admission charged; free 1st Wed of each month.

More than 10,000 selective examples of the genre, dating from the late 1700s to today, are lovingly curated and presented in 6,000 square feet of exhibition space. There's a children's gallery and an interactive CD-ROM show, as well. Check out the comically squeaking floorboards.

★★ Center for the Arts at Yerba Buena Gardens

701 Mission St. ☎ 415/978-ARTS. Tues–Sun 11am–6pm, 1st Thurs of each month 11am–8pm. Admission charged.

Two structures comprise the Center: the galleries, designed by Fumihiko Maki, winner of the 1993 Pritzker Prize; and the theater, created by James Stewart Polshek. The former, a corrugated aluminum-clad shiplike structure, houses the city's most adventurous series of changing, cross-cultural installations. (The Center's artistic director for visual arts, Renny Pritikin, headed the visionary New Langton Arts group for 13 years.) Equally challenging music, dance, and theatrical productions are staged in Polshek's cubist mass.

★★ Chinatown

See also "Neighborhoods in Brief" in "San Francisco . . . City by the Bay."

"A ward of the city of Canton set down in the most eligible business quarter of the place" was Rudyard Kipling's impression of Chinatown on a visit in the 1880s, and it still rings true. San Francisco's Chinese community has spread into other areas of the city, but an 8-block length of Grant Avenue is still the cultural and geographical nucleus of the biggest Chinese stronghold east of Taiwan. Guangzhou dialect is the first language of its residents, carved dragons entwine themselves around the lampposts, and buildings are adorned with arched eaves, ornate cornices, and filigreed balconies. Today, Chinatown's shops are crammed with art objects and curios. Restaurants, from award-winning temples of taste to dim sum teahouses, line the streets. The oldest Oriental-style building in Chinatown is the 3-tiered **Bank of Canton,** built in 1909. The **Bank of America** is ornamented with splendid golden dragons. Stockton Street, a block west of Grant, boasts an overwhelming 1,000-plus grocery stalls piled high with ginger root, shark fin, live chickens, and Peking duck—a much more genuine experience of the neighborhood is had along its crowded sidewalks than on Grant's tourist-oriented stretch.

Chinatown has had a checkered history. *Du Pon Gai,* as the area was known in the 19thC, had a reputation for tong wars, opium dens, and prostitution. The name of the 18th president of the United States was bestowed on the area's main thoroughfare as incentive for driving the neighborhood up-market. When Chinatown was decimated by the 1906 earthquake, City Hall schemed to relocate its inhabitants to a less desirable part of town, but residents rebuilt their homes and businesses with such alacrity that the plan had to be scratched. A resurgence in Asian gangs has recently bothered the community.

Chinese Culture Center

750 Kearny St. ☎ 415/986-1822. Tues–Sat 9am–5pm. Closed Sun and Mon. Admission free.

Attractions here include galleries of Chinese and Chinese-American art, historic exhibits, and cultural exchange exhibits from Asia. The Culture Center also sponsors programs aimed at visitors, including heritage and culinary walking tours of old Chinatown (see page 64 for tour details).

★ Chinese Historical Society of America

650 Commercial St. ☎ 415/391-1188. Tues–Sat noon–4pm. Closed Sun and Mon. Admission free.

This jewel box of a museum documents the remarkable contributions made by the Chinese to the gold rush, the building of America's transcontinental railroads, and the development of agriculture in California. (The derogatory term *coolie* stemmed from the Chinese word *kuli,* meaning "bitter toil.") Other exhibits illustrate how the Chinese have maintained their traditions in an alien land. Commentary is provided in English and Chinese.

★★ Civic Center Complex

Van Ness Ave. between McAllister and Grove streets.

San Francisco's Civic Center Plaza is one of the most impressive groupings of beaux arts buildings in the United States. The Civic Center was the creation of architect Daniel Burnham in 1904. In the aftermath of the 1906 earthquake and fire, Arthur Brown, Jr., and John Bakewell, Jr., won an international competition to design **City Hall,** whose dome is patterned after that of St. Peter's in Rome. Currently swathed in scaffolding, City Hall is undergoing a thorough structural renovation, as is the **War Memorial Opera House** across Van Ness Avenue; completed in 1932, it's due for some much-needed architectural attention. The Opera House is flanked by the curving contemporary glass facade of **Louise M. Davies Symphony Hall** to the south and the **Veteran's Building** to the north,

War Memorial Opera House in the Civic Center

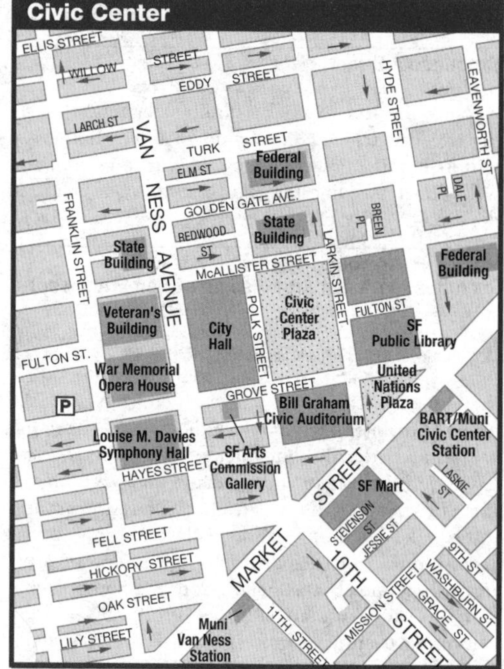

which is home to the Herbst Theatre, site of the signing of the United Nations Charter in 1945. Completing the Civic Center complex are the **Bill Graham Civic Auditorium,** the brand-new **San Francisco Public Library,** and the **Edmund G. Brown State Office Building.**

★ Coit Tower

Atop Telegraph Hill, east end of Lombard St. Daily 10am–4:30pm. Closed Jan 1 and Dec 25. Admission only for elevator service to the top.

Built with a $100,000 legacy from Lillie Hitchcock Coit and dedicated to "the purpose of adding beauty to the city I have always loved," the tower, designed in 1933 by the prolific Arthur Brown, Jr., is one of San Francisco's landmarks. An elevator takes visitors to the 210-foot open loggia with its a 360° panorama of the city and bay. The first relief work project for artists during the Depression, the tower's frescoes were created by 25 Social Realist painters, who each earned a monthly salary of $94 for their efforts. Completed in 1934 after 8 months' work, these impressive murals depict the lot of California's working class and at the time constituted one of the most politically confrontational public works projects funded by the American government.

Crookedest Street

Lombard St. between Hyde and Leavenworth streets.

Carving the sort of track a timid skier might make, this street switchbacks its way down a steep hill. Savvy visitors hop the Powell-Hyde cable car to its crest and walk down, avoiding the jam of automobile traffic at the top.

★★ M. H. de Young Memorial Museum (Includes the Asian Art Museum of San Francisco)

Golden Gate Park near 10th Ave. and Fulton St. ☎ 415/750-3600 or 415/863-3330 for recorded message. Wed–Sun 10am–5pm. Closed Mon and Tues. **Asian Art Museum:** ☎ 415/668-8921. Wed–Sun 10am–5pm. Closed Mon and Tues. Admission charged.

Established in 1895 with funds earned from the California Midwinter International Exposition, the de Young was named after the publisher of the *Daily Dramatic Chronicle* (forebear of today's daily *Chronicle*), one of the fair's leading lights. Michael Harry promptly instituted a vigorous—albeit eclectic—program of acquisitions, gathering paintings and sculpture, arms and armor, porcelain and *objets* from the South Pacific and American Indian cultures. From this motley beginning eventually grew today's highly respected collection of works from Oceania, Africa, and the Americas. The burgeoning museum soon outgrew its original home and, hastened by the 1906 earthquake, a new facility was built in 1917.

It was Mr. and Mrs. John D. Rockefeller III's 1979 gift of their exemplary collection of American paintings and works on paper that solidified the de Young as a locus for home-grown talents. Highlights of this survey, which spans from 1670 through the 20thC, range from Frederic Church's monumental 19thC landscape

M. H. de Young Memorial Museum

Rainy Season in the Tropics and John Singleton Copley's *William Vassall and His Son Leonard,* to *Dinner for Threshers* by Grant Wood and *From the Garden of the Château* by Charles Demuth.

The **Asian Art Museum of San Francisco,** housed in a separate wing of the de Young, is built around the legendary Avery Brundage Collection. The Chicago millionaire agreed to donate his extensive assemblage to San Francisco on the condition that the city construct a museum to contain it. Opened in 1966, it now features 12,000 objects from 40 countries and is the largest museum outside the Orient devoted exclusively to Asian art.

The first floor is devoted to works from China, with exhibits of Shang and Zhou bronzes and Neolithic painted pottery, plus Ming and Qing objects and jade. The upper floor encompasses Japan, Korea, India, and the rest of Asia as far as the Middle and Near East. Among its notable pieces are the oldest dated Chinese Buddha image (A.D. 338) and the largest collection of Japanese *netsuke* and *inro* in the country.

Over time, the structural problems of the de Young have grown too serious to ignore, and the decision was recently made to demolish the extant building (probably in 1999) and rebuild on the same location. The Asian Art Museum will relocate to the former Main Library as the much-needed reconstruction of the de Young gets underway.

★★ Exploratorium

In the Palace of Fine Arts, 3601 Lyon St. ☎ 415/561-0360 for recorded information. Tues, Thurs–Sun 10am–5pm; Wed 10am–9:30pm. Closed Mon, except holidays. Admission charged.

A huge cavern filled with first-rate lessons in science disguised as fun and games. Ingenious gadgets let children and adults measure their own eyes, ears and voices; others deal with broader questions of physics, exploring color, electricity, motion, weather, etc. There are more than 650 exhibits, so be prepared to spend hours here. Reservations are required to visit the Tactile Dome, where the sense of touch is explored in total darkness.

★ Ferry Building and Farmers Market

Embarcadero at Market St.

Modeled after Seville's Giralda Tower, the Ferry Building is the headquarters of the Port of San Francisco and the San Francisco World Trade Center. Though nondescript offices blandly occupy the building's

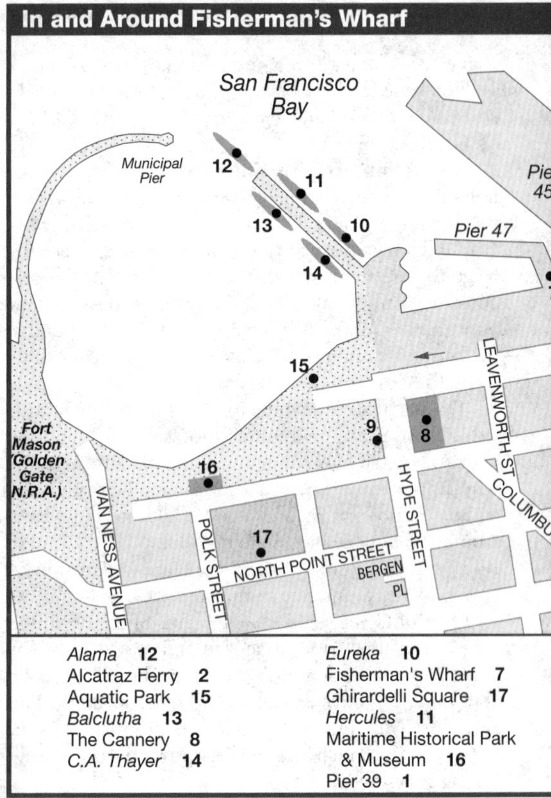

interior and the days when 50 million commuters passed through its portals are long gone (vanished with the construction of the city's 2 great bridges), the plaza in front of Arthur Brown's 1894 edifice is enlivened by a fabulous **Farmers Market** on Saturday mornings (9am–2pm). Ferries connect to Alameda, Oakland, and Marin County.

★★ Filbert Steps

Filbert St., on east side of Telegraph Hill between Coit Tower and Sansome St.

This series of precipitous boardwalks and stairways leads down (or up, for the masochistic) past some of the city's quaintest cottages—many dating from the 1870s—and prettiest flower patches. Off the steps, Napier Lane is a much sought-after address, one especially popular with artists, writers, and entertainers—and their cats, who roam the area freely.

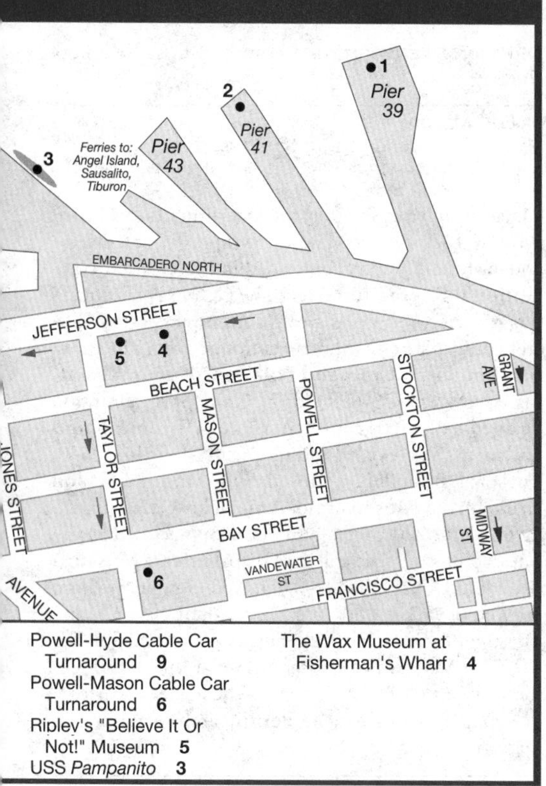

Fisherman's Wharf

Near the terminus of the Powell-Mason cable-car line at Taylor and Bay streets.

Rows of colorful fishing boats face off with an inexhaustible number of mostly middling seafood restaurants that are crowded by taffy stores and T-shirt shops at one of the city's most inexplicably popular tourist attractions. While it's become tantamount to a "Where's Waldo?" hunt to detect traces of the working harbor here, early-risers can watch the Dungeness crab catch being landed between mid-November and June.

Fisherman's Wharf is perhaps the city's prime spot for an irrepressible horde of street vendors, jugglers, and musicians, performing in what might look like unfettered chaos, but is not. Each is required to obey a set of rules created to ensure that their shows contribute to the favorable impression visitors get of the city. If the alfresco floor shows get to be a bit much, turn around and appreciate the pristine beauty of their backdrop: the Bay.

★ Fort Mason

Marina Blvd.. at Laguna St. Visitor's Center located in Building A, near main entrance. ☎ 415/441-5705. Daily 9am—5pm. Hours and admissions vary for each institution.

Once an embarkation port for American troops headed into the Pacific, Fort Mason now operates as a diverse and lively community center within **the Golden Gate National Recreation Area.** The GGNRA headquarters is currently here, as are a youth hostel, several theater companies, environmental groups, and 4 museums: **San Francisco Craft and Folk Art Museum** (Building A; ☎ 415/775-0990; daily 11am–5pm; admission charged); the **African-American Historical and Cultural Society** (Building C; ☎ 415/441-0640; Tues–Sat noon-5pm, closed Sun–Mon; admission charged); the **Museo Italo-Americano** (Building C; ☎ 415/673-2200; Wed–Sun noon–5pm, closed Mon–Tues; admission charged); and the **Mexican Museum** (Building D; ☎ 415/441-0404; Wed–Sun noon–5pm, 1st Wed of each month open noon–8pm; closed Mon–Tues; admission charged). Future plans call for the Mexican Museum to relocate to Yerba Buena Gardens some time in 1998, to a 50,000-square-foot structure designed by Mexican modernist architect Ricardo Legorreta.

★ Fort Point

Directly beneath the San Francisco end of the Golden Gate Bridge (access from Lincoln Blvd., 400 yards north of bridge approach). ☎ 415/556-1693. Daily 10am–5pm. Admission free.

This somberly handsome red brick structure was completed in 1861. Decommissioned in 1914, it now provides instructive images of an earlier military life through its architecture and troop drills (including artillery practice). The latter are staged by National Park Service personnel dressed in period uniforms. The fortress's sturdy seawall is an excellent fishing promontory, and the sight of the bridge from below is outstanding.

★★ Golden Gate Bridge

Pedestrian entrance near Fort Point. Toll for southbound cars, free for pedestrians.

If one image were to be chosen to symbolize San Francisco, it would likely be the Golden Gate Bridge, the first great suspension bridge (from 1937–59, it was the longest in the world) and an indelible element of the city's silhouette.

Golden Gate Bridge

A near-miracle of engineering, the Golden Gate Bridge spans a mile-wide strait that is the only cleft for nearly 600 miles in the coastal wall. Until this century, it was considered to be unbridgeable, and for very good reasons: The tides rip through the Golden Gate with 3 times the flow of the Amazon, 14 times that of the Mississippi. Add to this the 60-mile-per-hour currents, vicious winds that whip around the headlands, and the inevitable San Francisco fogs, and the scale of the challenge becomes clear.

The curve of soaring steel masterminded by engineer Joseph B. Strauss opened in May 1937, after a 2-decade battle to ignite the public imagination and a 4-year building program costing 11 lives and $35 million. Its 746-foot towers were the highest structures west of the Empire State Building. The 2 cables that suspend the bridge contain 80,000 miles of steel wire. Technically, the bridge is not "golden" at all; it is painted a high-visibility "International Orange."

The most breathtaking view is at the Marin County end of the bridge. Pedestrians and bicyclists can—and do, in throngs—cross for no fee. If you choose to drive, a $3 toll is charged at the bridge's south end.

★★ Golden Gate National Recreation Area

☎ 415/556-0560. Visitor's Center in Fort Mason open daily 9am–5pm.

The 39,000-acre GGNRA encompasses all of San Francisco's ocean beaches, the **Presidio,** and most of the city's waterfront from the Golden Gate east to Aquatic Park. The GGNRA also includes much of the Marin County shore from the Golden Gate, north to **Point Reyes National Seashore.** To fully understand

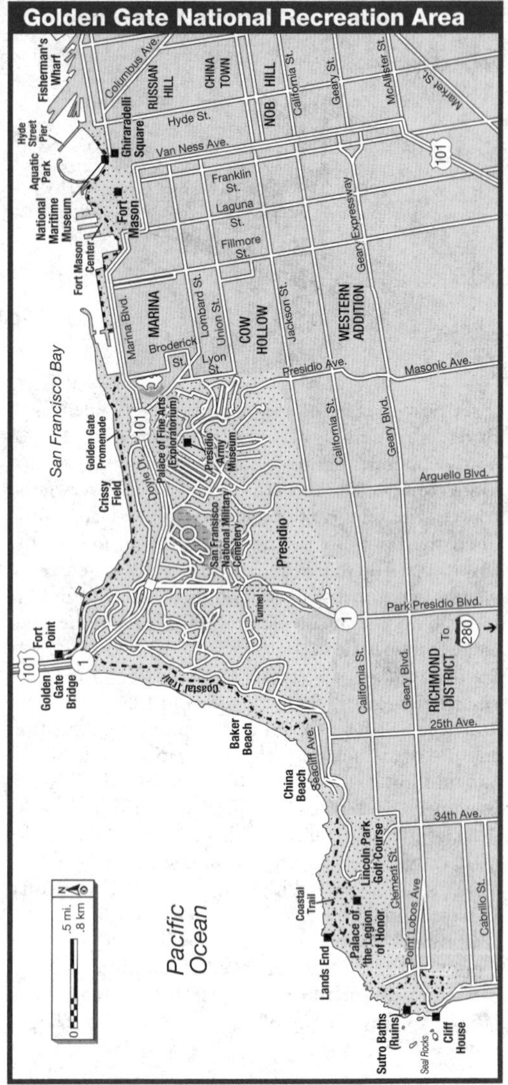

what makes the Bay Area so compelling, this unique wilderness shouldn't be missed.

See separate entries for Alcatraz, Fort Mason, Fort Point, and San Francisco Maritime National Historical Park.

★★ Golden Gate Park

Between Fulton St. and Lincoln Way, west of Stanyan St. Hours and admissions for the park's various museums and attractions vary.

This verdant enclave evolved from barren sand dunes and scrub oak largely through the determination of one John McLaren, a strong-willed Scotsman who spent more than a half century coaxing seedlings, shrubs, grass, and gardens out of its hostile soils. On the occasion of his 90th birthday in 1937, the still-superintendent of the park requested an unusual present: 10,000 yards of good manure. A likeness of "Uncle John" (he deplored the use of ornamental statuary, incidentally, and contrarily hid them in remote fringes of the park) stands at the entrance to the Rhododendron Dell, an area planted with more than 500 species of the horticulturist's favorite flower.

Four blocks wide and more than 40 blocks long, the park is home to the California Academy of Sciences, the M. H. de Young Memorial Museum, the Strybing Arboretum, and a host of outdoor and indoor recreational facilities. It is a paradise for bicyclists, skaters, and joggers (especially on Sunday, when cars are forbidden on JFK Dr.).

Many of the major attractions are in the easterly third of the park, between Stanyan Street and Tenth Avenue. These include:

A **playground** (near the Stanyan/Waller entrance), which has a fine merry-go-round with 62 animals.

The **Conservatory of Flowers** (JFK Dr., near Arguello Blvd./Fulton St. entrance; daily 9am–6pm; nominal admission) is modeled after the Palm House at London's Kew Gardens. Shipped around Cape Horn from Dublin in 1878, it is the park's oldest structure. It contains especially fine collections of orchids and other tropical plants, and the flower beds fronting it are kept in bloom much of the year.

The **Japanese Tea Garden** (adjoining the de Young Museum, near the 6th Ave./Fulton St. entrance; daily 8am–5pm; admission charged) dates from 1894. It comprises fine gardens and carp ponds (complete with a photogenic moon bridge), surrounding an open-air teahouse. Spectacular during cherry-blossom time in March.

The **Music Concourse** (bandshell between the de Young Museum and California Academy of Sciences), is the site of free concerts on Sundays in summer.

Shakespeare Garden (south of the Academy of Sciences), contains labeled specimens of every plant mentioned in the plays and sonnets of the Bard.

Stow Lake (directly west of the Japanese Tea Garden, also accessible from JFK Dr. or Martin Luther King,

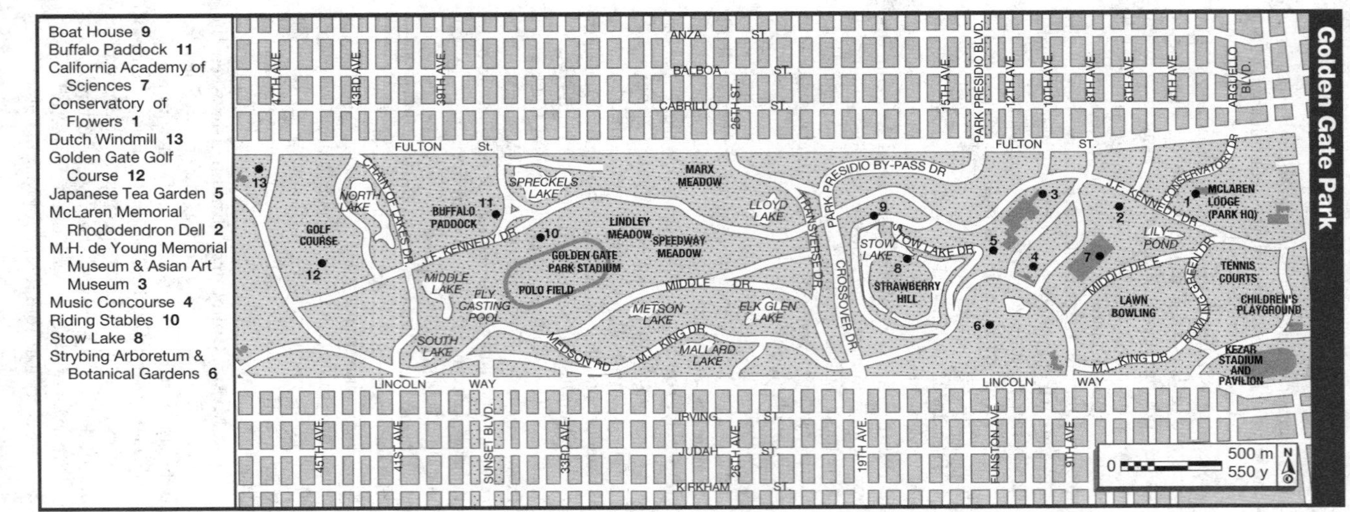
Golden Gate Park
Boat House 9
Buffalo Paddock 11
California Academy of Sciences 7
Conservatory of Flowers 1
Dutch Windmill 13
Golden Gate Golf Course 12
Japanese Tea Garden 5
McLaren Memorial Rhododendron Dell 2
M.H. de Young Memorial Museum & Asian Art Museum 3
Music Concourse 4
Riding Stables 10
Stow Lake 8
Strybing Arboretum & Botanical Gardens 6
ANZA ST.
BALBOA ST.
CABRILLO ST.
47TH AVE.
43RD AVE.
39TH AVE.
26TH ST.
15TH AVE.
PARK PRESIDIO BLVD.
12TH AVE.
10TH AVE.
8TH AVE.
6TH AVE.
4TH AVE.
ARGUELLO BLVD.
FULTON St.
FULTON ST.
CONSERVATORY DR
MCLAREN LODGE (PARK HQ)
J.F. KENNEDY DR
PARK PRESIDIO BY-PASS DR
MARX MEADOW
SPRECKELS LAKE
NORTH LAKE
CHAIN OF LAKES DR.
BUFFALO PADDOCK
GOLF COURSE
LLOYD LAKE
TRANSVERSE DR.
LINDLEY MEADOW
SPEEDWAY MEADOW
GOLDEN GATE PARK STADIUM
POLO FIELD
MIDDLE LAKE
FLY CASTING POOL
SOUTH LAKE
MIDDLE DR.
METSON LAKE
ELK GLEN LAKE
MALLARD LAKE
METSON RD
M.L. KING DR.
CROSSOVER DR.
STOW LAKE
STOW LAKE DR.
STRAWBERRY HILL
LILY POND
MIDDLE DR. E.
BOWLING GREEN DR
LAWN BOWLING
TENNIS COURTS
CHILDREN'S PLAYGROUND
KEZAR STADIUM AND PAVILION
LINCOLN WAY
IRVING ST.
JUDAH ST.
KIRKHAM ST.
45TH AVE.
41ST AVE
SUNSET BLVD.
33RD AVE.
26TH AVE.
19TH AVE.
FUNSTON AVE.
9TH AVE
0
500 m
550 y
N

Conservatory of Flowers

Jr. Dr. by a clearly identified loop road), offers rental rowboats and canoes for leisurely paddles around Strawberry Island (boat rentals daily 9am–4pm, fee charged).

Strybing Arboretum and Botanical Gardens (Martin Luther King, Jr. Dr., near the 9th Ave./ Lincoln Ave. entrance; ☎ 415/558-3622; Mon–Fri 8am–4:30pm; Sat, Sun, and holidays 10am–5pm; admission free) contains a collection of plants from every corner of the globe.

The **Tennis Center** (off JFK Dr., opposite the Conservatory of Flowers), has 21 hard courts open to the public daily. (See "Staying Active" for further details.)

In the wilder, more western parts of the park are a paddock with a small herd of buffalo, a children's zoo (daily 10am–5pm; admission charged), various lakes, a polo field, a stable, fly-casting pools, public golf course, and a restored Dutch windmill (it and a demolished twin were the original irrigation system for the park).

Grace Cathedral

At the top of Nob Hill, at California and Taylor streets.

Seat of the Episcopal Bishop of California, the cathedral is an impressive example of neo-Gothic architecture, begun in 1910 and not finished until after World War II. An undisguised concrete exterior gives the structure an air of enduring strength. Inside, its treasures include an 11thC French chapel altar; a Flemish 16thC carved oak reredos; Gabriel Loire's contemporary stained-glass windows portraying "The Human Endeavor," with likenesses of Albert Einstein, Robert Frost, Frank Lloyd Wright, and Franklin Delano Roosevelt, among other luminaries; and a carillon of 44 bells cast in Croydon, England.

★ Haas-Lilienthal House

2007 Franklin St. ☎ 415/441-3004. Wed noon–4pm; Sun 11am–5pm. Closed Mon–Tues, Thurs–Sat. Admission charged.

This is an immaculately maintained Victorian building in the Queen Anne style, dating from 1886. The

Haas-Lilienthal House

museum, which is the headquarters of the Foundation for San Francisco's Architectural Heritage, is the only fully furnished Victorian house in the city open to the public.

The house is also the starting point for excellent walking tours of the grand homes of Russian Hill and around the Pacific Heights neighborhood; ask one of the docents about schedules.

Hills

San Francisco has 42 hills, 10 of which are most frequently used to thrill the vertiginous visitor. To sample the sensation of pitching down a slope of 20% or more, or to give the brakes of your car an unrepeatable test, get out your map and head for Russian and Nob hills, and Pacific, Dolores, and Buena Vista heights, where all 10 hills are located.

According to the San Francisco Bureau of Engineering, the steepest grades are **Filbert** between Leavenworth and Hyde, and **22nd** between Church and Vicksburg, both an awesome 31.5%; **Jones** between Union and Filbert, 29%; **Duboce** between Buena Vista and Alpine, 27.9%; **Jones** between Green and Union, and **Webster** between Vallejo and Broadway, both 26%; **Duboce** between Divisadero and Alpine, **Duboce** between Castro and Divisadero, both 25%; **Jones** between Pine and California, 24.8%; and **Fillmore** between Vallejo and Broadway, 24%.

The city's finest white-knuckle ride, however, is to zoom down one-way **Filbert Street** (31.5%) then hurtle up intersecting **Jones Street** (29%), flaunting the very forces of gravitation.

Jackson Square

Near the intersection of Columbus Ave. and Washington St.

Bounded by Pacific, Washington, Sansome, and Montgomery streets, this area—not a square in the landscaping sense—is a collection of post–gold rush architecture that, despite being erected on 19thC landfill (which included the remains of previous occupants of the "land": sailing schooners), survived the 1906 earthquake. After decades of benign neglect the commercial structures underwent painstaking restoration in the early 1950s. Jackson Square is now an official historic district, with 17 of its 3-story brick buildings having landmark status. Most are occupied by antiques dealers and art galleries.

Japan Center

Post and Buchanan streets. Hours vary by establishment.

Stretching for 3 blocks—and a focal point of the Japantown area—this cultural and commercial complex has shops, hotels, theaters, sushi bars, and restaurants. Designed by Minoru Yamasaki in 1968, the sterility of the center is somewhat relieved by the 5-tiered Peace Pagoda, a gift from the Japanese people that is reminiscent of the Pagoda of Eternal Peace in Nara, Japan.

Jewish Museum San Francisco

121 Steuart St. ☎ 415/543-8880. Sun 11am–6pm, Mon–Wed noon–6pm, Thurs noon–8pm. Admission charged; free 1st Mon of each month.

"Understanding through art" could be the theme of this institution, which also displays Judaica from all eras. By 1998, the museum will relocate to more spacious quarters, designed by Willis Polk, near Yerba Buena Gardens.

★★ Mission San Francisco de Asis (Mission Dolores)

320 Dolores St. at 16th Street. ☎ 415/621-8203. Daily 10am–4pm. Closed Thanksgiving. Admission charged.

Its formal name was and is as given, but the church is nearly always called Mission Dolores. Founded in 1776, the year of American independence, this was the 6th of the 21 Franciscan missions established in California. Spanish baroque in style, its 4-foot-thick adobe walls are now sheathed in stucco for protection from the damp. Painted ceilings, carved wood appointments, and wrought-iron work enhance the church's ancient atmosphere. The garden cemetery is a roll call of San Francisco pioneers: Francisco de Haro, the city's first mayor, and Father Francisco Palou, the padre who designed the mission, lie here, alongside some flamboyant

Mission Dolores

monuments from later years when the Irish dominated the parish.

Morrison Planetarium
(See California Academy of Sciences)

Moscone Convention Center
Howard St. between 3rd and 4th streets. ☎ 415/974-4000.

As part of the Yerba Buena development, the Center was doubled in size; it now offers conventioneers 143,362 square feet of meeting space and 442,000 square feet of exhibit area.

★ Murals of the Mission
Enlivening walls and doors of the Mission District are more than 200 murals, some big, some small, some political, some religious, some global, some parochial—all wonderfully vivid. Some have been painted by individuals, while others are collaborative efforts of artists and members of the community. The Hispanic heritage of their creators is a strong motif in the paintings.

By car, 24th Street offers a good chance to view some of the larger works. On foot, walk 10 blocks along 24th Street between Mission and York streets. Informative guided tours (see page 63) are preceded by a slide show and historical talk.

★ Museum of the City of San Francisco
2801 Leavenworth St., in The Cannery, 3rd floor. ☎ 415/928-0289. Wed–Sun 10am–4pm. Closed Mon–Tues. Admission free.

A lively exhibit of historical items significant and not-so, many of them never previously shown. Among the more impressive is the 8-ton head of the statue of the Goddess of Progress, which adorned the dome of the old City Hall before its destruction in the Shake of 1906.

★★ Oakland Museum of California Art, Ecology, and History

Oak and 10th streets, Oakland. ☎ 510/238-3401. Wed–Sat 10am–5pm, Sun noon–7pm. Closed Mon–Tues. Admission charged. Lake Merritt BART stop.

With its exceptional mix of informative, involving displays on natural and cultural history and the fine arts, the Oakland Museum offers a great way to gain insight into the enigma that is California. The permanent collection of contemporary painting and sculpture is a Who's Who of the state's talents. The building is a work of art itself: Designed by Kevin Roche in 1969, with landscaping by Dan Kiley, its staggered planes of concrete and greenery are harmony made tangible.

"Painted Ladies" (See Victorian Homes)

★★ Palace of Fine Arts

Baker and Lyon streets, adjoining the Presidio.

In less than a decade from the devastation of 1906, San Francisco resurrected itself. In 1915, the world was invited to celebrate its rebirth (coincident with the opening of the Panama Canal) at the Panama-Pacific International Exposition. The Palace of Fine Arts was its centerpiece.

Architect Bernard Maybeck set the Palace, a Greco-Romanesque rotunda embraced by Corinthian colonnades, on the edge of an idyllic reflecting pond fringed with lush shrubbery. Crowning the freestanding colonnades, downcast female figures and their cohorts illustrate "life without art," adding a romantic pathos to the site. As were all the Exposition's buildings, the Palace was designed as a temporary structure, fabricated out of plaster; public sentiment demanded it be made permanent, and so in 1968 it was rebuilt in concrete. Appearance aside, the Palace is also notable as the home of the **Exploratorium** (see p. 79) and the **San Francisco Film Festival** (see p. 202).

Pier 39

Beach and Embarcadero streets. ☎ 415/981-8030. Daily from 10:30am–8:30pm.

There are plenty of man-made diversions at Pier 39, but the biggest draw has turned out to be one of nature's creations: the hundreds of male sea lions who have installed themselves on K-Dock. The pinnipeds come and go, so their presence isn't guaranteed. But if they are in residence, the show they put on is among the best—albeit noisiest—in town.

A recent addition to the pier is **Underwater World** (daily 10am–10pm, admission charged). Visitors follow a clear acrylic tunnel through the middle of a 700,000-gallon fish tank populated with 2,000 examples of aquatic life, including sharks, rays, and sea turtles.

Beyond these attractions, Pier 39 consists mainly of themed specialty shops, restaurants, arcades, and street performers, all of which have a hypnotic and irresistible appeal to children. It's also a hub for bay cruise operators.

★ St. Mary's Cathedral of the Assumption

1111 Gough St. at Geary St. Mon–Fri 7am–5pm; Sat–Sun 7am–6:30pm, except during special masses.

This replacement for the traditional cathedral of the Catholic Diocese of San Francisco, following its destruction by fire in 1962, was controversial throughout its construction because of its radical style. Completed in 1971 under the guidance of architect Pietro Belluschi and engineer Pier Luigi Nervi, the sleek marble structure rises to a height of 190 feet from concrete pylons. Officially described as a quartet of hyperbolic paraboloids, the church resembles a washing-machine agitator from the outside to some, but its soaring, cruciform interior is undeniably awesome. The cathedral's pipe organ is a grand sculpture as well.

St. Mary's Cathedral of the Assumption

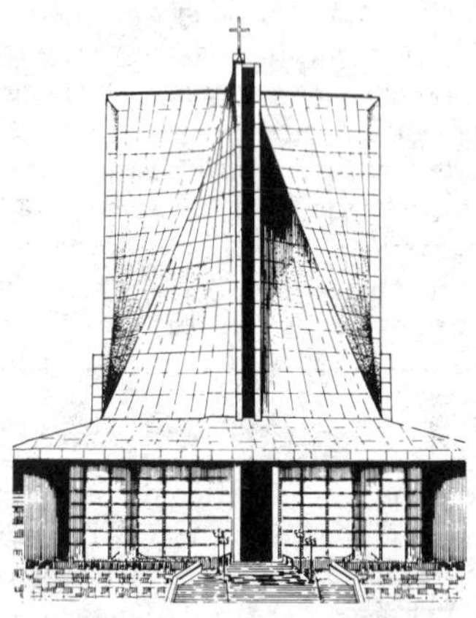

★ San Francisco Art Institute Galleries

800 Chestnut St. ☎ 415/771-7020. Walter McBean Gallery: Tues–Sat 10am–5pm, Thurs 10am–8pm; Diego Gallery: Mon–Fri 10am–5pm. Admission free.

This college of fine arts maintains 2 public galleries showing contemporary works. One boasts a mural by Diego Rivera. The buildings that house the galleries—one a 1926 Spanish colonial, courtyard-studded structure by Bakewell and Brown; the other a roughly elegant slab of concrete by Paffard Keatinge Clay done in 1969—are of interest both for themselves and for the views they offer across the city (have a cup of coffee at the student cafe and see for yourself). A new graduate studies structure, designed by Hodgetts & Fung of Los Angeles, is under construction at 2290 Taylor St.

★ San Francisco Fire Department Museum

655 Presidio Ave. ☎ 415/558-3891. Thurs–Sun 1–4pm. Closed Mon–Wed. Admission free.

Among fascinating displays of the history of local fire fighting are relics from the Great Earthquake and fire of 1906.

★ San Francisco Maritime National Historical Park

900 Beach St. ☎ 415/556-3002. Daily 10am–5pm with longer hours in summer. Admission free for museum; admission charged for ships.

The various components of the museum are all under the aegis of the National Park Service, as part of the **Golden Gate National Recreation Area.** Together they explain much of San Francisco's vibrant maritime era, through a pleasing mixture of grand and humble vessels.

The **Maritime Museum** building houses models, artifacts, photographs, and other naval memorabilia. Some of the most telling exhibits relate to the gold rush days. Linking the museum and Hyde Street Pier is **Aquatic Park,** a patch of lawn and garden, a beach, and, hidden away in trees near the base of Municipal Pier, some big-league bocce courts. **Municipal Pier,** accessible from Aquatic Park or the end of Van Ness Avenue, is a breakwater and heavily used fishing spot.

At the **Hyde Street Pier** (at the foot of Hyde, ☎ 415/556-3002, daily 10am–5pm) are moored the 1890 San Francisco–Oakland steam ferry ***Eureka,*** the 1895 lumber schooner ***C.A. Thayer*** (a common 19thC vessel), the 1891 scow ***Alma*** (a hay-hauler in the bay). Other ships in the museum fleet are the ***Balclutha,*** the **SS *Jeremiah O'Brien,*** and the World War II submarine

USS *Pampanito,* which is berthed at Pier 45 (☎ 415/929-0202).

The *Balclutha,* a typical iron-hulled, square-rigged ship from the end of the era of sail, was built in Scotland in 1886 and was the last of the Cape Horn fleet. Some below-deck areas look much as they did when the ship sailed the oceans in the 1890s, spending 20 years in the Alaskan salmon trade.

The SS *Jeremiah O'Brien* (temporarily berthed at Pier 32; ☎ 415/441-3101, Mon–Fri 9am–3pm, Sat–Sun 9am–4pm) is the last unaltered Liberty ship afloat. In 1941 American shipyards turned out 2,751 of these vessels, each completed in less than a week.

★★ San Francisco Museum of Modern Art

151 3rd St. ☎ 415/357-4000. Fri–Tues 11am–6pm, Thurs 11am–9pm. Closed Wed. Admission charged.

The new Mario Botta–designed museum—a chunky composition in red brick surrounding a black-and-white cylindrical skylight—opened in January 1995, anchoring the southeast corner of Yerba Buena Gardens. The building provides much-needed gallery space the old Civic Center edifice lacked, as well as being more aesthetically compatible with the collections of 20thC art, design, and photography. Among SFMOMA's holdings are major pieces by the Abstract Expressionists, among them Jackson Pollock, Willem de Kooning, Franz Kline, and Clyfford Still. Special attention (although some say not enough) is paid to contemporary Bay Area artists, including Nayland Blake, David Ireland, and Joan Brown. Streetside, there is an excellent gift/bookstore and **Caffè Museo** serves all day long, from breakfast to dinner.

★★ San Francisco Public Library

Larkin and Fulton streets. ☎ 415/557-4400. Tues–Thurs 10am–9pm, Mon, Fri, and Sat 10am–6pm, Sun 1–5pm.

Completed this year, the "New Main," designed by Pei Cobb Freed & Partners, turns 2 faces to passersby: the facades fronting the Civic Center tip their hat to the formal Beaux Arts buildings of the government complex, while those edging the bustling Market Street corridor assume a more commercial veneer. Step inside and survey the artworks that have been commissioned for the space, among them Alice Aycock's looping stairway and Nayland Blake's literary sconces. Across Fulton Street, the "old" library, a handsome 1917 structure by George Kelham, is being retrofitted to accommodate the Asian Art Museum, which will be displaced when the M. H. deYoung Memorial Museum is demolished.

★★ San Francisco Zoological Gardens

Sloat Blvd., near 45th Ave. ☎ 415/753-7083 (recorded message). Daily 10am–5pm. Admission charged.

The latest happening at the zoo: Cougars, jaguars, leopards, and other majestic felines have moved into their commodious new quarters. You can watch the big cats have their late lunch; it's served at 2pm (except on Mon). Primates, especially gorillas, are another premiere attraction. They live in the **Primate Discovery Center,** a $7 million home for 16 rare and endangered species, and **Gorilla World,** which, at an acre, is reputed to be the world's largest enclosed gorilla habitat, with 8 separate viewing platforms. There's much more to be seen: **Koala Crossing, Australian Walkabout, Penguin Island,** a tropical aviary, and of course a children's zoo, too.

★ Sigmund Stern Memorial Grove

Sloat Blvd. at 19th Avenue.

A beautiful natural amphitheater hidden in an urban forest of eucalyptus, redwood, and fir trees in a cozy valley below street level. On summer Sundays, join the crowd that picnics (reserve a table at ☎ 415/666-7027 on the preceding Mon) while listening to the free afternoon classical and jazz concert series.

Steinhart Aquarium
(See California Academy of Sciences)

Temple Emanu-El

Arguello Blvd. at Lake St.

The cultural and religious center of Reform Judaism in San Francisco. Its architect, Arthur Brown, Jr., also designed City Hall, and the contrast between these 2 massively domed buildings is indicative of Brown's versatility or malleability, depending on how you see it.

★ Tien Hou Temple

125 Waverly Place, 4th floor. Daily 10am–4pm.

This temple is dedicated to Tien Hou, the Queen of the Heavens. Offerings of fruit and flowers perfume the air, elaborate carvings and statuary fill the sanctuary's niches. A tip: Walk down the east side of Waverly Place to best appreciate its historic buildings.

Transamerica Pyramid

600 Montgomery St. at Columbus Ave. Observation Deck: Weekdays 10am–5pm. Admission free.

The tallest office tower in San Francisco, the sharp pyramid, 853 feet (260m) tall, was hardly greeted with universal huzzahs when built by William Pereira and Associates in 1972. But by today's design (non)standards, it's positively tame; distinguished, even. The highest occupied floor, number 48, is only 45 feet square. The observation deck is on the 27th floor.

★ Victorian Homes

Steiner St. between Fulton and Hayes streets. Also, Bush St. between Fillmore and Gough; 1200 block of Masonic St.; Liberty St. between Castro and Polk; 1834 California St.

At the first location, the 6 matching Victorian houses (also known as "Painted Ladies"), which border Alamo Square, are set against the backdrop of the modern cityscape and represent a must-shoot for visiting photographers. (If weather conditions preclude the shot, don't worry—the image is widely available on postcards and souvenirs.) The last address illustrates a typically San Franciscan architectural amalgam: Half the house is Italianate (circa 1876), half Queen Anne (1895), demonstrating the populace's fickle tastes.

Views

From the ritzy crest of residential **Nob Hill** (most easily reached by cable car), you can look down on the Bay Bridge, cradled between the towers of the Financial District and the pagoda roofs of Chinatown. Nearby **Russian Hill** offers a panorama of the Golden Gate Bridge and the bay. At the northeast corner of the city, **Telegraph Hill** also overlooks the water. One of the most spectacular hilltop vantage points is **Twin Peaks** (no kin to David Lynch's bizarre television series). A scenic drive leads to its 910-foot summit, where the vista is unobstructed. San Francisco looks especially uplifting from the water: Board a commuter ferry or drive to **Treasure Island,** or savor the liberating view from the confinements of **Alcatraz.**

★ Vintage Streetcars of Market Street

Market St., from Castro to Transbay Terminal (at 1st and Mission streets). Daily until 1am. Fee for riding streetcar.

These 17 restored streetcars, painted in the bright liveries of historic lines across the country, were put into service in September 1995 as part of the eternal effort to beautify Market Street. Built in 1947, the refurbished cars constitute Muni's new F-Market line.

★ Washington Square

Columbus Ave. at Union St.

Strictly speaking, this is not a "square" at all and has nothing to do with Washington, so North Beach, which is not a beach, is the perfect home for it. Washington Square is one of the city's nicest spots for an impromptu picnic lunch; perhaps some sourdough, prosciutto, and mozzarella from one of the many nearby delicatessens. Even the statuary in Washington Square is not what you would expect, for it is Benjamin Franklin who watches the crowds in the grassy expanse from his pedestal.

★ Wells Fargo History Room

420 Montgomery St. ☎ 415/396-2619. Mon–Fri 9am–5pm. Closed Sat, Sun, and bank holidays. Admission free.

Proudly centered around the Wells Fargo Overland Stagecoach, this museum, occupying 2 floors of the bank's headquarters, is dedicated to the rugged days of pioneer California, 1849–1906. The collection of Wild West artifacts (gold nuggets, miners' equipment, and assorted booty) and historical recountings of legendary stagecoach drivers and bandits is quite engrossing.

★★ Yerba Buena Gardens

3rd St. at Mission St.

A gleam in downtown developers' eyes in the early 1960s, the city's new arts complex is finally taking form, with several of the principal players—the Center for the Arts, the San Francisco Museum of Modern Art, and Moscone Convention Center—up and running (see the separate listings for more information on these 3 attractions). The core of the oasis is the 5-acre Esplanade, a grassy amphitheater defined by the Martin Luther King, Jr. memorial waterfalls. Slated to be in place by 2000: The Jewish Museum, the Mexican Museum, and a children's cultural center.

San Francisco Walks

It's something of an understatement to label San Francisco a "walking city," capitulating to a term that is so literally pedestrian. San Francisco is a promenading, wandering, huffing-and-puffing city. It's built on 42 hills, some of them merely steep inclines, others requiring stairways to ascend, as the song goes, halfway to the stars. These suggested routes aren't nearly that strenuous. They're designed to be walked in about an hour or so; if you have the time or inclination to linger at any of the sights along the way, so much the better.

Walk 1: Coit Tower—Filbert Steps—North Beach

Capping Telegraph Hill (so named for its 19thC use as a semaphore station, which signaled the approach of incoming clippers and schooners to the citizenry), (1) **Coit Tower** and its Depression-era murals are a must-see. Once you've finished your tour of the tower, find the Filbert Steps by crossing the parking lot to the Greenwich Street sign and descending a red brick stairway to Montgomery Street. For decades before the construction of Coit Tower, this area was inhabited by a progression of dockworkers, shanghaied sailors (the term originated in these parts), and artists in modest shingled cottages; with the advent of the monument, the neighborhood was "discovered" and gradually grew in prosperity. Proceed down the eastern side of Montgomery to the intersecting (2) **Filbert Steps.**

Walk down the wooden stairs towards the bay, enjoying the fruits of the residents' gardening efforts. One of the oldest homes on the hill is at (3) **224 Filbert;** built in 1863, it was finely restored in 1978.

Coit Tower

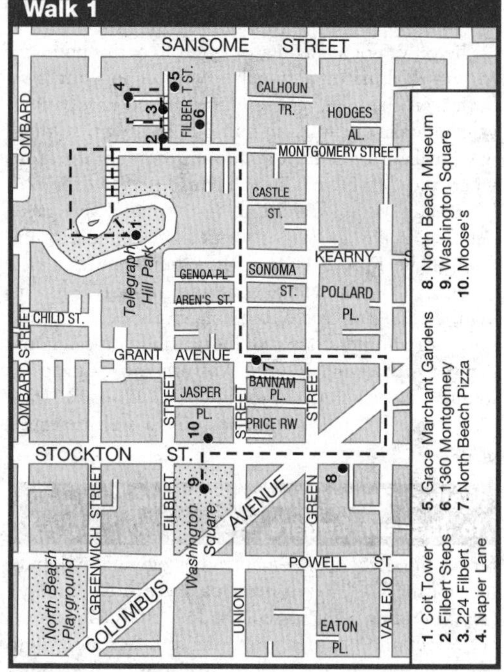

The rocky outcrop upon which these houses sit was once a convenient source of ballast for Gold Rush–era ships, which tied up in what was once the harbor at the base of the hill. Turn left onto flowery (4) **Napier Lane** for a chance to wander down one of the few remaining boardwalks in the city. At the end of the Filbert Steps, the (5) **Grace Marchant Gardens** are an urban idyll; on Halloween, hundreds of jack-o'-lanterns (carved by neighbors) glow eerily throughout the thick plantings here.

Retrace your path to Montgomery Street—catch your breath—and resume your downhill direction, noting (6) **no. 1360,** an Art Deco apartment building which was one of the settings for the Bogart-Bacall movie *Dark Passage*—and turn right on Union Street to reach the relative flatlands of North Beach. Make a left on busy Grant Avenue, where you can recharge over a snack at any number of cafes; try the pesto-topped pie at (7) **North Beach Pizza** *(1499 Grant Ave.; ☎ 415/433-2444)*. Browse the funky shops and boutiques until you come to Vallejo Street, where you'll bear right and cross the diagonal artery of Columbus Avenue; it's a block more to Stockton Street.

If you've got a craving for egg rolls at this point, go left into Chinatown (we'll leave you to your own devices, if that's the case—or better yet, urge you to wait and take our walking tour of Chinatown). Otherwise, make a right turn and look for 1435 Stockton, where the (8) **North Beach Museum** *(☎ 415/626-7070; open Mon–Thurs 10am–4pm, Fri until 5pm, closed Sat–Sun; admission free)* is located on the mezzanine level of the Eureka Federal Bank building. It's a rich repository of historic photos and artifacts illustrating the changing face of the neighborhood. Continue north for another couple of blocks, and you can command a park bench in (9) **Washington Square** for some bocce-watching, or slip into (10) **Moose's** *(1652 Stockton St.; ☎ 415/989-7800)* for a well-deserved drink.

Walk 2: Transamerica Pyramid to Jackson Square

Once your dizzy spell—incurred by ogling the sloping sides of the (1) **Transamerica Pyramid,** the city's tallest building—has passed, head north to Montgomery Street and bear left on Columbus Avenue, where the Pyramid's ancestral home still stands. A striking beaux arts flatiron structure clad in creamy terra cotta, (2) **4 Columbus Ave.** was built in 1909 for the Banco Populare Italiano Operaia Fugazi (whew!), which in a 1928 presaging of today's merger mania was subsumed by A. P. Gianninni's Bank of Italy. The bank's holding company, the Transamerica Corporation, made

Transamerica Building

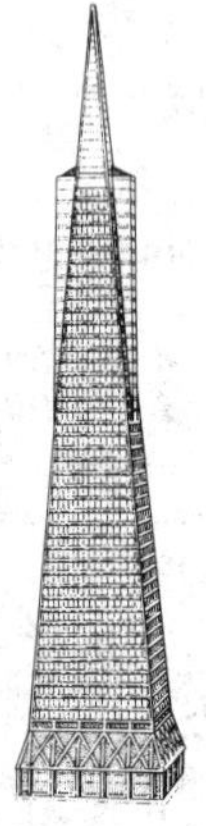

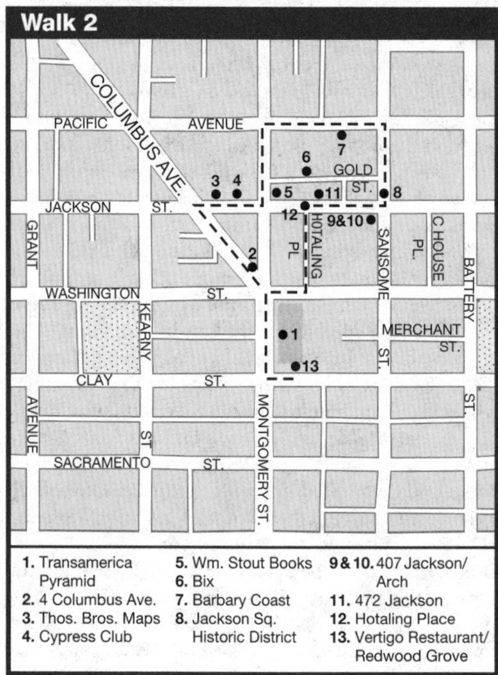

the building its headquarters in 1938; it remained there until the modern monolith was completed in 1972.

Up at the corner, make a right on Jackson Street. At no. 550, the (3) **Thomas Brothers Maps** store *(☎ 415/981-7520)* is a treat for cartography buffs. Depending on what time of day you choose to make this walk, it may be too early for a respite, but pop your head into the (4) **Cypress Club** *(500 Jackson St.; ☎ 415/296-8555)* for a visual tour de force of the surreal kind.

A left on Montgomery brings you to (5) **William Stout Architectural Books** *(804 Montgomery St.; ☎ 415/391-6757)*, in whose voluminous stacks of design books and periodicals you can easily and pleasantly blow the hour-plus we've allotted for this tour (not to mention a considerable bit of cash). The brick structure was built in 1853 as the home of the Bank of Lucas, Turner and Company, which for a while was directed by William Tecumseh Sherman.

Now, you can either backtrack a few feet and cut through the alley that is Gold Street or circle around on the 400 block of Pacific; either way, do slip into the neo-Deco (6) **Bix** *(56 Gold St.; ☎ 415/433-6300)* for a bite to eat. Assuming you're taking the Pacific route, in the mid-1800s this block was the heart of the infamous (7) **Barbary Coast.** The street teemed with unsavories of all types: thieves, kidnappers, prostitutes, crooked politicians, and gangs of vicious thugs—one type of which, known as the "Sydney Ducks," had a deadly penchant for torching large areas of the city. The Ducks were eventually one-upped by the fires of 1906.

When you reach Sansome Street, turn right, then right again on Jackson. The structures here survived the 1906 calamity by virtue of a pair of navy fire tugs, whose crew laid a mile-long hose, from the waterfront up over the shoulder of Telegraph Hill and down Montgomery Street, and flooded the area. In the 1950s, run-down and dilapidated, they were spared the wrecking ball owing to farsighted and faithful restoration by members of the interior design profession. The San Francisco Board of Supervisors declared (8) **Jackson Square** the city's first historic district in 1972.

At (9) **407 Jackson St.,** a rare 1860 example of commercial Italianate design, Domingo Ghirardelli once plied his chocolate trade before moving to the north shore of the city. Today, the building is occupied by (10) **Arch,** an art supply cum gift store that's worth a look. Wander past the many fine antiques showrooms that line the street to (11) **472 Jackson St.** (formerly the French consulate), which best typifies the straightforward architectural style favored by the merchants of the 1850s. Originally, salvaged ships' masts were used as its interior columns.

Midblock you'll encounter (12) **Hotaling Place,** a pedestrian shortcut through to Washington Street. The buildings at its entrance were part of the A. P. Hotaling distillery enterprise. It was the durability of the iron-shuttered Hotaling works which inspired the much-quoted jingle attributed to Charles Field. According to the chroniclers of the time, when local clergymen interpreted the 1906 disaster as divine retribution for the wickedness of the city, the writer irreverently queried:

If, as they say, God spanked the town
For being over-frisky,
Why did He burn His churches down
And spare Hotaling's whisky?

When you reach the end of Hotaling, you'll see you've made an irregular loop of sorts, as you're back at the (new) **Transamerica** edifice.

Go around to the Clay Street entrance and enjoy a bucolic surprise: a pocket park of 80 redwoods transplanted from the coastal mountains of Santa Cruz. This is a good place to contemplate what stood on this site before. Erected in 1853 on a raft of timbers sunk in the mud of the then-shoreline, the Montgomery Block was home to an extraordinary coterie of artists and industrialists. George Sterling, Samuel Clemens, Frank Norris, and other literati shared the 4-story structure with the U.S. Army Corps of Engineers, bullion vaults of the Adams Express Company, the offices of the Pacific and Atlantic Railroad, and 2 newspapers, the *Alta California* and the *Daily Herald*. Most days they gathered in the Bank Exchange Saloon over potent brandy concoctions that went by the sobriquet "Pisco Punch" to engage in what we can only assume to be highly spirited conversation. In 1959, the historic property was razed to make way for a parking lot. Step inside the aptly named (13) **Vertigo** restaurant *(☎ 415/433-7250)* at the base of the Pyramid and raise a toast to these luminaries of the past.

Walk 3: Chinatown

Even for first-time visitors, the appeal of Grant Avenue, Chinatown's most commercialized corridor, can wear a little thin after traversing its crowded blocks, lined as they are with a bright mosaic of unabashedly tourist-oriented curio shops and trinket stands. For a look at the more authentic, exotic side of the area, a trek through its backstreets is in order.

Bank of Canton

Walking north from the ceremonial portal, the ① **Dragon Gate** at Bush Street, turn right off Grant Avenue at Washington to study the old ② **Chinese Telephone Exchange** branch of Pacific Telephone and Telegraph *(743 Bush St., now the **Bank of Canton**)*. Built in 1909—remember, Chinatown, too, was completely destroyed in 1906—in an overtly Asian style intended to enhance the cultural identity of the neighborhood, this 3-tiered pagoda was manned by operators who were fluent not only in English, but also 5 dialects of Chinese. Until the development of direct-dial telephone service in 1949, these workers coped with the daunting task of manually putting through the calls of the hundreds of residents who disregarded phone numbers and asked for their parties by name; as the operators' directories were organized by street address only, this meant they had to essentially commit thousands of names and numbers to memory—in a total of 6 languages, no less!

If that nugget of mental dexterity temporarily overwhelms you, pay a visit to ③ **Li Po,** a few steps north of the corner at 916 Grant Ave. *(☎ 415/982-0072)*. At this cocktail lounge, with its extraordinarily exaggerated interior, you can bask in a comfortable time-warp of big-band music emanating from the jukebox.

Refreshed, continue west along Washington Street to Ross Alley on your right. It was along such hidden lanes as these that the lower-income families lived and opium dens prospered long ago. At 14 Ross Alley, the ④ **Sam Bo Trading Company** *(☎ 415/397-3958)* purveys all manner of Buddhist religious trappings: personal shrines, statues, lanterns, and more. Further down, the ⑤ **Golden Gate Fortune Cookie Company** *(56 Ross Alley; ☎ 415/781-3956)* is a 2-person enterprise where you're welcome to watch the fortune-making/baking process—and even more welcome to buy a bag of their wares.

Now go left on Jackson Street to Stockton, where you'll turn left again to experience a slice of the daily life of Chinatown's residents. Herb shops, bakeries, butcher stores, fish mongers, and vegetable stands proliferate. Between Sacramento and Clay streets, 2 buildings are worthy of note. Inside the post office at 855 Stockton St., the ⑥ **Kong Chow Temple** *(take the lobby elevator to the top floor; ☎ 415/434-2513)*, a 1977 creation by Ed Sue, is filled with antique furnishings and boasts a superlative view of the bay; and the

elaborate Technicolor facade of 843 Stockton St., the headquarters of the (7) **Chinese Six Companies,** a collective bargaining association of local merchants that was constructed in 1908.

A left on Sacramento leads to (8) **Waverly Place,** poetically known as "The Street of Painted Balconies." A walk down the east side of this 2-block stretch affords the best vantage point for admiring the ornate postearthquake structures, most of them family associations and benevolent societies. The building that houses the (9) **Eng Family Benevolent Association,** 53 Waverly Place, is an exuberant collage of everything *chinoise;* the 1907 edifice was remodeled in 1948, when the neon tracery (!) was applied. On the 3rd floor of 109 Waverly Place, another 1907 structure, the (10) **Norras Temple** is a tranquil sanctuary of incense and music, its altar surrounded by golden Buddha figures. The (11) **Tin How Temple** *(☎ 415/391-4841),* on the 4th story of the 1911 Lee Family Benevolent Association at 125 Waverly Place, is dedicated to the guardian of travelers—in both the physical and spiritual sense. Flickering oil lamps and offerings of fruit make it an especially serene rest stop. On the historically and numerically portent date of October 10 (the anniversary of the 1911 overthrow of the Manchurian regime in mainland China), many of these buildings are festively illuminated and bedecked with flags and banners.

Conclude your ramble with a plate of tasty dumplings and tea at the (12) **Pot Sticker** restaurant *(150 Waverly Place; ☎ 415/397-9985).*

Frisco for Kids

San Francisco and its environs offer ample ways for children to expend their pent-up energies in instructive—or ingenious—play. Some of these pursuits are obvious: riding the cable cars, screaming in the bleachers at a Giants or A's game, clambering around on historic schooners down at the docks. But there are other opportunities for fun only an insider would know; for instance, out on a bayside jetty lies the Wave Organ, a construction best described as a marine aeolian harp. Here, we've provided a quick-reference list of places and activities that kids will enjoy.

Educational Experiences

Animals: Zoos and Aquariums

Coyote Point Museum for Environmental Education (1651 Coyote Point Dr., San Mateo; ☎ 415/342-7755; Tues–Sat 10am–5pm, Sun 12pm–5pm; closed Mon; admission charged) A walk-through aviary, colorful gardens of indigenous plants and wildflowers, and more at this progressive facility.

Marine Mammal Center (Marin Headlands, Sausalito; ☎ 415/289-7325; daily 10am–4pm; admission free) Watch up close as volunteers nurse sea otters and other ailing marine mammals back to health.

Monterey Bay Aquarium (886 Cannery Row, Monterey; ☎ 408/648-4888; daily 10am–6pm; admission charged) If you've got the time (it's about a 3-hour drive from San Francisco) definitely visit this world-renowned aquarium, hard by Monterey Bay. Kids love to pet the manta rays in the tidepool exhibit and watch the sharks glide through the 3-story kelp forest. Call ahead to reserve tickets.

Pier 39 (Beach Street and Embarcadero; ☎ 415/981-PIER) Up to 600 sea lions haul out on K-dock. Just follow the barking.

San Francisco Zoo (Sloat Blvd. at 45th Ave.; ☎ 415/753-7083; daily 10am–5pm; admission charged) Welcome the big cats—cougars, cheetahs, and leopards—to their just-opened habitat.

Steinhart Aquarium (California Academy of Sciences; ☎ 415/750-7145) See page 73 for more information.

Underwater World (Pier 39; ☎ 415/623-5300; daily 10am–10pm; admission charged) Get a diver's-eye view of the ocean and 2,000 indigenous marine species from a 400-foot acrylic tunnel through the sea.

History Museums

California Historical Society (678 Mission St.; ☎ 415/357-1848) See page 73 for more information.

Fort Point (off Lincoln Blvd. at Long Ave.; ☎ 415/556-1373; daily 10am–5pm; admission free) Light the fuse on a Civil War–era cannon at this historic fortress.

Levi Strauss History Tour (250 Valencia St.; ☎ 415/565-9159; tours given Wed 10:30am and 1pm; reservations required; admission free) Learn everything you ever wanted to know about the famous work-pants at the birthplace of blue jeans.

Oakland Museum of California Art, Ecology, and History (Oak and 10th streets, Oakland; ☎ 510/238-3401; Wed–Sat 10am–5pm, Sun noon–7pm; closed Mon–Tues; admission charged) Giant 3-dimensional maps, Native American artifacts, and changing installations combine to give an indelible impression of the Golden State's heritage from pre-history to the current day. The concrete-terraced building was designed by Kevin Roche in 1969; its grassy plazas and koi pond are very much the urban oasis.

Wells Fargo History Room (420 Montgomery St.; ☎ 415/396-2619; Mon–Fri 9am–5pm; closed Sat and Sun; admission free) Stagecoaches and frontier memorabilia from "When the West was Young."

Science and Technology Museums

Audium (1616 Bush St.; ☎ 415/771-1616; Fri–Sat 8:30am; admission charged) For 75 awesome aural minutes, 169 high-tech speakers immerse listeners in sounds.

The Bay Model (Marinship Way, Sausalito; ☎ 415/332-3871; Tues–Sat 9am–4pm; closed Sun–Mon; admission charged) It's fun to watch the tiny tides roll in and out of this working model of the San Francisco bay and delta region.

Exploratorium (Palace of Fine Arts, 3601 Lyon St.; ☎ 415/561-0360; Tues and Thurs–Sat 10am–5pm, Wed 10am–9:30pm, closed Mon; admission charged) More than 650 whirling, ringing, and otherwise interactive exhibits demystify the wonders of science. The sense of touch is fully explored in the pitch-dark Tactile Dome; reservations are required (☎ 415/561-0362).

Lawrence Hall of Science (UC Berkeley campus; ☎ 510/642-5132; daily 10am–5pm; admission charged) Fabulous bay vistas can be had from this octagonal structure designed by Anshen and Allen in 1968. The building's shape represents the eight branches of physical science: astronomy, biology, chemistry, geology, mathematics, nuclear science, physics, and space science.

Morrison Planetarium (California Academy of Sciences; ☎ 415/750-7145; daily 10am–5pm, summer 9am–6pm admission charged).

Transportation Museums

Although contemporary San Francisco moves by automobile and airplane, it celebrates the contribution of railroads and sailing ships in two transit museums.

Cable Car Museum (1201 Mason St.; ☎ 415/474-1887; daily 10am–5pm; admission free).

San Francisco Maritime National Historical Park at Hyde Street Pier (900 Beach St.; ☎ 415/556-3002; hours vary by ship; admission free for museum, charged for ships).

Just for Kids

Bay Area Discovery Museum (557 East Fort Baker, Sausalito; ☎ 415/487-4398; Tues–Thurs 9am–3pm, Fri–Sun 10am–5pm, closed Mon; admission charged) Scramble underneath a house, broadcast your very own radio show; a wide range of exhibits taps into kids' creative abilities and curiosities.

Children's Fairyland (Lakeside Park, Grand and Bellvue, Oakland; ☎ 510/238-6876; 10am–4:30pm, open only Fri–Sun in winter, closed Mon–Tues except summer; admission charged) The innocent inspiration for Walt Disney's eponymous entertainment complex, this was the first themed children's park in the United States when it was built in 1950. No hulking costumed characters, no souvenir hawkers, just good and gentle fun in a lovely park setting.

Randall Museum (199 Museum Way; ☎ 415/554-9600; Tues–Sat 10am–5pm; closed Sun–Mon; admission free). On these 16 acres overlooking the bay, there's a petting corral and assorted arts and science programs.

The Arts and Hobbies

Carousel Museum (633 Beach St.; ☎ 415/928-0550). Call ahead to schedule a tour of the turn-of-the-century carved critters.

Cartoon Art Museum (814 Mission St.; ☎ 415/227-8666; Wed–Fri 11am–5pm, Sat 10am–5pm, Sun 1pm–5pm, closed Mon; admission charged) The only museum west of the Mississippi dedicated to the preser vation, collection, and exhibition of original cartoon art in all its forms, it features a children's gallery and an interactive CD-ROM room.

Musée Mécanique (1090 Point Lobos Ave.; ☎ 415/386-1170; 11am–7pm; admission free, most games 25¢) An arcade out of the past, this collection of antique coin-operated game machines is just as entertaining as anything Nintendo has produced.

Young Performers Theatre (Bldg. C, Fort Mason; ☎ 415/346-5550) Performance schedules change, so phone to see what's playing.

In a city that takes doesn't take its restaurants with a grain of salt, youngsters can get a head start on their culinary skill in the **cooking class** held at the Ferry Plaza Farmers Market every Saturday at 10:30am. "Tuition" is a mere dollar.

Budding Bobby Fishers hang out at the **chess club** (San Francisco Public Library, Larkin and Fulton streets; ☎ 415/557-4554): variations include international, Chinese, Vietnamese, Japanese, and Korean chess; also Go and Scrabble. Call to find out when meetings are held.

Again courtesy of the library: **Dial-a-Story** (☎ 415/626-6516).

Entertaining Experiences

Games

A word of caution: Right after lunch is *not* the best time to pay a visit to these places. All of these attractions can be found at Pier 39 at Beach Street and Embarcadero.

Cybermind Virtual Reality Center (Pier 39; ☎ 415/399-8950; daily from 10:30am; admission charged) The latest in video technology allows you to see the "world" from fantastic and hitherto unimaginable vantage points.

Frequent Flyers Bungee Trampoline (Pier 39; ☎ 415/207-5548; daily from 10:30am; admission charged) Even Michael Jordan doesn't have hang time like this 25-foot jump.

Q-Zar (2801 Leavenworth St.; ☎ 415/775-6700; daily from 10:30am; admission charged) Stalk your siblings through the maze, then zap them with harmless laser beams.

Turbo Ride (Pier 39; ☎ 415/392-8872; daily from 10:30am; admission charged) Two words: seat belts.

Shopping

Cell Block 41 (Pier 41; ☎ 415/249-4666) If the little darlings start to get out of hand, a visit to this store should plant some subliminal suggestions in their still-forming consciousness. T-shirts, silly postcards, and other Alcatraz-inspired items.

The Disney Store (Pier 39; ☎ 415/391-4119) Mickey, Donald, and friends are emblazoned on everything from toothbrushes to leather jackets.

Kite Flight (Pier 39; ☎ 415/956-3181) After a spree at this shop, head for the city's best kite-flying field, Marina Green.

Kitty City (Pier 39; ☎ 415/986-7684) From Krazy Kat to Felix to Garfield, there's something here to satisfy every feline fan.

Magnet P.I. (Pier 39; ☎ 415/989-2361) As if your fridge didn't have enough of these already.

Music Tracks Recording Studios (Pier 39; ☎ 415/981-1777) Record your favorite song and take home the tape.

Puppets on the Pier (Pier 39; ☎ 415/781-4435) Finger puppets, marionettes, and more.

Special-Interest Tours

Basic Brown Bear (444 DeHaro; ☎ 415/626-0781) Kids help design and stuff their new best friend here.

Ghiardelli Chocolate Manufactory (900 North Point; ☎ 415/771-4903).

Golden Gate Fortune Cookie Company (56 Ross Alley, ☎ 415/781-3956).

The Great Outdoors

Golden Gate Park Stow Lake for boat rentals, Spreckles Lake for model-ship sailing, the Buffalo Paddock for . . . bison, of course.

Wave Organ (Marina Blvd. at Baker St., at the end of the yacht club jetty) As the water rips through a series of buried tubes, an eerie but beautiful music emits.

Julius Kahn Playground in the Presidio (West Pacific Ave. at Spruce).

Steam Trains (Tilden Regional Park, Berkeley; ☎ 510/548-6100) Handmade and steam-powered, these diminutive engines carry riders through a rugged landscape.

Restaurants

Toy Boat Dessert Cafe

401 Clement St. ☎ 415/751-7505. No credit cards. **$**.
More bang for your parental buck here, with 2 kid-pleasing emporiums in one. Playthings from Power Rangers to Punch and Judy dolls share space with a soda fountain that features Double Rainbow ice creams.

Isobune

1737 Post St. ☎ 415/563-1030. MC, V. **$$**.
More boats . . . only this time the cargo is sushi.

Mel's Drive-In

3355 Geary St. ☎ 415/387-2244. No credit cards. **$**.
Straight out of *American Graffiti*, with jukeboxes in every booth to divert the young ones while they wait for the decent burgers and shakes.

Planet Hollywood

2 Stockton St. ☎ 415/421-7827. AE, MC, V. **$**.
Props and costumes from San Francisco–set movies—*Star Trek IV, 48 Hours, Dirty Harry*, and more—are the draw.

Hard Rock Cafe

1699 Van Ness Ave. ☎ 415/885-1699. AE, MC, V. **$**.
No artifacts from Smashing Pumpkins or Nine Inch Nails grace the walls yet, but you'll find stuff from Van Halen and other rockers of earlier eras.

MacArthur Park

607 Front St. ☎ 415/398-5700. AE, MC, V. **$$**.
You'll enjoy the baby back ribs (and the full bar); the kids occupy themselves creating Crayola masterpieces on the butcher paper table-coverings.

Staying Active

Beaches

Aquatic Park (Hyde St. on the Bay, ☎ 415/556-3002) The water is warmest in September at this domesticated inlet situated at the western end of Fisherman's Wharf.

Baker Beach (Lincoln Blvd. at 25th Ave., ☎ 415/556-8371) This mile-long sandy shore is popular with surf fishers, strollers, and picnickers, who in fair weather gather at the tables and grills at the east end of the parking lot. However, waves and currents here are perilous for swimmers. Sunbathers who prefer catching their rays *au naturel* congregate at the beach's north end.

China Beach (28th Ave. and Sea Cliff, ☎ 415/556-8371) The only safe place to swim in San Francisco proper aside from Aquatic Park, this tiny cove is patrolled by lifeguards during the summer months. Tucked between Baker Beach and Lands End, you'll find showers and changing rooms available.

Ocean Beach (Geary Blvd. to Fort Funston on the Pacific Ocean; ☎ 415/556-8371) A formidable undertow makes its waters too dangerous for swimming, but walkers and joggers have plenty of room to amble along the esplanade that tops this beach's 3-mile seawall. From the foot of Ortega Street you can see the remains of one of the many ships that have met their end upon the submerged rocks; the *King Philip* sank on this spot in 1878. Ocean winds whip down this segment of the Pacific coast; to the north, the breakers are ripe for surfing, while along the southern cliffs, the upwelling breezes attract flocks of hang gliders.

Biking: City and Mountain

For bicycle, helmet, and accessory rentals, **Marina Cyclery** (3330 Steiner St., ☎ 415/929-7135) and **Start**

to Finish (2530 Lombard St., ☎ 415/202-9830) are local merchants of good repute.

On Sundays, John F. Kennedy Drive in Golden Gate Park is closed to cars, giving cyclists 7.5 miles of free-wheeling to such sights as the Japanese Tea Garden, the Dutch windmill, and Stow Lake. If you're feeling strong of leg, continue west to the Great Highway, the coastal route that parallels Ocean Beach (stash a windbreaker in a backpack for this stretch). Three dedicated bicycle lanes ensure safe passage.

A couple of tips for riders who venture into downtown territory: Wide tires are much more compatible with slick cable-car tracks than are narrow treads. And when crossing them, make sure you do so at a right angle.

Mountain bikers take off for the trails that thread through the Marin Headlands and around Mount Tamalpais. Crossing the Golden Gate Bridge to these areas can be a workout in itself, owing to the relentless crosswinds.

Billiards and Parlor Games

More than a pool hall, **The Great Entertainer** (975 Bryant, ☎ 415/861-8833) offers plenty of family entertainment: table tennis, shuffleboard, darts, and more. **Chalker's Billiards Club** (101 Spear, Rincon Center, ☎ 415/512-0450) is an upscale parlor, with 30 custom and antique tables. **South Beach Billiards** (270 Brannan, ☎ 415/495-5939) is a cavernous place popular with the SoMa set; they serve good food, better beer, and have an indoor bocce court amidst the 37 pool tables.

Boating and Water Sports

Boating

The San Francisco skyline is perhaps most memorable when seen from the sea. The least expensive aqueous excursions are the commuter ferry lines, which connect San Francisco with ports north and east. Contact the **Blue & Gold Fleet** (☎ 510/522-3300); **Golden Gate Ferries** (☎ 415/332-6600); **Harbor Bay Maritime** (☎ 510/769-5500); or **Red & White Fleet** (☎ 415/546-2628) for routes and schedules. Another option is to take one of the many commercial tours offered. **Pacific Marine Yachts** (☎ 415/788-9100) and **Adventure Cat Sailing Charters** (☎ 415/

777-1630) are but two; most of these feature dinner and brunch cruises. Finally, there are private charter operations offering crafts of all kinds for rent, with a skipper or on a bareboat basis; one, **Rendezvous Charters/Spinnaker Sailing** (Pier 40; ☎ 415/543-7333) has more than 40 vessels from which to choose, from classic sailing schooners to luxury motor yachts.

Visitors who really want to get their feet wet may want to consider the following pursuits.

Jet Skiing

Sausalito Jet Ski (85 Liberty Way, Sausalito, ☎ 415/331-1133) Everything from wet suits to towels is provided for renters of these noisy but mobile speedsters.

Sea Kayaking

Sea Trek Ocean Kayaking Center (P.O. Box 561, Woodacre, CA 94973, ☎ 415/488-1000) An otter's-eye view of the world is had from these small, stable craft, which can hold one or two people.

Windsurfing

Cityfront Sailboards (2233 Larkspur Landing Circle, Larkspur, ☎ 415/925-8585) Instruction and equipment for first-timers and experienced boarders alike.

Camping, Climbing and Hiking

There's certainly an argument to be made that scaling the fabled hills of San Francisco constitutes hiking rather than walking. But if you're looking for a respite from concrete underfoot, there are peaceful redwood forests that are laced with well-maintained trails only minutes away. In the Berkeley hills, the paths of **Tilden Park** (☎ 510/562-7275) are popular, while to the north, **Mount Tamalpais State Park** (☎ 415/388-2070) is a favorite getaway.

Campers can find many sites in the immediate vicinity that are remarkable for their natural beauty: **Kirby Cove** sits virtually underneath the Golden Gate Bridge on the Marin County side; **Angel Island** boasts solitude in the middle of the bay, and just south of Stinson Beach; **Steep Ravine** offers rustic cabins with an ocean vista. Contact the **California Department of Parks and Recreation** (☎ 916/653-4000) for further information; reservations can be made through **DESTINET** (☎ 800/444-7275). Tents, sleeping bags, and other back-country necessities can be rented from **REI** (1338 San Pablo Ave., Berkeley, ☎ 510/527-4140).

Climbing Gyms

Should your hotel concierge frown on your brushing up on your rappelling techniques in the comfort and privacy of your room, there are a few climbing gyms in the area. Day passes hover in the area of $15, with nominal shoe and harness rental fees additional. Call for hours and class information.

City Rock (1250 45th St., Emeryville, ☎ 510/654-2510) In the East Bay, this facility has 8,000 square feet of climbing terrain, with 40-foot walls. Bouldering (climbing without ropes) practice available.

Mission Cliffs (2295 Harrison St., ☎ 415/550-0515) This club boasts a 12,000-square-foot climbing area and 50-foot walls; weight room and sauna use included with day pass.

Golf

Limber up at **Mission Bay Golf Center** (1200 6th St., ☎ 415/431-7888). At this bayside driving range, 2 floors of duffers aim for the 400-yard mark. There's a putting green and cafe, too. If your game requires a more intensive tune-up, **Driving Obsession** (310 Grant Ave., Suite 402, ☎ 415/397-4653) provides digital video analysis of your swing and stance, along with more in-depth instruction.

When you're ready for the real thing, there are several 9- and 18-hole public and semi-private links in and near the city.

Golden Gate Park Course (47th Ave. at Fulton St., ☎ 415/751-8987) Nine holes, 1,357 yards, par 27. Greens fees are very reasonable.

Harding Park (Skyline Blvd. at Harding Rd., ☎ 415/664-4690) has two courses: the Fleming course has 9 holes (2,316 yards, par 32), and the more challenging Harding Park links (6,743 yards, par 72), which occupy a peninsula embraced by Lake Merced.

Lincoln Park Golf Course (Clement St. at 34th Ave., ☎ 415/221-9911) This 5,150 yard-par 68 course is rated 64.3; some of its 18 holes feature the Golden Gate Bridge in the background.

If you're going to pay a visit to the wine country, go ahead and bring your clubs: the **Chardonnay Golf Club** (2555 Jameson Canyon Rd., Napa, ☎ 707/257-8950) opens one of its two 18-hole courses to the public.

Horseback Riding

Golden Gate Park Stables (JFK Dr. and 36th Ave., ☎ 415/668-7360) Pony rides for kids, and guided trail treks through Golden Gate Park for equestrians of all abilities.

Jogging and Fitness

The iron-men and -women among you can follow all or part of the route of the **San Francisco Marathon** (☎ 415/391-2123 to request a map). Miles 6 through 8 make up a scenic but demanding (translation: hilly) section of the race: from Leavenworth Street, go south on Columbus to Grant, then turn left on Bush and left again on Kearny. Bear right at Jackson and you'll end up at the Embarcadero. Because this path runs through the heart of Chinatown, it's best to tackle it in the early hours, well before streets and sidewalks become congested.

Mere mortals can enjoy a noon-time sprint along the Embarcadero, cooled by bay breezes and views all the way from Market Street to Marina Green. It's a flat dash, and round-trip mileage is approximately 4 miles. At Marina Green (Scott St.), there's a fitness parcourse. On your return, remember to detour out along Pier 7 (at Broadway) for the great skyline silhouette. This circuit is also favored by in-line skaters.

Workouts and Renewals

With locations throughout the city, 24-hour **Nautilus Fitness Centers** (☎ 800/24 WORKOUT for addresses) make it nigh impossible to miss a day on the Stairmaster or treadmill. Aerobic classes are offered around the clock, accommodating the most extreme schedules. In addition to strength-training apparatus and cardiovascular equipment, **Club One** (350 3rd St., ☎ 415/543-8466) features a heated outdoor lap pool.

For a speedy recovery from the rigors of exercise—physical or mental—the most aesthetic massage experience in San Francisco is found at **Body Work** (155 South Park, ☎ 415/896-2224) where Marc Ellyn Garth practices an integrated massage system in a tranquil, Zen-influenced studio. If your aches are simply superficial, a soak in the traditional Japanese baths at **Kabuki Hot Springs** (1750 Geary St., ☎ 415/922-6000) should ease the pain.

In-Line Skating

Just a half-block from Golden Gate Park, **Skates on Haight** (1818 Haight St., ☎ 415/752-8376) is *the* place to be outfitted with in-line skates, pads, and other protective gear.

Tennis

In San Francisco, the Recreation and Park Department maintains more than 100 hard courts that are free and available on a first-come, first-served basis; for locations, call 415/753-7101. An exception are the 21 courts in Golden Gate Park (off JFK Drive opposite the Conservatory of Flowers), which require reservations on weekends (☎ 415/753-7101) and charge a small fee for hourly play. The courts at Alamo Square have the best view of the city—but keep your lobs low at this hilltop playground, or you'll be chasing balls past the picturesque Victorians down Steiner Street!

Shopping

While Main Street has been replaced in many cities by the mall, San Francisco has preserved its neighborhood shopping streets, allowing local businesses to give each area a distinctive character and flavor.

Whether browsing bookstores in North Beach, searching for souvenirs in Chinatown, bargain-hunting South of Market, or perusing the boutiques along Union Street, shopping in San Francisco is not just about finding what you're looking for. It's also about having a good time in the process. Depart from the "shop 'til you drop" mind-set and take a midday break to admire the panoramic vista from atop Russian Hill, or linger over a cappuccino at a cafe—spending time here is just as enjoyable as spending money.

Where to Go

Union Square, so named because a pro-Union rally was held here during the Civil War, is San Francisco's most prestigious shopping address. Surrounding the park are such pillars of the department store realm as **Macy's** (101 Stockton St., at O'Farrell St.), **Saks Fifth Avenue** (384 Post St.), **Neiman Marcus** (150 Stockton St.), and **Nordstrom** (San Francisco Shopping Centre, Market and 5th streets).

On **Maiden Lane,** a 2-block upscale alley off the Stockton side of the Square, you'll find many designer boutiques. Once the throbbing heart of the city's red-light district, the lane acquired its current name after the 1906 earthquake and fire destroyed its bordellos. Local merchants rechristened the street "Maiden Lane" in an effort to improve its character and reputation.

San Francisco is at once a cosmopolitan international city and a coalition of distinct communities. This dual heritage can be appreciated by visiting **Chinatown,** which begins just a few blocks from Union Square. Pass through the red-tiled gateway adorned with lions and dragons at Grant and Bush streets: Chrome and glass give way to carved wood and bamboo, Gucci shoes to ginseng teas. Born as a ghetto for Chinese laborers who arrived at the turn of the century to work on the railroad, Chinatown has been constantly renewed by new waves of immigrants. The 8-block stretch of Grant between Bush and Broadway is lined with dozens of stores selling jade jewelry, silks and linens of serviceable quality, and a curious jumble of trinkets and souvenirs.

After industry moved out of the area **South of Market,** factory outlets moved in. On Saturdays, parking in this area can be problematic; it's best to take a cab.

The cows that used to graze along **Union Street** when it was farmland on the perimeter of the city have long since moved on to greener pastures, but the area is still referred to as Cow Hollow. Today, Union Street runs through the heart of one of San Francisco's most exclusive neighborhoods. Former stables now house antique stores; Victorian homes have been converted into restaurants, art galleries, and boutiques.

The cramped streets of **North Beach** are home to a vibrant miscellany of merchants—Italian delis and bakeries, hat shops, woodworkers, the odd gallery—that cater to both residents and visitors. Down by the Civic Center, **Hayes Valley** has emerged as the locus of hip, with dozens of clothing shops, furniture designers, and hair salons crowding its blocks. **Haight Street** is still headquarters for free spirits; its poster shops and record stores democratically displaying such icons of the 1960s as Jimi Hendrix black-light posters alongside Green Day T-shirts, while the vintage clothing emporiums have racks upon racks of bellbottoms and fringed vests that to some of us look all too familiar.

Museum Shops

The **Exploratorium Store** (3601 Lyon St.; ☎ 415/561-0390) has all sorts of fascinating gifts and learning tools. Pick up a copy of Charles and Ray Eames's classic "Powers of Ten" video or a wristwatch that whimsically illustrates Einstein's concept of relativity (hours are marked "1ish, 2ish", etc.).

For a Helgi Tomasson–autographed pair of toe shoes or Nutcracker dolls year-round, the **San Francisco Ballet Shop** (455 Franklin St.; ☎ 415/553-4688) is your place.

The shops at the various Fort Mason museums are also good bets. Handicrafts of many cultures abound at the **San Francisco Craft and Folk Art Museum** (Bldg. A; ☎ 415/775-0990). The **African-American Historical and Cultural Society** (Bldg. C; ☎ 415/441-0640) and the **Mexican Museum** (Bldg. D; ☎ 415/441-0445) specialize in their own ethnic expressions.

At the San Francisco Museum of Modern Art, **MuseumBooks** (151 3rd St.; ☎ 415/357-4035) stocks much more than its name implies. It has a fine selection of local artists' creations. Berkeley industrial designer Sigmar Willnauer's ingenious Zip Light—a table lamp of conical constructions that zips together—is packaged flat, making it simple to transport. The fog dome (the local variant of the snow dome) commemorating the new museum is . . . well, let's just say it's unique.

Auctions

The most active auction house in town is **Butterfield & Butterfield** (220 San Bruno St.; ☎ 415/861-7500). Sales are held regularly, most all of them subject to previews. They specialize in California concerns: wine lots, decorative arts, and local estates.

The San Francisco branch of **Christie's** (3516 Sacramento St.; ☎ 415/346-6633) holds less frequent sales of fine art.

Not an auction house, but a tremendous resource for prints, paintings, and sculpture is **Art Exchange** (77 Geary St.; ☎ 415/956-5750), where private collectors and museums put their unwanted treasures on the resale market. The artists are first-rate: Robert Indiana, Michael Heiser, Ed Ruscha, and many others.

Fast Facts

Shopping Guides Personal shoppers are available in many of the major department stores; they can be a real help if you're in town only briefly or during the holidays and need to pick up some quick gifts. For customized consumer binges on a grander scale, try these on for size:

- **Gift Guides of San Francisco** (44 Montgomery St., Suite 500; ☎ 415/955-2733).
- **Shopper Stopper Discount Shopping Tours** (P.O. Box 535, Sebastopol, CA 95473, ☎ 707/829-1597).

Shipping Virtually every store can arrange this service. Not only does it save you the trouble of lugging your packages around town and across the country, but sending your purchases out of state exempts you from anteing up the 8.5% San Francisco sales tax.

Shopping A to Z

Antiques

Founded as a Spanish mission in 1776, San Francisco was a small backwater until the 1849 Gold Rush suddenly brought the city tremendous prosperity. The new elite built mansions and furnished them with the best that Europe had to offer. This legacy, combined with the city's historic ties to the Far East, makes the Bay Area a great place to find both European and Asian antiques.

Antonio's Antiques

445 Jackson St. and 701 Bryant St. ☎ 415/781-1737.

Tour 300 years' worth of fine Continental and English furniture at this premiere dealer's 2 properties.

Argentum—The Leopard's Head

414 Jackson St. ☎ 415/296-7757.

Silver is the specialty of this beautiful shop.

Evelyn's Antique Chinese Furniture

381 Hayes St. ☎ 415/255-1815.

Seventeenth- and eighteenth-century works from China are well represented.

John Doughty Antiques

619 Sansome St. ☎ 415/398-6849.

English antiques from the 1700s and 1800s; the writing desks are particular objects of desire.

Therien & Company

411 Vermont St. ☎ 415/956-8858.

Preferred customers are chauffeured via Rolls-Royce to this rarefied showroom of 17th and 18thC European pieces.

Zentner Collection

5757 Landregan, Emeryville. ☎ 510/393-9917.

The most extensive collection of tansu—intricate, multidrawered Japanese chests—in the Bay Area.

Apparel and Accessories

One doesn't need a guidebook to shop the usual suspects—Chanel, Versace, Armani, and the rest of the haute clan all have boutiques in town, with the major specialty and department stores (Macy's, Saks, Neiman Marcus, and Nordstrom) supplying work by 2nd-tier designers for all tastes and budgets. And the ubiquitous clone-chains of casual wear—the Gap, Banana Republic, Bennetton, ad infinitum—have infected the globe, so you won't read about them in these pages, either. The uncommon denominator of these entries is that they reflect the San Francisco sensibility.

Apparel for Women

Babette

28 South Park ☎ 415/267-0280.

A flurry of Fortuny pleats mark this designer's outfits and outerwear, constructed of shimmery polyester microfiber and chiffons.

Behind the Post Office

1504 Haight St. ☎ 415/861-2507.

Local Isaac Mizrahi–wanna-bes send their samples and experiments to this hip hole-in-the-wall store. Expect an avant-garde slant.

Bella Donna

539 Hayes St. ☎ 415/861-7182.

Fragile, very feminine dresses, but not of the ruffles and lace ilk—think loose-fitting linen. If you're headed down the aisle, ask about the very special wedding gowns by Camille De Pedrini.

Brava Strada

3247 Sacramento St. ☎ 415/567-5757.

An uptown shop with correspondingly up-market prices, their selection of leather goods merits a stop.

Diana Slavin

3 Claude Lane. ☎ 415/677-9939.

Combining a feminine fit with haberdasher styling, the trousers, jackets, skirts, and dresses designed by Slavin inspire a fierce loyalty among her chic customers.

Haseena

526 Hayes St. ☎ 415/252-1104.

Dark and delicate, these long slinky dresses would be right at home in Edith Piaf's armoire.

Japanese Weekend

500 Sutter St. ☎ 415/989-6667.

These youthful fashions for mothers-to-be are distinguished by a wide cotton waistband that supports both belly and lower back; quite a departure from "Le Look du Sack" so typical of maternity togs. The line is designed and manufactured in San Francisco.

Jeanne-Marc

262 Sutter St. ☎ 415/362-1121.

Husband Marc Grant and wife Jeanne Allen collaborate on their women's wear collection; she designs the Asian-inspired fabrics, he crafts them into eye-catching clothing. Be sure to check out **Jeanne-Marc Downs** (508 3rd St.; ☎ 415/243-4396) for great buys on samples and out-of-season items.

Lava 9

542 Hayes St. ☎ 415/552-6468.

Leather pared down to sewing pattern–simplicity: The vests and jackets sport no buckles, studs, or chains; the closures are hidden zippers. Emma Peel for the 1990s.

Max Nugus

2237 Union St. ☎ 415/346-9474.

Nugus revels in complex cocktail frocks and counts among his clients the more free-spirited ladies of San Francisco society.

Métier

50 Maiden Lane. ☎ 415/989-5395.

You're not quite sure if you've stepped into an art gallery or a dress shop. Take a peek at the dressing rooms with bud vases embedded in the walls.

Mio

2035 Fillmore St. ☎ 415/931-5620.

The Hino & Malee ensembles toe the cutting edge, but still have enough restraint to find a home in a worldly woman's wardrobe.

Mizani Venturo

402 Sutter St. ☎ 415/693-9400.

Sculptural cut and sensuous drape are the signature characteristics of the women's wear offered by this just-opened shop.

Obiko

794 Sutter St. ☎ 415/775-2882.

A solid catalogue of some of San Francisco's brightest designers is prominently stocked at this stark shop.

One By Two

418 Hayes St. ☎ 415/252-1460.

The clothing here defies categorization; fashionably boxy garments in offbeat materials—a bowling-style shirt in pinstriped seersucker, for example—comprise the current stock. Among the featured designers: homeboy Al Abayan.

Siri Boutique

7 Heron St. ☎ 415/431-8873.

Housed in a faux Italian villa South of Market, this collection focuses on classic yet contemporary women's outfits.

22 Steps

280 Sutter St. ☎ 415/398-7797.

An inspired gathering of footwear, reached by descending—you guessed it—22 steps from street level.

Worldware

336 Hayes St. ☎ 415/487-9030.

Shari Sant, a former stylist for Ralph Lauren, creates clothes with a conscience: They're fashioned from pure fibers and colored with low-impact, natural dyes.

Apparel for Men

Billy Blue

73 Geary St. ☎ 415/781-2111.

Spiffy suits and separates for men that can go from office to gallery opening with no one being the wiser.

Cronan Artefact

11 Zoe St. ☎ 415/543-5222.

Graphic designer Michael Cronan crosses over to the rag trade with his own line of consciously casual menswear dubbed "Walking Man." They're pretty costly for sweats, but cool has its price.

Diagonale

352 Sutter St. ☎ 415/397-3633.

A sophisticated cross-section of designer duds—Gianfranco Ferre, for instance—for men.

Politix

21 Stockton St. ☎ 415/788-6044.

Moderately priced Italian suits and sportswear for men, displayed in a minimalist environment of concrete and steel.

Rolo

2351 Market St. ☎ 415/431-4545.

For gents who've had to repress their radical side for appearance's sake, here's the place to cut loose.The racks are filled with handsome yet high-profile clothes created by one of the city's free spirits.

Apparel for Both Men and Women

Bulo

437A Hayes St. ☎ 415/864-3244.

These statement-making shoes for men and women make Doc Martens look pedestrian.

Lat Naylor/Think Tank

349 9th St. ☎ 415/255-9313.

The men's and women's fashions by this home-grown talent are smartly tailored; fabrics are of the highest quality. If you're in town for one of his biannual sales (call for dates), your wardrobe will be forever altered.

MAC

1543 Grant Ave. ☎ 415/837-1604.

The initials stand for Modern Appealing Clothing, and there's plenty for both men and women at this North Beach storefront. Hank Ford's versatile designs are standouts.

Wilkes Bashford

375 Sutter St. ☎ 415/986-4380.

Mr. B has set the sartorial standard for the Bay Area's best-dressed men and women for 30 years. His clientele—many of whom spend their lives in the public eye as politicians, entertainers, and power-brokers—are wooed with wine and music as they shop.

Apparel for Children

Coulars

327 Hayes St. ☎ 415/255-2925.

Although the retro floral dresses are fo
witty appliquéed black velvet slippers f
the fancy at this closet-sized store in

Kidiniki
2 Embarcadero Center. ☎ 415/986-5437.
Colorful, durable clothes for youngsters from ages 4 through 7.

Mudpie
1694 Union St. ☎ 415/771-9262.
Doting grandparents can find lots of fetching pint-sized outfits here.

Apparel Outlets and Bargains

Bernie Bernard Hotel Robes
1525 Tennessee St.; ☎ 415/550-1188.
Here's where slightly flawed monogrammed hotel robes get a second chance. If you're lucky, you'll walk away with a "souvenir" of the Plaza or the George V for a song. A phone call first to check on the stock could save you a trip to this out-of-the-way outlet.

Esprit Outlet
499 Illinois St. ☎ 415/957-2500.
Great savings on a great selection of all of Esprit's stuff, from the career-oriented Susie Tompkins line to their colorful trademark T-shirts. Bed linens, shoes, and cartloads of accessories are also here at drastically reduced prices—would you believe a pair of desert boots for $5? Go.

Goodbyes
3464 Sacramento St. ☎ 415/346-6388.
If you're partial to high style but recoil at high prices, this upscale consignment shop may be just your ticket. Armani, Donna Karan, Calvin Klein, and other top contemporary designers are offered here at substantial savings for both men and women.

Vintage Apparel

Buffalo Exchange
1555 Haight St., ☎ 415/431-7733 and 1800 Polk St., ☎ 415/346-5726.
These stores have been in the vanguard of the recycled clothing movement for years, as their slave-to-funky-fashion customers willingly attest.

Sugartit
1474 Haight St. ☎ 415/552-7027.

of the season: a limited-edition Chanel promo-nal bracelet marked at $25. The merchandise is chosen with a discerning yet playful eye, and tends toward the theatrical.

Books

Befitting its literary (non)traditions—from Ambrose Bierce to Jack London to Armistead Maupin—the Bay Area's bookstores are a varied lot. See "Shopping the East Bay" in this chapter for additional listings.

Bound Together
1369 Haight St. ☎ 415/431-8355.
Left-leaning political tomes and manifestos.

City Lights
261 Broadway, ☎ 415/362-8193.
Poet Lawrence Ferlinghetti is the proprietor of this historic Beat haven, which, not surprisingly, excels in poetry.

A Clean Well-Lighted Place for Books
601 Van Ness Ave. ☎ 415/441-6670.
Local literati gather here for frequent readings and signing parties.

Comix Experience
305 Divisadero St. ☎ 415/863-9258.
Collectible and contemporary examples of the genre.

A Different Light
489 Castro St. ☎ 415/431-0891.
Both gay and lesbian literature are featured.

Fields Books Store
1419 Polk St. ☎ 415/673-2027.
Truth-seekers in religion, metaphysics, and mysticism look for inspiration here.

Limelight
1803 Market St. ☎ 415/864-2265.
Film and theater titles take center stage.

The Magazine
920 Larkin St. ☎ 415/441-7737.
An offbeat backlist of periodicals dating from the turn of the century.

Richard Hilkert, Bookseller, Ltd.
333 Hayes St. ☎ 415/863-3339.
A superb library specializing in titles on the decorative arts; M. Hilkert is a proverbial fount of knowledge.

San Francisco Mystery Bookstore

746 Diamond St. ☎ 415/282-7444.

In Dashiell Hammett's town, it's hardly puzzling that this is a popular haunt indeed.

Sierra Club Books

730 Polk St. ☎ 415/923-5600.

Pick up your Bay Area nature books and trail guides at this in-town source.

William Stout Architectural Books

804 Montgomery St. ☎ 415/391-6757.

A floor-to-ceiling complement of volumes on the built environment, the graphic arts, and landscape architecture.

Cameras and Photo Equipment

Home to such pioneers of modern photography as Ansel Adams and Brett Weston, San Francisco still supports a thriving community of professional and amateur shooters.

Adolph Gasser

181 2nd St. ☎ 415/495-3852.

New and used cameras, lights and flashes, and a complete inventory of film and accessories.

Photographer's Supply

576 Folsom St. ☎ 415/495-8640.

Film at good prices, camera accessories and supplies, and processing.

Note: The camera stores along Market Street are exactly what they seem—junky—and are not to be trusted.

Gifts and Amusements

See "Shopping the East Bay" for additional listings.

Arch

407 Jackson St. ☎ 415/433-2724.

This Jackson Square business expanded on its original role as an art supply store to include all sorts of nifty items that are ideal gifts for the desk-bound artiste: appointment books, designer pens, and the like.

Artrock

1153 Mission St. ☎ 415/255-7390.

If you know who Stanley Mouse is, you must pay a visit to this veritable Mouse Museum. And if you don't, come anyway to peruse the gallery's stock of original rock-and-roll posters dating from the psychedelic era to more contemporary visions.

Bell'occhio

8 Brady St. ☎ 415/864-4048.

Imported silk ribbons, dried flowers, and other accoutrements of the romantic lifestyle are found in this charming place, situated on a block-long street with other, more evanescent retail ventures.

Chew Chong Tai & Co

905 Grant Ave. ☎ 415/982-0479.

Reputedly the oldest store in Chinatown, it offers everything needed to try your hand at traditional Asian calligraphy (except instruction): bamboo brushes, a variety of inks, and art papers.

---

de Vera

384 Hayes St., ☎ 415/861-8480 and 334 Gough St., ☎ 415/558-8865.

The high-caliber, collectible art glass at the Hayes address has gotten a lot of notice. Around the corner at the Gough store, you'll encounter a greater diversity of merchandise; articles of a found-object character are displayed on the basis of their aesthetic attributes.

Forma

1715 Haight St. ☎ 415/751-0545.

A tongue-in-cheek boutique of the bizarre, with vending machine art (that is, artworks dispensed from a vending machine) and assorted novelties designed to amuse.

General Bead

637 Minna St. ☎ 415/255-2323.

Sample boards of thousands of beads of all shapes and sizes cover the walls at this no-nonsense, obscure outlet. Don't worry about counting your tiny treasures into muffin cups, either—a clerk fills your order from behind the counter.

Gump's

135 Post St. ☎ 415/982-1616.

Founded in 1861, this elegant local landmark is famous for its marvelous Orientalia, jade and pearl jewelry, and china and crystal departments.

Joseph Schmidt Confections

3489 16th St. ☎ 415/861-8682.

The liqueur-laced truffles and fanciful chocolates made here are internationally known.

La Parisienne

460 Post St. ☎ 415/788-2255.

In a precious art nouveau setting that could have come straight from the 7th arrondissement, reproduction baubles based on fin de siècle designs are enticingly displayed.

Lady Luck Candle Shop

311 Valencia St. ☎ 415/621-0358.

Looking for love? Want to succeed in business? Burning one of the dedicated candles from this Mission shop could be the key to these and other dreams coming true.

Narumi

1902 Fillmore St. ☎ 415/346-8629.

An unusual stock of Japanese dolls dating from the 18th and 19thCs exhibit exquisite details in their strange melding of realism and caricature.

Oggetti

1846 Union St. ☎ 415/346-0631.

Fabulous Florentine marbled papers cover desk accessories in a rainbow of Renaissance hues.

Polonco

393 Hayes St. ☎ 415/252-5753.

Behind the red double doors there's a trove of traditional *santos* and *retablos,* as well as more contemporary examples of Mexican artwork.

Quantity Postcards

1441 Grant Ave. ☎ 415/986-8866.

This self-explanatory shop carries thousands of cards depicting sites and scenes of near-limitless subjects. Confuse the folks back home by sending them a picturesque greeting from Baton Rouge or Machu Picchu.

Shige Antiques and Vintage Kimonos

1581 Webster St. ☎ 415/346-5567.

The glorious array of traditional silk and cotton robes here may tempt you to abandon your tattered terrycloth model; resist the urge, as these rare wraps are of heirloom quality.

Skin & Bones, Sticks & Stones

210 Fillmore St. ☎ 415/864-2426.

For that outré look: a curious melange of skulls, crystals, and other of life's not-so-necessities.

Ten Ren Tea Company, Ltd.

949 Grant Ave. ☎ 415/362-0656.

An exotic aura—and aroma—pervades this store, where you can take your pick of more than 40 different types of loose tea.

Terra Mia

2122 Union St. ☎ 415/921-0239.

Choose a piece of unfinished pottery, don a smock, and paint and glaze it as you like (a personalized gift, maybe?). Within a week, Terra Mia takes care of the firing in their on-site kiln, and voila, you're an instant ceramist. They'll ship, too.

Ujama

411 Divisadero St. ☎ 415/252-0119.

Choice African arts, crafts, and clothing.

Yankee Doodle Dandy

1974 Union St. ☎ 415/346-0346.

Collectors of Americana come to ogle the antique quilts, one of the largest assemblages in the country.

Zeitgeist

437B Hayes St. ☎ 415/864-0185.

Time stands still at this emporium of vintage clocks, watches, and jewelry. Expert repair services are offered, as well.

Home and Garden

See "Shopping the East Bay" for additional listings.

AD 50

601 Laguna St. ☎ 415/626-4575.

Museum-collection modern furniture by Charles Eames, Eero Saarinen, Alvar Aalto, and others in a spare, cubist setting that would do the designers proud.

Biordi Italian Imports

412 Columbus Ave. ☎ 415/392-8096.

Hand-painted ceramic platters and planters to brighten any table, featuring the Capodimonte line from Naples.

City Green

500 Hayes St. ☎ 415/431-5822.

Complementing the fresh cut flowers here are Catherine Merrill's terra-cotta plates and goblets that bridge the gap between functional craft and ornament.

Cookin'

339 Divisadero St. ☎ 415/861-1854.

Not a single Cuisinart is in evidence at this emporium of vintage kitchenware, all culled from the days when microwaves were but phenomena in outer space. Pots and pans with a past and esoteric culinary gadgets make this store a browser's paradise.

Country Stark Java

572 Hayes St. ☎ 415/552-2767.

The head-turning hybrid of quasi–Empire style furniture with Indonesian upholstery is curiously pleasing and altogether different. A+ for originality.

Darbury Stenderu

541 Hayes St. ☎ 415/861-3020.

Sexy pillows, throws, and clothing of black silk touched with amber, turquoise, amethyst, and other jewel tones in an alluring fairy-tale ambiance.

Fillamento

2185 Fillmore St. ☎ 415/931-2224.

Materialism is alive and flourishing at this trend-following store, crammed with every conceivable object for the home. The glut of style is intriguing, albeit a tad overwhelming.

Isak Lindenauer

4143 19th St. ☎ 415/552-6436.

Around the turn of the century, the California Mission–style was all the vogue, its sturdy, hand-hewn aesthetic emphasizing the role of the craftsman. This Castro merchant's forte is lighting and furniture dating from 1895 to 1916.

Kris Kelly

174 Geary St. ☎ 415/986-8822.

If you're in the market for a banquet-sized tablecloth, look no further: Super-scaled linens are a specialty of the house.

Lumbini

158 South Park. ☎ 415/896-2666.

Award-winning landscape architect Topher Delaney has named her shop after the birthplace of Buddha. She selects her merchandise—mirrored gazing globes, seeds from around the world, and more—to spark an awareness of the restorative powers of gardens and plants.

The Open Door

548 Union St. ☎ 415/765-0488.

Shawn E. Hall fashions new functions out of old materials by collaging odd fragments of salvaged building materials into one-of-a-kind settees, tables, and case goods.

Paint Magic

2426 Fillmore St. ☎ 415/292-7780.

Disciples of Jocasta Innes's preternatural skill with a paintbrush will find inspiration and instruction here; 1- and 2-day classes in decorative painting and finishing techniques are offered, along with a complete line of pigments and equipment.

Pomp and Circumstance

516 Hayes St. ☎ 415/864-1830.

A plethora of plaster castings of classical architectural ornaments and statuary. Heaped all over the floor in an array that suggests a pan-historical archaeological dig, you'll discover corbels, pediments, and gargoyles galore.

R.H.

2506 Sacramento St. ☎ 415/346-1460.

Tabletop topiary, bent willow baskets, and other natural knickknacks abound at this cottage-aesthetic storefront.

Shabby Chic

3075 Sacramento St. ☎ 415/771-3881.

How long the hand-me-down fad in upholstered furniture will last is anybody's guess. This shop continues to ride the rumpled-look wave with calculatedly ill-fitting covers in a spectrum of fabrics.

Slips

1534 Grant Ave. ☎ 415/362-5652.

Both couture and casual slipcovers are the stock in trade at this engaging storefront; Owner Sami Rosenzweig has branched out into furniture design lately, and also features the creations of other designers, such as whimsical paper-wrapped chandeliers.

Sue Fisher King

3067 Sacramento St. ☎ 415/922-7276.

The diva of au courant dinnerware always sets a beautiful spread in her store—a visit is like a free tutorial in tabletop design.

Victorian Interiors

575 Hayes St. ☎ 415/431-7191.

Everything for the architecturally accurate Victorian: decorative tiles from the English firm Minton Hollins, authentic upholstery fabrics and trims, plaster ornaments, and reference books on the period.

The Wok Shop

718 Grant Ave. ☎ 415/989-3797.

Woks of all shapes and sizes, with a mind-boggling array of Asian cooking utensils.

Zinc Details

906 Post St. ☎ 415/346-1422.

A small, select showcase for emerging industrial and interior designers, some of them just out of school, this store provides a good opportunity to collect their work before their reputations exceed your grasp.

Zonal

568 Hayes St. ☎ 415/255-9307.

There's a kind of visual lyricism to this well-curated clutter of furniture and accessories; the deliciously decrepit lawn gliders could have been snatched from William Faulkner's front porch.

Music

See "Shopping the East Bay" for additional listings.

Reckless Records

1377 Haight St. ☎ 415/626-4075.

The best of the Haight's many sources for new and used recordings. The staff may be a bit breezy if you're not wearing a nose ring, but don't let that deter you from digging through the stock.

Star Classics

425 Hayes St. ☎ 415/552-1110.

A few blocks behind the Opera House, this store's repertoire focuses on Mahler, Mozart, and company.

Tower Records Outlet

660 Third St. ☎ 415/957-9660.

Not too much in the way of mainstream music here; instead, there's an odd-couple mix of modern rock and classical tapes and CDs available at prices that are more than fair.

Shopping the East Bay

Where to Go

College Ave., Oakland

A BART ride away (get off at the Rockridge station) is Oakland's College Avenue, which links the California

College of Arts and Crafts with UC Berkeley. Here at the Oakland end of the street, **Saturn Records** (5488 College Ave., ☎ 510/655-0335) and **Diesel, a Bookstore** (5433 College Ave., ☎ 510/653-9965) cover one's cultural needs, while for corporeal sustenance, there's rustic Italian fare at **Oliveto** (5655 College Ave., ☎ 510/547-4382); the world's best pizza (no lie—order the stuffed pesto pie and you'll agree) at **Zachary's** (5801 College Ave., ☎ 510/655-6385); and California/French cooking at **Citron** (5484 College Ave., ☎ 510/653-5484).

Piedmont Ave., Oakland

If one were to subscribe to the notion that retailers reflect the lifestyles of consumers, you could conclude that the denizens of Piedmont Avenue do nothing but eat and drink . . . and do so very well. **Bay Wolf** (see page 19) is at the forefront of the neighborhood culinary pack. At **John A. Brown Kitchenwares** (4029 Piedmont Ave., ☎ 510/654-6462), you can pick up any equipment you might need to try and duplicate the delectables found at **Just Desserts** (4001B Piedmont Ave., ☎ 510/601-7780) or **Fenton's Creamery** (4226 Piedmont Ave., ☎ 510/658-7000). **Don't Eat the Furniture** (4024 Piedmont Ave., ☎ 510/601-7387) isn't a restaurant—it's a combination homeware/pet-supply store that's always in a state of convivial chaos. If you're in a walking mood, head east up to **Mountain View Cemetery,** where many of the old-money families of San Francisco are entombed in elaborate mausoleums. Stop at **Cato's Ale House** (3839 Piedmont Ave., ☎ 510/655-3349) on your return for a pint of any of their always-changing roster of 22 handcrafted brews.

4th St., Berkeley

In a move that might seem to contradict the community's reputation for free-for-all enterprise, the developers of Berkeley's 4th Street have exercised a high degree of selectivity in leasing storefronts to merchants. As a result, the atmosphere of this 4-block stretch is cultured in a low-key kind of way. **Elica's Paper** (1801 4th St., ☎ 510/845-9530) sells handmade fine art and wrapping papers by the sheet. At **Hear Music** (1809 4th St., ☎ 510/204-9595), you're encouraged to try before you buy via CD listening stations. Despite its flat-footed name, **Restoration Hardware** (1733 4th St., ☎ 510/526-6424) carries some of the more well-crafted and hard-to-find accessories for the home and garden. Unusual gifts of an architectural nature are found at **Aerial** (1840 4th St., ☎ 510/644-1566), while **Devony's** (1816 4th St., ☎ 510/540-8553) purveys antique and offbeat linens. **Builders Booksource** (1817 4th St., ☎ 510/845-6874) carries a full range of books and periodicals devoted to environmental design. Across the street, **The Gardener** (1836 4th St., ☎ 510/548-4545) has a sublime mix of utilitarian and ornamental pieces for gracious living.

Among the street's eateries, the competition is distractingly good: **Bette's Oceanview Diner** (1807 4th St., ☎ 510/644-3230) is renowned for their scones and breakfast baked goods; **Ginger Island** (see page 28) draws raves; **Spenger's Fish Grotto** (1919 4th St., ☎ 510/845-7771) is a hardy holdover from decades past; and **O Chamé** (1830 4th St., ☎ 510/841-8783) is an avant-garde Japanese tea house.

Telegraph Ave., Berkeley

Despite its proximity to the University of California campus, Telegraph Avenue is depressingly thick with decidedly uncolorful characters; the scene cleans up a bit on Sundays, when the legendary street market closes the thoroughfare to all but foot traffic. That's the best time to visit the neighborhood's unparalleled book and record stores. The former includes **Cody's** (2454 Telegraph Ave., ☎ 510/845-7852) and **Moe's** (2476 Telegraph Ave., ☎ 510/849-2087); the latter **Amoeba** (2455 Telegraph Ave., ☎ 510/549-1125) and **Rasputin's** (2401 Telegraph Ave., ☎ 510/848-9004). The area is about a 10-block walk southeast from the Berkeley BART stop.

The Arts

Last year, with the realization of the first phase of the Yerba Buena Gardens Cultural Center, San Francisco attracted international attention to its arts facilities. Now the question looms: Can the city deliver on its newly expanded artistic promise? Even after decades of planning, it's still too early to tell.

For just as the initial wave of Yerba Buena tenants settled into their new homes, other major arts organizations started playing a game of musical chairs that will last through the next several years. Upgrading the War Memorial Opera House sends both the San Francisco Opera and the San Francisco Ballet to temporary quarters around the Bay Area. Impending demolition of the M. H. de Young Memorial Museum has the Asian Art Museum slated to move into the old Main Library building (the de Young collections will be the sole occupant of its new facility, located on its present site). And the potential of the Presidio—the recently decommissioned army base—is being hotly contested by nonprofit arts groups and private-interest parties.

Another issue is raised by the development: What will be its effect on the community's smaller, independent galleries, dance companies, and theaters? Will they share the Yerba Buena limelight or fade into its shadow? Until all the pieces are in place, this too remains to be seen; right now the Bay Area continues to offer the culturally curious visitor a satisfying, stimulating experience on all fronts.

Not all of the Bay Area's performance companies have the luxury of owning their own venue (indeed, many of those that do are currently displaced due to building renovations); depending on their production needs, schedules, and budgets, shows are presented in a variety of settings. Our listings reflect this condition by providing a phone number for the box office, which can provide current location information.

Tickets

TIXBay Area (on the Stockton Street side of Union Square: Tues–Thurs 11am–6pm, Fri–Sat 11am–7pm, ☎ 415/433-7827) is the source for half-price, day-of-performance tickets for select theater, dance, and music performances. Sales are made on a cash-only basis.

BASS Tickets has many convenient outlets throughout the city. For information on events and to charge tickets by phone, call 415/776-1999 or 510/762-BASS.

Should you have your heart set on a sold-out event, **Mr. Ticket** (2065 Van Ness Ave., ☎ 415/775-3031 or 800/424-7328 outside area codes 415 and 510) is a broker who secures premium seating for prices greater than face value.

Arts listings can be found in the "Datebook" section of the *San Francisco Chronicle*. The *San Francisco Bay Guardian* and *SF Express*, both weeklies published on Wednesdays, are also good sources for information.

Cinema

The city has a good number of art and repertory movie houses, some of them—notably the Castro in San Francisco and the Paramount in Oakland—marvels of movie palace fantasies as practiced by architect Timothy Pflueger. Among the places where you won't see *Rambo IX* on the marquee:

Artists' Television Access (992 Valencia St., ☎ 415/824-3890) Lots of avant-garde videos by local auteurs.

Casting Couch (950 Battery St., ☎ 415/986-7001) No sooner do you sink into a plush couch or love seat at this micro theater, than a waiter glides up to take your order for gourmet snacks. Contemporary cult films and unusual new releases.

Castro Theatre (429 Castro St., ☎ 415/621-6120) When there's a Joan Crawford flick playing or an outbreak of *Eraserhead*, this is the best audience participation venue in town. The Spanish baroque interior, circa 1922, is pure eye candy.

Cinémathèque (480 Potrero Ave., ☎ 415/558-8129) A state-of-the-art screening room at the

San Francisco Art Institute in its 35th season of presenting artist-made films.

Pacific Film Archive (2625 Durant, Berkeley, ☎ 510/642-1124) Serious cinema buffs will appreciate the University of California theater's bill of rare and obscure films.

Paramount Theater (2025 Broadway, Oakland; ☎ 510/465-6400) No better setting for the "Hollywood Classics" series exists than this theater, where the Mighty Wurlitzer rises from the orchestra pit. Art Deco aficionados can't miss this magnificently restored example of Pflueger at the height of his creative powers. If there's no film showing during your stay, sign up for a guided tour of the building.

The Red Vic Movie House (1727 Haight St., ☎ 415/668-3994) High-spirited revivals and offbeat premieres in the heart of the Haight, appropriately.

Roxie (3117 16th St., ☎ 415/863-1087) Foreign flicks, documentaries, and art films. Site of the Werner Herzog festival.

If you want to catch a first-run film and can't drag yourself to the newsstand to get a paper, a supremely convenient way exists to find out what's playing where and when. A call to **MovieFone** (☎ 415/777-FILM) gives you instant access to theaters and show times; you can even charge tickets to select shows on the American Express card.

Concerts

Audium (1616 Bush St., ☎ 415/771-1616) A total sound environment with "spatial compositions" performed through an ear-boggling 169 speakers.

Chanticleer (☎ 415/896-5866) Based in the Bay Area, the only full-time classical vocal ensemble in the country travels the world singing a cappella arrangements of music from many cultures and historical eras: Italian madrigals, American spirituals, 20thC jazz. Their concerts typically take place in churches and missions.

Kronos Quartet (☎ 415/731-3533) Internationally renowned for their tuneful abstractions, this string ensemble calls San Francisco home. Their local performances (often held at UC Berkeley's Zellerbach Hall), are frequently sold-out affairs.

Grace Cathedral

San Francisco Symphony (Davies Symphony Hall, Grove St. at Van Ness Ave., ☎ 415/864-6000) Longtime musical director Herbert Blomstedt handed off his baton to Michael Tilson Thomas last season. Get a behind-the-scenes peek at the new maestro by attending one of the Wednesday morning open rehearsals—following complimentary doughnut service (!), noted musical authorities offer insights into the program; the music begins at 10am. Tickets for these run-throughs are available through the regular box office.

San Francisco Taiko Dojo (☎ 415/928-2456) This group's thundering outdoor demonstrations of traditional Japanese drumming are real crowd pleasers.

Organ recitals are held at **Episcopal Church of St. John the Evangelist** (1661 15th, ☎ 415/861-1436), **St. Mary's Cathedral of the Assumption** (1111 Gough St., ☎ 415/567-2020), **Old First Church** (1751 Sacramento St., ☎ 415/474-1608), **Grace Cathedral** (California and Taylor streets, ☎ 415/258-6524), and **Old St. Mary's Cathedral** (660 California St., ☎ 415/288-3840). A bit of organ-oriented trivia: With 9,235 pipes, the concert keyboard at Davies Symphony Hall is the largest such instrument in North America.

Dance

Joe Goode Performance Group (☎ 415/648-4848) High velocity, postmodern partnerings characterize the demanding dances of this innovative group.

ODC San Francisco (3153 17th St.; ☎ 415/863-6606) Original choreography of an adventurous bent—think Twyla Tharp with classical ballet underpinnings—has kept the former Oberlin Dance Collective on its toes for 25 years.

San Francisco Ballet (☎ 415/865-2000) With the closing of the Opera House for renovation, the corps is dividing its performances between several venues: the Palace of Fine Arts, the Center for the Arts at Yerba Buena Gardens, and Zellerbach Hall at UC Berkeley. Artistic Director Helgi Tomasson likes to mix it up, with dances from Mark Morris's *Drink to Me Only with Thine Eyes* to *Swan Lake* highlighting the repertoire.

Third Wave Dancehouse (3316 24th St.; ☎ 415/282-4020) This African-inspired dance group sponsors a weekly "Barefoot Boogie" in which the public is invited to participate.

Opera

Pocket Opera (☎ 415/989-1855) The English translations of classic operas staged by this group emphasize the literary value of the libretto rather than the spectacle of costumes and scenery, making their productions ideal for the beginning listener. For musical accompaniment, there's the Pocket Philharmonic: a string quartet, woodwind combo, and piano.

San Francisco Opera (☎ 415/864-3330) Until the refurbishing of the Opera House is completed, Lotfi Mansouri's crew is setting up camp at the **Orpheum Theatre** (1192 Market St.) and the **Bill Graham Civic Auditorium** (99 Grove St.), which is being outfitted with festival-style seating for the engagement. Both venues feature supertitles; in fact, owing to the configuration of the stage and orchestra pit, the Graham Auditorium has two projection screens flanking the performance area. The concierge at the **Inn at the Opera** (see page 53) can sometimes do the impossible when you simply must have seats at *Don Giovanni*—but it helps if you're staying at the hotel.

Theater

American Conservatory Theater/A.C.T. (415 Geary St., ☎ 415/749-2228) One of the country's most respected thespian groups, the Tony-award winners return to a newly-restored Geary Theater to mark their 29th season.

Asian American Theater Company (403 Arguelo Blvd., ☎ 415/751-2600) Two stages for contemporary productions about the Asian-American experience.

The Best of Broadway series (☎ 415/474-3800) brings national touring companies and pre–New York shakedown runs to 2 major venues: the **Golden Gate Theatre** (1 Taylor St.) and the **Curran Theatre** (445 Geary St.).

Bindlestiff Studio (185 6th St., ☎ 415/974-1167) Modern dramas by established and emerging talents.

Black Repertory Group (3201 Adeline St., Berkeley, ☎ 510/652-2120) Plays by or about African Americans constitute the program here, from Langston Hughes' *Mulatto* to *Bubbling Brown Sugar* to Quincy Jones' adaptation of *The Wiz*.

George Coates Performance Works (110 McAllister St., ☎ 415/487-6960) Multimedia productions that challenge perception by crossing technology with very untraditional theater.

42nd St. Moon (☎ 415/861-8972) Admirably bucking the juggernaut that is Andrew Lloyd Webber, this ensemble is dedicated to revivals of classic musicals from the 1920s forward.

Lamplighters (☎ 415/227-0331) For more than 40 years, the catalogue of Gilbert and Sullivan has been faithfully and often fancifully recreated by this company.

Magic Theatre (Bldg. D, Fort Mason, ☎ 415/441-8822) At this intimate, 100-seat theater, prominent playwrights, such as Sam Shepard and Michael McClure, premiere their latest works.

San Francisco Mime Troupe (☎ 415/285-1720) Political issues are broached with a chain-saw wit by this once-revolutionary, now-classic group.

Theatre Artaud (450 Florida St., ☎ 415/621-7797) Experimental works by visiting dance and theater companies, some of which are produced in the **Noh Space** (2840 Mariposa St., ☎ 415/621-7978).

Theatre Rhinoceros (2926 16th St., ☎ 415/861-5079) Stagings by gay and lesbian playwrights run the gamut from satirical to philosophical in content.

Visual Art Galleries

Art spaces have a tendency to come and go with little warning; this is a list of progressive galleries with staying power.

Site-Specific Installations

Capp Street Project (525 2nd St., ☎ 415/495-7101)

Headlands Center for the Arts (Bldg. 944, Fort Barry, Sausalito, ☎ 415/331-2787; call for directions) with interior spaces designed by David Ireland, Mark Mack, and the Interim Office of Architecture.

New Langton Arts (1246 Folsom St., ☎ 415/626-5416)

Painting, Print Media, Mixed Media, Sculpture

Gallery Paule Anglim (14 Geary, ☎ 415/433-2710)

Rena Bransten Gallery (77 Geary, ☎ 415/982-3292)

John Berggruen (228 Grant, ☎ 415/781-4629)

Bomani Gallery (251 Post, ☎ 415/296-8677)

Galeria de la Raza (2857 24th St., ☎ 415/826-8009)

Jack Hanley Gallery (41 Grant, ☎ 415/291-8911)

Modernism (685 Market, ☎ 415/541-0461)

Daniel Weinberg (49 Geary, ☎ 415/982-0180)

Stephen Wirtz Gallery (49 Geary, ☎ 415/433-6879)

Photography

Fraenkel Gallery (49 Geary, ☎ 415/981-2661)

Photo Metro (17 Tehama, ☎ 415/243-9917)

SF Camerawork (70 12th St., ☎ 415/621-1001)

The Bay Area After Dark

These days, as it draws closer to the millennium, San Francisco seems to specialize in reinventing entertainment, rather than generating new forms of it; witness the revival of jazz and the craze for nostalgic supper clubs. This shouldn't be seen as a wholesale cultural retread, though; the city puts its distinctive stylistic stamp on its amusements while retaining an admittedly rose-colored sense of its history. In other words, you would be hard-pressed to confuse a London or Miami dance club with its SoMa counterpart—for better or worse, the urban edge here is always tempered with a well-disguised sentimentality for the past.

To see what's happening on a given night, consult the "Datebook" section of the *San Francisco Chronicle.* Published on Wednesdays, the weekly papers, the *San Francisco Bay Guardian* and *SF Express* are especially good resources for detailed information on left-of-center events.

Cabaret and Comedy

Whether your taste runs to brash cabaret productions or the caustic humor of alternative comedy, there is plenty to keep you smiling in Baghdad by the Bay.

Club Fugazi (678 Green St.; ☎ 415/421-4222) has been home to the "Beach Blanket Babylon" spectacle for nearly 20 years. An ever-changing revue skewers timely subjects with the extreme visual aid of outrageous hats and costumes. Lead diva Val Diamond always gets a standing ovation, even from folks who've seen the show a dozen times. Newcomer **Josie's Cabaret and Juice Joint** (3583 16th St.; ☎ 415/861-7933) offers one-man and one-woman shows, interspersed

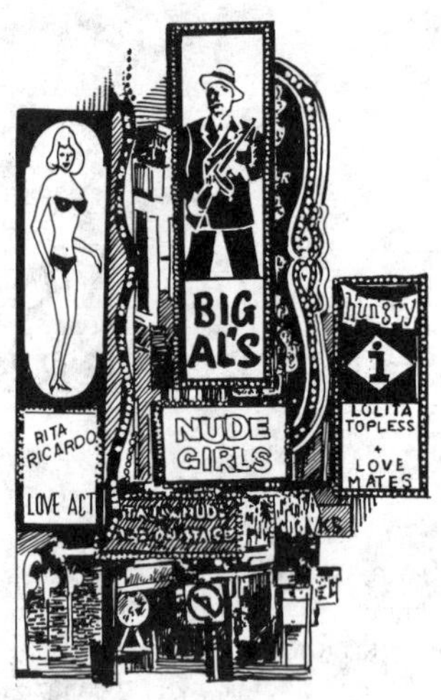

with comedy nights and ensemble performances. For comedy of the conventional stand-up type, the **Punch Line** (444 Battery St.; ☎ 415/397-7573) books established comedians and locals on the rise Wednesday through Saturday; on Sundays, anyone in the audience is free to take (or make) a crack at the open mike. On Monday nights, **Cobb's Comedy Club** (2801 Leavenworth St.; ☎ 415/928-4320) presents a marathon showcase of 14 professional wits that's guaranteed to take the sting off starting a new week.

Dance Clubs

For those who thrive on the spontaneity of the moment (and like to stay up really late), there are several party lines you can call to find out where and when last-minute gatherings occur: **Rave** (☎ 415/626-4087); **Fatline** (☎ 415/207-3668); and **Pirate DJs** (☎ 415/469-2081).

At the **DNA Lounge** (375 11th St.; ☎ 415/626-1409) unfettered DJs unencumbered with Jurassic rock syndrome keep the alternative atmosphere going; at **Trocadero** (520 4th St.; ☎ 415/995-4600) dancers move to a more industrial-gothic beat. After-hours, the crowd at **177 Townsend** (177 Townsend St.; ☎ 415/974-1156) dresses to excess. It's less formal over at the **Paradise Lounge** (1501 Folsom St.; ☎ 415/861-6906), where 3 separate stages allow for freedom of expression.

Gay and Lesbian Clubs

Men gather in the Castro, women call Valencia Street their own. Further entertainment listings can be found in the gay publication the ***Bay Area Reporter;*** the ***Bay Times*** is aimed at a lesbian readership.

For Boys

You won't find 501s and T-shirts at **Alta Plaza** (2301 Fillmore St.; ☎ 415/922-1444). A hangout for peacocks and fashion plates, it's kind of like GQ comes to life. Dressing up in an entirely different sense, **Esta Noche** (3079 16th St.; ☎ 415/861-5757) stages Latino drag shows. Over at **The Pendulum** (4146 18th St.; ☎ 415/863-4441) the clientele swings to mostly African American men. If you're a highly sociable sort, cruise the **Jackhammer** (290 Sanchez St.; ☎ 415/252-0290) for company.

For Girls

Despite its name, **Wild Side West** (424 Cortland St.; ☎ 415/647-3099) is a relaxing sort of place; on warm evenings, the backyard, replete with tiki torches and porch swing, is funky and homey. **Club Confidential** (600 Polk St.; ☎ 415/885-0842) is a lively spot for mingling and conversation. If you're looking to be entertained, **The Bearded Lady** coffeehouse (485 14th St.; ☎ 415/626-2805) features acts of a cabaret nature. In a more intimate setting, **Comme Nous** (139 8th St.; ☎ 415/553-8719) also has bands and solo performers. Get there early if you want a seat—it's that small.

Music Clubs

Blues

If you're looking for an ungentrified blues experience, **Eli's Mile High Club** (3629 Martin Luther King Jr. Way, Oakland; ☎ 510/655-6661) is the place to go. Yes, it's in a part of town where you probably wouldn't want to dally on your evening constitutional, but the music is what you're here for, right? In San Francisco, the **Blue Lamp** (561 Geary St.; ☎ 415/885-1464) is fairly funky, with a small stage that burns (and not because of the fireplace) 7 nights a week. **Jack's Bar** (1601 Fillmore St.; ☎ 415/567-3227) has been around since 1932, hosting the likes of John Lee Hooker and Earl King. As you may be able to glean from its moniker, **Biscuits & Blues** (401 Mason St.; ☎ 415/292-BLUE) has more style than soul; the

Southern cooking usually has more guts than the featured performers.

Folk and Ethnic

Those with a wee dram of Scottish blood might want to hit **Edinburgh Castle** (950 Geary St.; ☎ 415/885-4074), where live bagpipers drone dissonant tunes into the foggy night. And 2 spots stand out in the East Bay area. Over the years, the wood-paneled walls of the venerable **Freight & Salvage** (1111 Addison, Berkeley; ☎ 510/548-1761), the oldest acoustic music club in the western United States, have seen their share of famous folkies; some of them, like Janis Ian, continue to drop in, but mostly it's up-and-coming troubadours on the bill. Mondays at **Starry Plough** (1301 Shattuck, Berkeley; ☎ 510/841-2082) feature traditional Irish music and dance.

Jazz

Currently the form of musical entertainment most in vogue, it's played—sometimes with more enthusiasm than skill—in a wide variety of settings. The clubs have their own policies: At some, if you arrive before 9pm or so, you may not have to pay a cover charge; at others, advance tickets may be necessary for some acts.

Julie Ring's Heart & Soul (1695 Polk St., ☎ 415/673-7100) is a swanky interpretation of a 1940s' nightclub. Still in the supper club vein, but with a loftlike ambiance, **Eleven** (374 11th St.; ☎ 415/431-3337) dishes up Italian food to accompany the sets by chanteuses or small groups. **330 Ritch Street** (330 Ritch St.; ☎ 415/541-9574 or 415/522-9558) puts an international spin on things; Latin- and acid-flavored bands stretch the limits of the genre to varying degrees of success.

True connoisseurs of the established jazz scene rate a pair of East Bay venues as the Bay Area's best: Stanley Turentine, Peabo Bryson, Bobby "Blue" Bland, and others of their caliber are regulars at **Kimball's East** (5800 Shellmound St., Emeryville; ☎ 510/653-5300). Part Japanese restaurant–part jazz club, **Yoshi's** (510 Embarcadero, Oakland; ☎ 510/652-9200) has played incongruous host to such top international performers as Joe Sample, the Brecker Brothers, and Benny Carter.

Mixed Bag

A former speakeasy, **Cafe du Nord** (2170 Market St.; ☎ 415/252-7842) is a basement-level dive where the nights bring quality rockabilly, world beat, bebop, or who-knows-what-next to the stage. Over in the Mission, the **Elbo Room** (672 Valencia St.; ☎ 415/552-7788) presents similar fare above ground. If you like a little salt air with your salsa or some sea breezes with your blues, **Pier 23** (Pier 23, between Greenwich and Filbert streets; ☎ 415/362-5125) is a waterfront spot with fine food and drink, and a bayside terrace to boot. Back on terra firma, the **Bottom of the Hill** (1233 17th St.; ☎ 415/621-4455) holds an unbelievably cheap and tasty barbecue on Sunday afternoon; original rock music is the typical aural accompaniment. And the granddaddy of eclecticism, **Hotel Utah** (500 4th St.; ☎ 415/421-8308), continues to cut its individualistic path with country one evening, techno-pop the next.

Spirited Standards

Just when it seemed that classic lounge performers had run out of venues that suited their style, along came the aptly named **Plush Room** (York Hotel, 940 Sutter St.; ☎ 415/885-6800), its natty environs recalling the Good Old Days of Yore. Even its opulence pales, though, by comparison to the latest addition to the salon circuit, **Harry Denton's Starlight Room** (Sir Francis Drake Hotel, 21st floor, 450 Powell St.; ☎ 415/395-8595). Swagged gold brocade cascades from the ceilings, cushy red velvet booths envelop couples—you get the picture. Another swell spot is the **Coconut Grove** (1415 Van Ness Ave.; ☎ 415/776-1616), which books headliners who are on their way to or from Reno or Las Vegas (Tom Jones opened the room last year). In its stylized-palm-studded space, it's easy to imagine Ricky Ricardo taking a curtain call with a howling version of "Babbaloo."

Spoken-Word Performances

The current affair with the spoken word rages on all over the Bay Area, whose residents will happily remind you is one of the last bastions of free speech. Taking this to an extreme is **Java Source** (343 Clement St.; ☎ 415/387-8025), which holds a weekly "open shout." A less frenetic experience is offered by the **Luggage Store Annex** (1007 Market St.; ☎ 415/255-5971), where the poetry readings are given in a smoke- and alcohol-free environment. The **Coffee Zone** (1409 Haight St.; ☎ 415/863-2443) features an open fiction mike on Tuesday evenings.

In a more professional category, **Intersection for the Arts** (446 Valencia St.; ☎ 415/626-2787) attracts writers from around the world. Readings by more established authors are also held at virtually all the major independent booksellers; both **A Clean Well-Lighted Place for Books** (601 Van Ness Ave.; ☎ 415/441-6670) and **Black Oak Books** (1491 Shattuck, Berkeley; ☎ 510/486-0698) in the East Bay present particularly cohesive programs.

XXX

Few would contest that AIDS has proved a significant motivation in the taming of the former Barbary Coast's adult entertainment arena. The once-infamous bathhouses closed in the 1980s; a couple of years ago, seminal stripper Carol Doda watched as her Condor Club was turned into a G-rated coffee shop, its Broadway neighbors reduced to a few rote strip joints and peep shows, ugly vestiges of lustier and looser days.

At **Stocks and Blondes** (1484 Market St.; ☎ 415/621-6900) highly decorative females flirt with the customers in a slick environment; the formula is duplicated over at **Centerfolds** (932 Montgomery St.; ☎ 415/834-0661) in an upscale, pseudo–men's club atmosphere. Things get a lot seedier—oops, that's steamier—at the **Mitchell Brothers' O'Farrell Theatre** (895 O'Farrell St.; ☎ 415/776-6686). (I love the tony spelling of "Theatre"—a real touch of class.) Twenty-seven years in the adult entertainment biz, the brothers primly keep their doors closed until 5pm on Sundays; the rest of the week the action starts at lunchtime.

For gay men, the **Eros Club** (2051 Market St.; ☎ 415/864-3767) bills itself as the first safe-sex male club, with massage rooms, saunas, and more inventive environments.

Only in San Francisco

At night, **Momi Toby's Revolution Cafe** (528 Laguna St.; ☎ 415/626-1508) puts politics aside and transforms into a charming, mellow place that's reminiscent of North Beach 20 years ago.

Some may prefer the microcosmic view of the city garnered from rooftop cocktail lounges, but for our money, the best vantage point is on the west shore of **Treasure Island.** From the midpoint of the Bay Bridge, the sea-level panorama of San Francisco's skyline has an impact that just can't be captured from 30th-floor window seats.

Take an evening stroll around the grand **Palace of Fine Arts,** which recently benefited from a campaign to restore and refine its lighting design. The new scheme washes Bernard Maybeck's 1915 rotunda with a balance of ambient and spot illumination, allowing a full appreciation of its monumental arches and intricate friezes.

We'd be remiss if we didn't mention the **Tonga Room** (Fairmont Hotel, 950 Mason St.; ☎ 415/772-5000), where the Polynesian theme—thatched roofs, fake orchids trailing down lava rock walls, and pu-pu platters—is breathing perhaps its last gasp. Every 20 minutes a tropical monsoon blows through the auditorium-sized space, complete with rain, thunder, and lightning. Order a Blue Hawaii and hum along with the ukulele band on the "boat" stage that's permanently marooned in a sea of dining tables.

The Wine Country

An hour's drive north of the Golden Gate Bridge, skyscrapers and office buildings give way to cottages and barns; asphalt grids dissolve into a verdant patchwork of fields; the cacophony of traffic is replaced by a bird's song. Welcome to the wine country.

Whether you like it elegant or easygoing, time spent here rejuvenates both the mind and the body. Sleep late in your own vineyard-surrounded bungalow, or tee off early in the morning at a world-class resort. Make supper a spontaneous picnic in a quiet meadow or slip into a chic little black something for a 5-course repast. Cultivate a new appreciation for petit sirah—or blanc de noirs. For visitors to this Bay Area arcadia, there are no routines to follow.

Wine Country Tours from San Francisco

Great Pacific Tour Company (☎ 415/626-4499) supplies a picnic lunch on its 1-day, 13-passenger minivan excursions through Napa and Sonoma.

Pure Luxury Limousines (☎ 800/626-5466) offers door-to-door service via chauffeured stretch limo. Choose from 4-, 6-, or 8-hour customized itineraries to wine country vineyards and restaurants.

Red & White Fleet (☎ 415/546-2700 or 800/229-2784) provides a different perspective—from the water, specifically—on its day-long cruise to the Carneros area wineries in Napa.

About Wineries

It's estimated that between them, Napa Valley and Sonoma County are home to more than 200 wineries.

This admittedly selective roster identifies those noted for unique facilities, exceptional siting, and superb wines.

The wineries are open for public tastings, tours, and/or sales unless otherwise indicated. A "by appointment" designation shouldn't put you off in the least; it frequently refers only to scheduling a tour, which if anything means you'll enjoy a high level of personal attention—likely from the wine-maker. Also, in the winter months (approximately November–April) a few close their doors an hour earlier than in the summertime, another good reason to call ahead. During this time, too, the crowds thin considerably, making the overall experience more leisurely.

A final word: Economic realities being what they are, the days of complimentary tastings are behind us. Most (but not all) vintners ask a nominal fee for their samples, and often you get to go home with a glass that bears the winery's logo.

A thrifty alternative has recently emerged. You may want to consider purchasing a VIT (Very Important Taster) card to help combat the rising costs of sampling. Good for a year, it entitles the bearer(s) to free tastings at more than 100 wineries in both Napa and Sonoma, and discounts up to 20% on a single-bottle as well as by-the-case purchases. The price of the VIT is $20 ($25 for 2 people)—a most reasonable fee if you're intending to spend a few days in the area. Contact VIT Marketing, P.O. Box 174, Napa, CA 94559 (☎ 707/255-1639).

The Napa Valley

Driving Directions

From San Francisco: Cross the Golden Gate Bridge, going north on California Highway 101. Exit on Route 37; follow it to Route 12/121 East, which leads to Route 29; head north. Driving time to Napa proper is a little more than an hour; if you're going to the top of the valley (Calistoga) allow an additional 40 minutes.

From the East Bay: Take Interstate 80 north over the Carquinez Strait to Route 37 in Vallejo. Follow Route 29 to the valley. Driving time to Napa is approximately 1 hour.

As the main commercial thoroughfare, Route 29 (sometimes called the St. Helena Hwy.) is the most-traveled road through the valley; once it fades from divided freeway status, traffic (mostly on weekends, and throughout the crush season, which is usually in September) can get thick. A more tranquil driving alternative on the east side of the valley is the Silverado Trail, which courses through plenty of vineyards, but none of the area's small towns.

Useful Numbers

Napa Valley Conference and Visitors Bureau, 1310 Napa Town Center, Napa, CA 94559; ☎ 707/226-7459; fax: 707/255-2066.

Towns of the Napa Valley

Since the 1850s, the working side of the wine business has been at the heart of the town of **Napa,** where many of its 64,000 residents are involved in viticultural side-industries such as construction, shipping, and manufacturing. As the gateway to the valley, it offers plenty of lodging and dining opportunities.

The little village of **Yountville** sits quietly to the side of Route 29. A sprinkling of fine bed and breakfast inns, small hotels, and restaurants dots its primarily residential streets. Several intimate shopping centers have sprung up over recent years, with a shifting tenancy of boutiques and galleries.

Best not to blink if you're looking for **Oakville** and **Rutherford.** Defined by little more than a couple of crossroads, the plats are home mostly to prime acreage of cabernet sauvignon vines.

Continuing up-valley, **St. Helena** is an enclave of turn-of-the-century charm: Its bustling Main Street features many architecturally interesting municipal buildings and no shortage of interesting shopping and eating establishments.

Calistoga retains a spunky dash of western flavor, perhaps due to its host of mineral hot springs that have been rejuvenating visitors since the 1800s. Beyond downtown's array of restaurants and gift stores, there's ample Victorian-era accommodations.

Alternative Transports

Napa Valley Model "A" Rentals (Washington Square, Yountville, ☎ 707/944-1106) can set you up with "classic" automobiles. Car buffs can't resist taking these replicas of the 1929 Model A Roadster and the 1930 Phaeton for a spin. Both models are convertibles and seat 4 (the Roadster does so with the aid of a rumble seat, no less). The Phaeton is painted a warm burgundy; the Model As pale parchment. In a bow to modern convenience, the cars have automatic transmissions and stereo tape players. Rates range from $35 per hour to $280 for a full day.

The restored 1917 Pullman cars of the **Napa Valley Wine Train** (1275 McKinstry, Napa, ☎ 707/253-2111) gently chug through 36 miles of vineyards in 3 hours. Brunch, lunch, and dinner trips are the main attractions, although you can hitch a meal-less ride for a lesser price (and get bumped into ordinary coach seats). The train makes no stops save for its Napa terminus. It's hard to shake the suspicion that this enterprise is secretly owned by Disney.

Napa Valley Wineries

Natural forces blessed Napa with an intimate scale; vineyards roll across its narrow floor and up into canyons whose convoluted walls are often a mere 800 yards apart. And yet, for all its compactness, the climate changes so radically within its 25-mile stretch that it provides suitable growing conditions for an astonishing variety of grapes.

Calistoga

Chateau Montelena

1429 Tubbs Lane, Calistoga. ☎ 707/942-5105.

The clock seems to tick a little slower at this tranquil winery at the foot of Mount St. Helena. Part of that impression is perhaps due to the chateau itself, a hundred-year-old castle complete with turrets and crenulated parapet. Out of this peacefulness comes some remarkably spirited and consistent premium cabernet sauvignon and chardonnay; of the latter, it was a 1973 vintage that captured the crown in the seminal 1976 blind tasting of French vs. California bottlings. The valley's prime picnic spot—under the pagoda on the island in Jade Lake—requires advance reservations.

Clos Pegase

1060 Dunaweal Lane, Calistoga. ☎ 707/942-4981.

Many visitors come to Clos Pegase not only to sample the chardonnay, cabernet, and merlot, but to behold the compound of benchmark postmodern buildings designed by architect Michael Graves in 1987. A bold geometry of colonnades and courtyards, the classically-inspired, earth-toned structures also house owner Jan Schrem's far-ranging art collection, from which a slide program on wine in art has been culled for presentation.

Sterling Vineyards

1111 Dunaweal Lane, Calistoga. ☎ 707/942 3344.

Sterling's eye-catching icon of a winery—a contemporary affair in white stucco, it's most often likened to a Mediterranean monastery—sits atop a 300-foot knoll that's scaled via aerial tramway. The view it affords of the surrounding patchwork quilt of vineyards always evokes a frenzy of camera-shutter clicking. With a whopping 1,200 acres of vineyards at its disposal, Sterling produces a full spectrum of red and white wines. Tastings are held in a glass-walled room that frames yet another panoramic valley vista.

Napa

Carneros Alambic Distillery

1250 Cuttings Wharf Rd., Napa. ☎ 707/253-9055.

If you've had enough of winery tours that conclude by confronting rows of sterile stainless steel tanks, the experience offered at this North American offshoot of Remy Martin is guaranteed to rekindle your romance with the grape. Blessedly off the beaten path, the handsome complex of masonry buildings houses 8 hammered-copper brandy stills that resemble burgundy-enameled Aladdin's lamps. Visits culminate in the Barrel House, where recorded Gregorian chants fill the air—as also does the intoxicating perfume (called the "angel's share" of the brandy) emitted by 4,000 Limousin oak barrels reposing in the damp darkness. Certified

alambic aficionados should inquire about the private blending program. A tip: It's worth timing your visit to join one of John Sapata's tours; he truly knows the place from the ground up.

Codorniu Napa

1345 Henry Rd., Napa. ☎ 707/224-1668.

An architecturally monumental winery in the minimalist vein, this deliquescent structure echoes the rolling Carneros terrain in both its shape and substance. Essentially pyramidal in profile, its sloping walls are planted with native grasses, effectively rendering it invisible from a distance. Inside, sample the sparkling wines in futuristic rooms fitted with cutting-edge Italian furniture.

Domaine Carneros

1240 Duhig Rd., Napa. ☎ 707/257-0101.

When Taittinger was constructing their California outpost in 1989, the chateau took it on the chin from many in the design community who saw the 18thC-style building as wholly alien to the vernacular of the area. A few years have since passed, and while you still won't confuse the property with a centuries-old chateau, the lovingly-tended landscape has asserted itself nicely; Domaine Carneros has acquired some character and evolved into a thoroughly pleasant place to while away an afternoon sipping bubbly on the umbrella-shaded terrace. The wines, on the other hand, suffered no such growth pangs, and have been outstanding since day one, in no small part thanks to the vision of managing director Eileen Crane and the organization's prescient recognition of the potential of the Carneros region.

The Hess Collection

4411 Redwood Rd., Napa. ☎ 707/255-1144.

One would never guess that on a back-country road within the vine-bound limestone walls of this modest 1903 winery hangs a world-class collection of contemporary art; Francis Bacon, Gilbert & George, Morris

Louis, Robert Motherwell, and Frank Stella are but a few of the modern masters represented in the spacious galleries. But then Swiss entrepreneur Donald Hess has always appreciated the spectacular over spectacle, an attitude that's also evident in his powerful but understated cabernet sauvignon and chardonnay vintages.

Seguin Moreau Napa Cooperage

151 Camino Dorado, Napa. ☎ 707/252-3408.

Five thousand American oak barrels are handmade each year at this outgrowth of the pedigreed French cooperage. Stop by and see what's usually a behind-the-scenes stage in wine-making.

Oakville

Chateau Potelle Winery and Vineyard

3875 Mount Veeder Rd., Oakville. ☎ 707/255-9440.

The views from this Mount Veeder aerie are superlative—and so are several of its wines, which, in a departure from common viticultural methods, are fermented with the grape's own natural yeasts in a time-consuming and costly practice. The 1991 VGS Chardonnay, tasting of soft honey and fruit, has gotten high marks for its balance and long finish.

Groth Vineyards & Winery

750 Oakville Cross Rd., Oakville. ☎ 707/944-0290. *By appointment.*

The pink stucco sprawl of a California Mission–style building gives architectural expression to the pioneering Western spirit behind Groth and its feisty cabernets, chardonnays, and sauvignon blancs. Normally cool connoisseurs sat up and took notice of the winery's work when Robert Parker bestowed a perfect 100 on the 1985 cabernet sauvignon, a standard that wine-maker Michael Weis, who joined Groth in 1994, is determined to uphold.

Opus One

7900 St. Helena Hwy., Oakville. ☎ 707/963-1979. *By appointment.*

This joint vision of Robert Mondavi and Baron Philippe de Rothchild produces exclusively ultrapremium Bordeaux-style red wines, and the opportunity to taste these coddled bottlings shouldn't be missed. The sleek building, designed by Los Angeles architects Johnson, Fain, and Pereira, slopes gradually up from the earth, and relies on a radiant cooling system to insulate the cellars from the surrounding geothermal springs. The central rotunda recalls Mondavi's innovative flange-top bottles. Inside, in a further reflection of

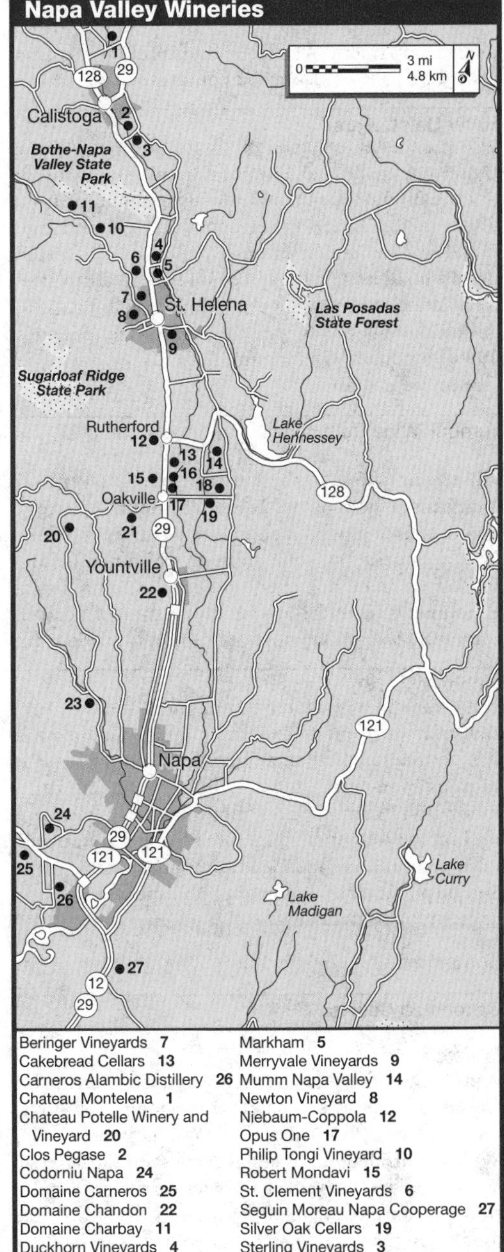

Beringer Vineyards **7**
Cakebread Cellars **13**
Carneros Alambic Distillery **26**
Chateau Montelena **1**
Chateau Potelle Winery and Vineyard **20**
Clos Pegase **2**
Codorniu Napa **24**
Domaine Carneros **25**
Domaine Chandon **22**
Domaine Charbay **11**
Duckhorn Vineyards **4**
Groth Vineyards & Winery **18**
The Hess Collection **23**
Markham **5**
Merryvale Vineyards **9**
Mumm Napa Valley **14**
Newton Vineyard **8**
Niebaum-Coppola **12**
Opus One **17**
Philip Tongi Vineyard **10**
Robert Mondavi **15**
St. Clement Vineyards **6**
Seguin Moreau Napa Cooperage **27**
Silver Oak Cellars **19**
Sterling Vineyards **3**
Turnbull Wine Cellars **16**
Vichon Winery **21**

the Franco-American collaboration, spaces are a sophisticated pastiche of classic and contemporary.

Silver Oak Cellars

915 Oakville Crossroad, Oakville. ☎ 707/944-8808.

By seasoning their voluptuous cabernet sauvignons in oak for 30 months, then bottle-aging them for up to 2½ years to develop the bouquet, Silver Oak creates wines that can satisfy serious wine-cellarers as well as those who don't have the space—or the self-discipline—to hold the vintages to their full potential. The 1992 Alexander Valley version is due to release in August 1996; boasting a 95 rating from *The Wine Advocate,* it's sure to cause a clamor.

Turnbull Wine Cellars

8210 Hwy. 29, Oakville. ☎ 800/TURNBUL. *By appointment.*

Change is afoot at the former Johnson Turnbull Vineyards; a new owner brings additional acreage to the party, giving wine-maker Kristin Belair (a holdover from the earlier era) some fresh opportunities. This fall marks the debut of the 1994 merlot, with future experiments centering around the creation of a proprietary red, possibly a sangiovese/cabernet sauvignon mix.

Vichon Winery

1595 Oakville Grade, Oakville. ☎ 800/VICHON-1.

A hairpin-turn off the Oakville Grade leads to this hillside winery, where chevrignon—a proprietary blend of sauvignon blanc and semillon—is the signature innovation. Another interesting oenologic avenue is Vichon's series of Mediterranean-inspired varietals, malbec, mondeuse, and Gewürztraminer, among them. Shaded picnic tables surround a bocce court, with views of canyon vineyards beyond.

Rutherford

Cakebread Cellars

8300 St. Helena Hwy., Rutherford. ☎ 707/963-5221.
By appointment.

A profusion of perennials greets you upon entering the Cakebread premises, where contemporary low-slung redwood structures, designed by architect/vintner William Turnbull, Jr., fit comfortably into the agrarian landscape. The vineyards have been a friendly, family-run affair for more than 20 years. Jack Cakebread is the founder of the winery; his wife, Dolores, is its culinary director; sons Bruce and Dennis are responsible for wine-making and sales and marketing, respectively.

Cakebread's cabernet, chardonnay, and sauvignon blanc are regulars on better wine lists.

Mumm Napa Valley

8445 Silverado Trail, Rutherford. ☎ 707/942-3434; 800/686-6272.

The barnlike appearance of this *méthode champenoise* winery might raise some eyebrows over in Épernay—there's not a chandelier in sight—but the laid-back architecture is right at home in the Napa Valley. Refresh yourself on the patio with a flute of sparkling blanc de noirs, blanc de blanc, or the commemorative Winery Lake Cuvée, made exclusively of fruits from its namesake Carneros vineyard. On display are 32 silver gelatin prints by Ansel Adams (commissioned by Seagram & Sons in 1959) that document "The Story of a Winery" from grape bud to glass.

Niebaum-Coppola

1991 St. Helena Hwy., Rutherford. ☎ 707/967-3493.

More noteworthy for its current owner—filmmaker Francis Ford Coppola—than its recent oenological efforts, this historic property is undergoing a renewal. Coppola finally realized his dream of acquiring the entire parcel founded by Finnish sea captain Gustave Niebaum (née Nybom) in 1879. To this point, the proprietary "Rubicon" bottlings have been interesting but erratic; with the restoration of the estate completed, attention can be totally focused on fulfilling the promise of its classic cabernet sauvignon, cabernet franc, and merlot formula.

St. Helena

Beringer Vineyards

2000 Main, St. Helena. ☎ 707/963-4812.

Guests at Beringer are escorted through the historic winery (including a visit to the original storage tunnels hand-dug by Chinese laborers in the 1880s) and gather in the Rhine House to cap off the experience with a sampling of current releases. The 17-room, slate-roofed Tudoresque mansion was modeled after the Beringer family home in Mainz, Germany; built in 1884, it is a showplace of the woodcarver's art. The Founders' Room, on the 2nd floor, is the elegant environment where rare and reserve bottlings are poured upon request.

Domaine Charbay

4001 Spring Mountain Rd., St. Helena. ☎ 707/963-9327; 800/634-7845. *By appointment.*

Beringer Vineyards

Intriguing specialty spirits crafted by Miles Karakasevic, a 12th-generation master distiller who hails from Yugoslavia, are more than worth the steep mountain drive. His "Charbay" is a dessert blend of chardonnay and brandy liqueur; "Nostalgie" infuses black walnuts into oak-aged brandy. New is a pinot noir marc, a smooth and aromatic concoction that is being poured by some A-list restaurants around the country.

Duckhorn Vineyards

3027 Silverado Trail, St. Helena. ☎ 707/963-7108.

Marvelous merlots have come from these skillfully minded vineyards for many years; recently, wine-maker Tom Rinaldi directed Duckhorn's first varietal culled completely from the formidable *terroir* of Howell Mountain. Released in the spring of 1995, the 1991 vintage (it's forthrightly named "Napa Valley, Howell Mountain") comprises 49% merlot, 43% cabernet sauvignon, and 8% cabernet franc in a full-bodied, traditional Bordeaux-style wine that has great aging potential.

Markham

2812 St. Helena Hwy., St. Helena ☎ 707/963-5292.

Merlot mavens are doubtless on a first-name basis with Markham's goods; the current blend of the ruby-colored wine, with its characteristic flavors and nose of black cherry, raspberry, and herbal grace notes can be sampled at the revamped tasting room, a slick wing of redwood and glass that is set off by the original, rustic lava-rock cellar, constructed more than a century ago.

Merryvale Vineyards

1000 Main, St. Helena ☎ 707/963-2225.

A range of red and white varietals, along with reserve bottlings of chardonnay, meritage, and the winery's "Profile" (a heady blend of cabernet sauvignon, merlot, and cabernet franc) can be sipped in one of Napa's most evocative settings; the Tank Room is erected within a 22,000-gallon wooden cask. On Saturdays, tasting seminars are given (reservations required) that will attune your palate to tannins, sugars, alcohol, and tartaric acid.

Robert Mondavi Winery

7801 St. Helena Hwy., St. Helena. ☎ 707/259-9463.

With missionary fervor, Robert Mondavi and family have spread the good life gospel of fine wine and food for decades. To this end, the tours of his winery are both innovative and comprehensive; you can take the standard version given daily, or reserve a spot on one of the scheduled in-depth tours, which last from 3 to 4 hours and detail all aspects of wine growing, from viticultural research to the ins and outs of extended barrel aging. Inside the stylized Mission structure, designed by Cliff May in 1966, the To-Kalon Room is where you'll sample the good stuff: the reserves and older vintages.

Newton Vineyard

2555 Madrona, St. Helena. ☎ 707/963-9000.

Deep beneath the boxwood hedges, herbs, and roses of the formal parterre garden cut into the side of Spring Mountain, the workings of this winery lie in disguise. Su Hua and Peter Newton pursue the perfect merlot—and chardonnay and cabernet sauvignon—from this idyllic site, and consistently come close to achieving their goal. Their best wines go from barrel to bottle without artificially tweaking the acidity or filtering away natural proteins, resulting in mouth-filling, collectible elixirs.

Robert Mondavi Winery

St. Clement Vineyards

2867 St. Helena Hwy., St. Helena. ☎ 707/963-7221.

A refined 1878 Victorian mansion high on a hillside serves as the hospitality center for this producer of full-bodied and full-flavored sauvignon blanc and excellent chardonnay, cabernet sauvignon, and merlot. Library wines are aged in the original stone cellar, which was bonded in 1879, just the 8th to be so designated in Napa Valley.

Philip Tongi Vineyard

3780 Spring Mountain Rd., St. Helena. ☎ 707/963-3731.
By appointment.

The complex, opulent cabernets that come from the 10-acre peak tended by Philip Tongi (who honed his skills at Chateau Lascombes, among other prestigious houses) are crafted for long-term cellaring. Owing to their labor-intensive, limited production (the 1-man winery releases about 2,500 cases annually) these are rare prizes indeed; consistently high praise from critics Robert Parker, Frank Prial, and company further ensure this status.

Yountville

Domaine Chandon

1 California Dr., Yountville. ☎ 707/944-2280. Closed Mon and Tues.

Enter the pastoral grounds of this American cousin to Moët et Chandon and enjoy 1 of 2 tour options: The self-guided walk is intelligent and informative; the guided excursion takes visitors through a model vineyard for an up-close peek at the pinot noir, chardonnay, and pinot blanc grapes used in the house's sparkling wines. Of course, there's a 3rd choice, and that's to go directly to Le Salon, where flutes of the 5 varieties are served with complimentary hors d'oeuvres. For lunch or dinner, resident chef Phillipe Jeanty's cuisine (see page 173) is not to be missed; many consider his to be among the most exceptional restaurants in northern California.

Other Diversions in the Napa Valley

Spas

Should you be feeling the effects of a buildup of tannins of your own after an intense bout of wine tasting, Calistoga is the ideal place to right the wrongs of excess. Its natural confluence of hot springs and mineral-water pools attracted the attention of 19thC entrepreneur Sam Brannan, who set about developing these indigenous attributes into a complete resort spa. Today you'll find a variety of treatments available from a dozen different purveyors, some sticking to the classic regimens, others expanding on these with more holistic therapies. Here are a few that offer singular experiences of their own.

The elegant choice is the **Mount View Spa** (1457 Lincoln, Calistoga, ☎ 707/942-5789). Fango mud—volcanic soils blended with pine oil and salicyl—is but one of the baths offered in the 13 private rooms, where marble trim, soft lighting, and music enhance the mood. Various body wraps and massages are available à la carte or as packages; services for couples are also offered.

Nance's Hot Springs (1614 Lincoln, Calistoga, ☎ 707/942-6211) is the spa that time forgot. The neat, motel-like lodgings project a wholesome, 1950s' type of clinical efficiency.

Indian Springs (1712 Lincoln, Calistoga, 707/942-4913). This is the property that first caught Sam Brannan's eye in 1860. Hammocks hang throughout the grounds, giving them a summer-camp feel.

White Sulphur Springs (3100 White Sulphur Springs Rd., St. Helena, ☎ 707/963-8588), a stone's throw down the road from Calistoga, is the most secluded of the area's spas. Outdoor massages are proffered at the edge of a forested canyon; the sulfur hot springs bubble up at year-round temperatures of 85° to 92° at the foot of a mountain.

The Great Outdoors

Bothe-Napa Valley State Park (3 miles south of Calistoga on Hwy. 29, ☎ 707/942-4575) contains more than 1,800 pine- and redwood-forested acres ranging in elevation from 400 to 2,000 feet. For those who prefer sleeping under the stars, the 50 campsites have barbecues, rest rooms, and hot showers—reserve well in advance of your visit by calling 800/444-PARK.

Aerial Amusements

Balloon Aviation of Napa Valley (P.O. Box 2500, Yountville, ☎ 800/367-6272) is a good choice for a hot-air balloon ride. The thermal currents are optimal at dawn, which is why when the sun rises, so do the balloons. Upon landing, you're met by a chase vehicle that totes all the necessities for a champagne brunch. Don't let the $165 ticket burst your bubble, though—it's pretty much the going rate among all the flight operators.

Calistoga Gliderport (1546 Lincoln, Calistoga, ☎ 707/942-5000) provides a happy compromise between the gentle drifting of a balloon and the daredevil antics of an airplane.

Biking and Horseback Riding

The knowledgeable folks at **St. Helena Cyclery** (1156 Main, St. Helena, ☎ 707/963-7736) can suggest routes compatible with both your interests and your endurance, while outfitting you with all the gear (helmets, panniers, locks) you'll need.

Napa Valley Trail Rides (P.O. Box 877, Glen Ellen, ☎ 707/996-8566) arranges guided horseback sojourns through the hilly forests of Bothe-Napa Valley State Park for equestrians of all levels of experience.

Accommodations in the Napa Valley

★ Ambrose Bierce House

1515 Main, St. Helena, CA 94574. ☎ 707/963-3003. 4 rooms. No credit cards; accepts personal checks. **$$**.

Bedding down in the last known abode of Ambrose Bierce is an edifying experience. The unprepossessing house is brimming with artful memorabilia displays about the author, in a pleasing combination of history and hospitality. It's especially gratifying to come across a bed-and-breakfast library that has genuine literary significance, rather than acting as a period diorama. Spare brass beds are the focus of the 4 subdued suites, which bear the names of some of the writer's more illustrious acquaintances: Lillie Langtry, Eadweard Muybridge, and Lillie Hitchcock Coit (of Coit Tower fame).

★★ Auberge du Soleil

180 Rutherford Hill Rd., Rutherford, CA 94573. ☎ 707/963-1211; 800/348-5406; fax: 707/963-8764. 48 rooms. AE, D, MC, V. **$$$$**.

Amidst 33 hillside acres of olive trees sit a sprinkling of earth-colored dwellings at a resort dedicated to peace, privacy, and luxury. If you're fortunate enough to call one of the 48 suites home for your wine country stay, you'll enjoy oodles of amenities: Frette linens on the bed, a refrigerator stocked with local wines and cheeses, fresh cut flowers, a fire laid in the hearth daily. Shuttered French doors lead from the Michael Taylor–designed interiors out to a sun-drenched deck with a vineyard view. The restaurant (which predates the hotel) is so renowned that discerning "outsider" diners often outnumber the resort's guests at meals; savvy serenity-seeking visitors will opt for a twilight cocktail on the terrace. *Amenities:* Large health club, exercise room, outdoor pool, restaurant, conference facilities, 3 out-door tennis courts, in-room VCRs, 4 rooms wheelchair accessible.

Brannan Cottage Inn

109 Wapoo, Calistoga, CA 94515. ☎ 707/942-4200. 6 rooms. MC, V. **$$**.

Brannan Cottage Inn

The quintessential cottage: gingerbread architectural trim; shady, wraparound porch; white picket fence out front. Built in the 1860s as part of Sam Brannan's resort, the inn is within walking distance of all of Calistoga's attractions. Intricate white wicker furnishings contribute to the Victorian country ambi-ance. In fair weather, a home-made breakfast is served in the manicured garden. *Amenities:* 1 room wheelchair accessible.

Calistoga Inn

1250 Lincoln, Calistoga, CA 94515. ☎ 707/942-4101; fax: 707/942-4914. 18 rooms, all with shared bath. AE, MC, V. **$**.

Rooms at this wine country bargain are smallish and spotless, Spartanly rendered in grey and white paint. If you're on a whirlwind trip through the valley (a shame, that), the 1-night minimum stay policy here can offer relief from the 2-night rule that pervades the area. There's a tradeoff for the 2nd-floor front rooms (try number 19) that occasionally catch some street noise: They sport cool little wooden balconies. The winter dining room is a real charmer, appointed with antiques in a graceful indication of the inn's 90-year history. In summer, the Napa Valley Brewing Company (see page 175) opens its riverside patio for meals. *Amenities:* 2 restaurants.

★ Churchill Manor

485 Brown St., Napa, CA 94559. ☎ 707/253-7733; 800/799-7733; fax: 707/253-8836. 11 rooms. AE, D, MC, V. **$$**.

Reminiscent of the grand mansions of Newport, this stately 1889 structure, its entrance marked by 2-story Ionic columns, is an enclave of old-fashioned sophistication. Canopied beds, mirrored armoires, claw-footed tub/showers and pedestal sinks, and tiled fireplaces are typical of the interior's finery. Start the morning with a hearty breakfast in the sunroom, with its original marble mosaics, or take your meal out on the verandah. Guests have free use of tandem bicycles and croquet equipment—live out your Gatsby fantasies. *Amenities:* Conference facilities, 1 room wheelchair accessible.

El Bonita Motel

195 Main, St. Helena, CA 94574. ☎ 707/963-3216; 800/541-3284; fax: 707/963-8838. 41 rooms. AE, D, MC, V. **$**.

If you're willing to forego European feather comforters, plush bathrobes, and nightly turn-down service for the sake of saving beaucoup bucks (families, are you listening?), consider the El Bonita. Its clean, well-maintained rooms sport motel-mode furnishings, but the pool and garden area have been recently relandscaped, and are really quite pleasant. The location poses a Hobson's choice: St. Helena is central to all the valley, but the Bonita sits right on busy Highway 29. *Amenities:* Outdoor pool, exercise room, conference facilities, 2 rooms wheelchair accessible.

Hotel St. Helena

1309 Main, St. Helena, CA 94574. ☎ 707/963-4388; fax: 707/963-5402; 18 rooms, 14 with private bath. AE, MC, V. **$$**. Even though it's situated smack in the heart of St. Helena, it's possible to overlook this establishment; you pass through a small arcade to the entrance, set back off the street. The rooms are done up in fairly standard Victoriana. What's really unusual is the wine bar adjacent to the lobby. It's populated by a bizarre cast of marionettes and costumed dolls in a vignette that's far more crazy than quaint. *Amenities:* Conference facilities.

The Ink House

1575 St. Helena Hwy., St. Helena, CA 95474. ☎ 707/963-3890; 800/553-4343; fax: 707/963-2195. 4 rooms. MC, V. **$$**. A concert grand piano in one parlor and a restored antique pump organ in another—it's immediately apparent that the Ink House is a cultured home (in fact, one of the hosts is the former director of the Honolulu Symphony). The buttercup-yellow Italianate structure was constructed in 1884, and is listed on the National Register of Historic Places. A mix of English, American, and French antiques lend the 2nd-story bedrooms a nostalgic mood. At day's end, retreat to the intimate 3rd-floor observatory with a bottle of the local product and watch the shadows fall over the surrounding hills and vineyards.

★ The Inn at Southbridge

1020 Main St., St. Helena, CA 94574. ☎ 707/967-9400; 800/520-6800; fax: 707/967-9486. 21 rooms. AE, D, MC, V. **$$$$**. The restrained hand of architect William Turnbull, Jr. touches this property with an elegant, updated agrarianism; the L-shaped building is textured with trellises and French doors. Fireplaces warm the Shaker-simple guest rooms, which are furnished with cherrywood pieces and finished in a soothing autumnal palette of ocher, olive, and black. Bathrooms harbor a spatial surprise: Their skylit ceilings rise 20 feet. Chef Michael Chiarello, the guiding light behind nearby Tra Vigne (see page 176), works his magic at the mammoth brick oven that's the heart of the restaurant, Tomatina; after a leisurely dinner at one of its courtyard tables, stroll into town for a nightcap or a round of window-shopping. *Amenities:* Privileges at Meadowood resort, restaurant, conference facilities, 21 rooms wheelchair accessible.

★ La Residence Country Inn

4066 St. Helena Hwy. North, Napa, CA 94558. ☎ 707/253-0337; fax: 707/253-0382. 20 rooms. AE, D, MC, V. **$$$**. The uncommonly large rooms and suites at this oak-shaded property are divided between 2 buildings: Quarters in the

La Residence Country Inn

French Barn, a contemporary construction, are designer variations on the French-country theme, while those in the Mansion, an 1870 gothic revival work, are more period in flavor. Most rooms have fireplaces and balconies; all are thoughtfully provisioned with CD players, in lyrical lieu of televisions. Innkeepers David Jackson and Craig Claussen are to both the manor and the manner born, hosting breakfasts and afternoon wine receptions with friendly authority and ease. *Amenities:* Outdoor pool, spa.

★ Maison Fleurie

6529 Yount St., Yountville, CA 94599. ☎ 707/944-2056; 800/788-0369. 13 rooms. AE, MC, V. **$$$**.

Anchored by a vine-covered, 100-year-old brick building, this compound of 3 rustic structures, while sited in the vineyards of Yountville, is redolent of Provence. The Old Bakery and the Carriage House enclose a verdant courtyard and swimming pool; 5 rooms in these buildings feature fireplaces and baths with Roman tubs. Relaxed breakfasts are served in a cheery common room, and there are bicycles available for use gratis, for pedaling through the surrounding fields of pinot noir. Visitors who are also touring San Francisco and Monterey may take advantage of a frequent guest program by staying in the inn's sister properties in these locations. The reward? Discounted or even free lodging. *Amenities:* Outdoor pool, spa, 2 rooms wheelchair accessible.

★★ Meadowood

900 Meadowood Lane, Rutherford, CA 94574. ☎ 707/963-3646; 800/458-8080; fax: 707/963-3532. 85 rooms. AE, D, MC, V. **$$$$**.

Sequestered amongst more than 250 rolling acres of oak and madrone trees are the superlative facilities of Meadowood. Accommodations are in contemporary interpretations of classic New England architecture, and are spread throughout the property; you can opt to bunk near the venue of your sport of choice or in one of the forested hideaway cottages. Spend a Saturday with the resident wine tutor, John Thoreen, and learn the nuances of fine vintages in a guided tasting session of more than a dozen wines while enjoying a 3-course lunch. And after a workout on the tennis courts, croquet lawns (bring your whites), or golf links, head for the spa to recuperate with a chardonnay gel body wrap. *Amenities:* Large health club, exercise room, 2 outdoor pools, 2 restaurants, conference facilities, 2 croquet courts, 7 outdoor tennis courts, 9-hole golf course, in-room VCRs, 2 rooms wheelchair accessible.

Mount View Hotel

1457 Lincoln, Calistoga, CA 94515. ☎ 707/942-6877; fax: 707/942-6904. 33 rooms. AE, MC, V. **$$**.

Owing to a recent remodeling, the once Art Deco guest rooms now have a Victorian disposition. If peace and quiet are a big part of your plans, avoid the street-side chambers; they sit atop the wildly popular Catahoula Restaurant and its adjoining saloon, where the live and loud music from the weekend "Blues Brunch" festivities can wake even the soundest sleeper. Play it safe and splurge on one of the comfortable cottages, which come equipped with private patio, hot tub, and wet bar. *Amenities:* Full-service spa, outdoor pool, restaurant, conference facilities.

★ Rancho Caymus Inn

1140 Rutherford Rd., Rutherford, CA 94573. ☎ 707/963-1777; 800/845-1777; fax: 707/963-5387. 26 rooms. AE, MC, V. **$$$**.

Beds crafted of black walnut, stoneware basins, wrought iron lamps, carved parota wood dressers, and rugs and textiles hand-woven by Salazaca and Otavalon Indians imbue this gracious hacienda with a rich artistic character. Encircling a profusely-planted Spanish-style courtyard, rooms feature either a private garden patio or balcony. The sitting areas of all the suites save four are warmed by beehive adobe fireplaces. The larger quarters have kitchenettes, making them ideal for extended wine country siestas. *Amenities:* Restaurant, conference facilities, 2 rooms wheelchair accessible.

RustRidge

2910 Lower Chiles Valley Rd., St. Helena, CA 94574. ☎ 707/965-9353; fax: 707/965-9263. 5 rooms. AE, MC, V. **$$**.

Combining a thoroughbred-horse farm, a working winery, and a bed & breakfast operation isn't a job for the faint of heart (not to mention the weak of back). For their fortunate visitors, the folks at secluded RustRidge are old pros at each pursuit. Guests are housed in contemporary Southwestern quarters, with a choice of valley, vineyard, or pasture views. The grapes come into bud in the spring, coincident with the arrival of the new crop of foals, who spend their pretrack years being trained and exercised amidst the vines. *Amenities:* 1 room wheelchair accessible.

★ Silverado Country Club & Resort

1600 Atlas Peak, Napa, CA 94558. ☎ 707/257-0200; 800/532-0500; fax: 707/257-5400. 280 rooms. AE, D, MC, V. **$$$$**.

For some, relaxation means a good book and an empty beach; for others, a dawn to dusk regimen of golf, tennis, and swimming is in order. If you hold the latter preferences dear, Silverado's abundant facilities will keep you busy unwinding for days on end. The Robert Trent Jones, Jr.–designed links are up to the demanding standards of the PGA, which holds its annual Transamerica tournament here. The 6,500-yard South Course confounds with more than a dozen water crossings; the North Course, at 6,700 yards, is longer but the terrain is more forgiving. The illuminated plexipaved tennis

Vintage Inn

courts are randomly set into the landscape, allowing for picturesque playing until well after dark. Accommodations are in club members' private units, which are comfortable, but basically undistinguished—small consequence when you're running around all day, anyway. *Amenities:* 8 outdoor pools, 3 restaurants, conference facilities, 23 lighted tennis courts, 2 18-hole golf courses, 150 downstairs rooms wheelchair accessible.

Vintage Inn

6541 Washington, Yountville, CA 94599. ☎ 707/944-1112; 800/351-1133; fax: 707/944-1617. 80 rooms. AE, D, MC, V. **$$**.

If you've had the occasion to stay at Ventana, the posh retreat in Big Sur, the master planning at the Vintage Inn may seem familiar; designer Kipp Stewart created both getaways. Clusters of shingle-roofed villas dot the property; the guest rooms complete the California casual look with bleached-wood cathedral ceilings, wicker and rattan furniture, louvered window treatments, and oversized fireplaces. *Amenities:* Outdoor pool, conference facilities, 2 outdoor tennis courts, 4 rooms wheelchair accessible.

Restaurants in the Napa Valley

★ All Seasons Cafe

1400 Lincoln, Calistoga. ☎ 707/942-9111. MC, V. Reservations recommended. Wheelchair accessible. Closed Wed; open only Sat and Sun for breakfast. AMERICAN. **$$**.

Maybe—just maybe—there's reason beyond the Dungeness crab cakes and the spinach-smoked chicken salad that keeps locals and enlightened visitors coming back to this comely establishment. Possibly it's the sagacious stand the cafe has adopted with regard to their wine cellar/shop: You select a bottle from the well-stocked on-premises retail store, and then pay only a modest corkage fee, thus avoiding the usual usurious restaurant markup.

Armadillo's

1304 Main, St. Helena. ☎ 707/963 8082. MC, V. Wheelchair accessible. MEXICAN. **$**.

If the piquant huevos rancheros don't open your eyes, the colorful folk-industrial sculptures standing guard at this Mexican eatery certainly will. Although the menu tends to stick to the standard taco/tostada/burrito litany, there are a few flavorful departures worthy of mention: *huajalote,* a plump grilled turkey breast marinated in tequila and chiles; and for an appetizer, the "Mexican won ton"—shredded pork and cheese wrapped in a flour tortilla and deep fried.

★ Bistro Don Giovanni

4110 St. Helena Hwy., Napa. ☎ 707/224-3300. AE, MC, V. Reservations recommended. Wheelchair accessible. ITALIAN. **$$**.

On the site of the much-missed Table 29, this is an upbeat, sophisticated spot for a better-than-average Italian repast. Saffron pappardelle tossed with grilled rabbit ragout and baby artichokes, the ever-honest pizza Margherita, and other straightforward dishes from the open kitchen are all potentially amicable partners with any of the offerings on the extensive wine list. At night, the abundantly windowed room glows brightly among the surrounding Trefethen vineyards, making a table on the trellised terrace worth the probable wait.

Bosko's Ristorante

1364 Lincoln Ave, Calistoga. ☎ 707/942-9088. Wheelchair accessible. ITALIAN. **$$**.

Despite the fact that it's been around for more than 10 years, this nonetheless popular haunt has yet to acquire much in the way of ambiance; what keeps the customers satisfied is the moderately priced menu of Italian favorites, particularly the fresh pastas that are cooked to order. Among the selections, spinach fettuccine with scallops and mushrooms in a basil cream sauce is a standout. Assorted salads, pizzas, and sandwiches round out the picture. Bosko's is one of the relatively few restaurants in the area where children won't feel out of place.

★★ Brava Terrace

3010 St. Helena Hwy., St. Helena. ☎ 707/963-9300. Reservations recommended. Wheelchair accessible. CALIFORNIA. **$$$**.

Dinner at Brava Terrace is a quintessential California wine country experience, for all the right reasons: ingenious cooking, graceful service, and a sylvan environment. Any table on the expansive stepped patio, shaded by canvas umbrellas and surrounded by lush walls of greenery, is a good one, especially when it's laden with a selection of chef Fred Halpert's repertoire of winners. Delicate rings of fried calamari is a de rigueur appetizer; for an entree, if the risotto studded with a dice of peaches, corn, grilled chicken, chili flakes, and scallions is offered, don't hesitate. Should the weather ever be less than perfect, the indoor dining room, with its skylights and river rock hearth, is just as pleasant. Ask about seeing the restaurant's herb and vegetable garden, the origin of many of its ingredients.

Cafe Pacifico

1237 Lincoln, Calistoga. ☎ 707/942-4400. MC, V. Wheelchair accessible. MEXICAN. **$$**.

This commodious cantina is especially appealing during Fiesta Hour, when icy margaritas, tacos, and taquitos plunge in price.

★★ Catahoula Restaurant & Saloon

1457 Lincoln, Calistoga. ☎ 707/942-2275. MC, V. Reservations recommended. Wheelchair accessible. Closed Tues and the month of Jan. AMERICAN. **$$$**.

A couple years back, Jan Birnbaum packed up his well-traveled toque (most recently he was executive chef at

Campton Place; previous stints include the Quilted Giraffe, the Rattlesnake Club, and K-Paul's Louisiana Kitchen) to open a restaurant that would allow him to put into practice his straightforward philosophy that good food "has to make you want to take the next bite." A meal at Catahoula can compel even the most jaded to take that one step further, and make you want to lick the plate. Southern-inspired American fare, earthy and assertive in taste, is Birnbaum's passion. Start with a bowl of spicy rooster gumbo, then delve into one of the wood-fired entrees—roasted lamb chops with garlic mashed potatoes and chipotle sauce, maybe, or the capon salad with caramelized pears. Desserts are impossible to pass up, what with the likes of Meyer lemon-mango meringue tart and a spiced chocolate cake with coffee and chicory offered. Once satiated—no, make that stuffed—you can relax and contemplate the curiously friendly decor, the walls scattered with a hodgepodge of rusty corrugated siding, weathered plywood, and other salvaged materials. And what of the sonorous, Southern "Catahoula," evocative of an obscure Tennessee Williams character? It's actually the name of a breed of hound dog, a native Louisiana canine whose soulful visage stares out at diners from photographs throughout the room.

Checkers Pasta & Pizza Restaurant

1414 Lincoln, Calistoga. ☎ 707/942-9300. MC, V. Wheelchair accessible. ITALIAN. **$**.

The bustle of this modish neighborhood place is mirrored by the vivid abstract paintings that cover the walls. More than a dozen thin-crusted pizza recipes tantalize; at dinner the choices are further complicated by the addition of several well-prepared chicken dishes to the menu.

★ The Diner

6476 Washington, Yountville. ☎ 707/944 2626. Wheelchair accessible. Closed daily from 3–5:30pm. AMERICAN. **$**.

Pretensions are checked at the door of this proven valley favorite, where the counter is long and the booths roomy. Brightly-hued Fiestaware lines the walls. They serve 3 squares here, and breakfast is the biggest draw; the cornmeal pancakes and smoky links are allegedly addictive. The buttermilk shake has proved the delectable downfall of many a waist-watcher—go ahead, we won't tell.

★★ Domaine Chandon

1 California Dr., Yountville. ☎ 707/944-2892; 800/736-2892. AE, D, MC, V. Reservations recommended; jacket for dinner preferred. Wheelchair accessible. Nov–Apr; closed Mon–Tues. CALIFORNIA. **$$$$**.

This enclave of modern elegance and culinary excellence was one of the valley's first fine dining rooms, opening in 1977. At midday, the mood is relaxed; the glass walls slide open to the flagstone patio. Come dinner, candles light the linen-covered tables and service is more formal, focusing attention on chef Phillippe Jeanty's marriage of French and Californian cuisines. Although many dishes are naturally geared to the house's sparklers, there's a complete selection of still wines from other vintners available, as well as a captain's list of rare bottles that are no longer found on the market.

★★ The French Laundry

6640 Washington, Yountville. ☎ 707/944-2380. AE, MC, V. Reservations recommended. Wheelchair accessible. Closed Mon. FRENCH. **$$$$**.

Since assuming command of this rustic stone building and its pastoral gardens in 1994, chef Thomas Keller hasn't rested for a moment on his considerable culinary laurels; he's constantly developing 4- and 5-course prix fixe menus that showcase the seasonal bounty of the region. His creations are nothing short of sensual—visually, as well as in taste and texture. Through his deft orchestrations of dishes (for example, a warm fricassée of artichokes, leading to a filet of John Dory with Provençal olives, followed by pan-seared skirt steak, then a cheese course), diners experience a remarkable sequence of flavors. Desserts give Keller a chance to indulge his humorous side, with items like "coffee and doughnuts" (actually a sinful cappuccino semi-fredo paired with tiny cinnamon-sugared beignets). It would be a mistake to pass the French Laundry by based on any preconceived notions about prix fixe meals; Keller provides a wide choice of courses that surpasses that of many à la carte establishments.

Jack Hunter's Smokehouse Cafe

1458 Lincoln, Calistoga. ☎ 707/942-6060. Wheelchair accessible. AMERICAN. **$$**.

The owners urge you to "Eat American" at this fun, farmhouse-style place, replete with Bob Wills on the jukebox and an O-scale model train chugging above the oilcloth-covered tables. Their breakfasts will more than stoke you for a long day of wine country touring, and the Slow Pig Sandwich is toothsome testimony to the kitchen's skill in the smokehouse. The ample servings can all be kid-sized upon request.

Magnolia Café

1118 Hunt Ave., St. Helena. ☎ 707/963-0748. MC, V. Wheelchair accessible. AMERICAN. **$**.

When was the last time you saw croissant sandwiches listed on a menu . . . 1983? Well, if you happen to harbor fond memories of those crumbly days, relive them at this well-intentioned but otherwise clueless establishment that misses the mark on several counts. Besides the unimaginative food (stromboli, anyone?), the brick walls are covered with tiers of garish, Basquiat-esque paintings; one canvas is titled "You Never Get a Third Chance to Make a Second Impression." Indeed.

Mustards Grill

7399 St. Helena Hwy., Napa. ☎ 707/944-2424. D, MC, V. Reservations recommended. Wheelchair accessible. AMERICAN. **$$**.

This is the country cousin of San Francisco's Fog City Diner: The two are similar in both spirit and casual menu. You'll no doubt notice platters of oak-smoked baby back ribs and onion strings on more than one of the tables. At busy times, the staff can get a little too zealous when clearing the dishes to make way for the next round of diners; in other words, lingering is not encouraged.

Napa Valley Brewing Company

1250 Lincoln, Calistoga. ☎ 707/942-4101. AE, MC, V. Wheelchair accessible. Closed daily 3-5:30pm. AMERICAN. **$$**.

Daring to be different in the heart of the wine country, the folks at this small brewery produce a wheat ale, a golden lager, and a red ale. Cool down with a frosty mug on the creekside patio, which sparkles at night by the glow of Japanese paper lanterns. Better yet, order a plate of the pork tenderloin that's finished with a fiery Thai chili glaze and conduct your own personal taste test of all three brews.

Rutherford Grill

1180 Rutherford Rd., Rutherford. ☎ 707/963-1792. Wheelchair accessible. AMERICAN. **$$**.

In a spacious environment that might be well described as "rusticated postmodern"—black concrete floor, tailored red leather and matte wood booths, angular lighting fixtures—the food strikes a decidedly down-home note. Spit-roasted chickens are a big draw, the succulent birds also appearing as sandwiches and salads. A dish of the house-marinated olives, a side of skillet corn bread, and the Caesar salad makes a satisfying light meal indeed. Definitely drop by the patio for a glass of wine (the restaurant pours a generous 7-oz. serving); a series of simple limestone fountains gurgle pleasantly from the perimeter. Choose a table near the fireplace if there's a chill in the air.

★ Showley's

1327 Railroad St., St. Helena. ☎ 707/963-1200. AE, D, MC, V. Reservations recommended. Wheelchair accessible. Closed Mon. CALIFORNIA. **$$$**.

Never underestimate the ladies who lunch. They (and other locals who appreciate attention to dining details) are out in force at Showley's, a refined spot away from the fracas of Main Street. A collection of airy, casual rooms bedecked with bright contemporary watercolors is the setting for some serious cooking, much of it centered around seasonal indigenous ingredients. The pasilla chile stuffed with a mixture of pork tenderloin, pine nuts, and chutney is ethereal (the recipe is credited to the film *Like Water for Chocolate*), and the fresh peach pie with bourbon ice cream just as heavenly. On a warm night, a table under the spreading, century-old fig tree is an enchanting spot from which to enjoy the restaurant's soft jazz trio.

★ Stars Oakville Cafe

7848 St. Helena Hwy., Oakville. ☎ 707/944-8905. AE, MC, V. Reservations recommended. Wheelchair accessible. CALIFORNIA. **$$**.

Jeremiah Tower has exported his particular brand of big-city culinary celebrity to this little wine country burg with sensitivity, checking his theatrical tendencies in favor of a toned-down enterprise that's more compatible with the local culture. The dining room is clean-lined and simple, albeit a bit snug; the terrace is bordered by a gorgeous formal garden limned by olive and lemon trees. Meals, though, retain the fresh sophistication of their urban compatriots and celebrate the bounty of California: Fish and seafood entrees are unerring, pastas inspired, and desserts sublime.

Susie's Bar

1365 Lincoln, Calistoga. ☎ 707/942-6710. Wheelchair accessible. **$**.

Nothing special here, and that's the point. If you hanker for a break from the très gentile ways of the wine country, Susie understands. A classic Schwinn 3-speed dangling from the rafters, sports schedules plastering the walls, a few pinball machines, and a no-frills barkeep who drawls, "What can I do you for?" make this a most cordial dive.

Taylor's Refresher

933 Main, St. Helena. ☎ 707/963-3486. Wheelchair accessible. AMERICAN. **$**.

The neighborhood's changed quite a bit since this drive-in roadside spot was founded in 1949, but Taylor's endures, its tidy green-and-white awning acting as a beacon for locals hungry for burgers, fries, and a shake. Picnic tables are scattered around the broad carpet of lawn, so you can liberate the kids from the confines of the car while you eat.

Terra

1345 Railroad Ave., St. Helena. ☎ 707/963-8931. MC, V. Reservations recommended. Wheelchair accessible. Closed Tues. ECLECTIC. **$$$**.

The 1884 fieldstone structure that houses Terra has found its true calling. Formerly a foundry, then a chicken hatchery, later a museum, its potential has been beautifully realized with the addition of tall arching windows, saltillo tile floors, and wrought-iron sconces illuminating the rocky walls. The menu combines the sunny flavors of southern France and northern Italy with tastes from the Orient, a balancing act that chef Hiro Sone manages with flair and aplomb. The grilled tuna sauced with tahini and pine nuts or quail and polenta napped with a mushroom-rosemary mixture are palatable proof of his proficiency. The wine list is one of the valley's best, organized not just by varietal, but also by stylistic and technical characteristics; for instance, you can select a sauvignon blanc that is grassy or floral, a barrel or malolactic fermentation.

★ Tra Vigne

1050 Charter Oak, St. Helena. ☎ 707/963-4444. D, MC, V. Reservations recommended. Wheelchair accessible. ITALIAN. **$$**.

Thirty-foot ceilings, gold-leafed crown molding, amber glass-beaded lampshades—the dining room at Tra Vigne is not what you'd call an exercise in subtlety. Michael Chiarello's lusty Italian/Californian fare is parallel in its philosophy: Flavors are vigorous, presentations have impact. Outside, a grove of mulberry trees canopies the terrace; at night, they're an earthbound constellation of tiny lights. Across the courtyard, Cantinetta Tra Vigne (☎ 707/963-8888; **$**) is great for grabbing a quick bite or take-out dish; it carries an attractive stock of kitchen gifts as well, including the restaurant's line of signature food products.

Trilogy

1234 Main, St. Helena. ☎ 707/963-5507. MC, V. Reservations recommended. Wheelchair accessible. Closed Mon and for lunch on Sat and Sun. CALIFORNIA. **$$$**.

You'll eat well at this small establishment, and you'll be in good company—it's frequented by some prominent area vintners who may be taking advantage of the opportunity to taste the competition in Trilogy's prix fixe dinner menu, which features a different wine with each course. Rock shrimp-tomato-asparagus terrine in saffron-orange sauce is paired with a Schloss Vollrads Spätlese Rheingau, while a venison chop is coupled with a 1992 La Jota cabernet sauvignon.

★ The Wine Spectator Greystone Restaurant

2555 Main, St. Helena. ☎ 707/967-1010. MC, V. Reservations recommended. Wheelchair accessible. Closed Tues. MEDITERRANEAN. **$$**.

A menu of Mediterranean-inspired *meze* ("little plates") gives chef Paul Sartory, the first-place finisher in 1994's U.S.A. Bocuse d'Or competition, a wide field on which to create savories such as spit-roasted seafood, grilled pizzas, and roasted vegetables (of the latter, many are cultivated on the premises in the Culinary Institute of America's own gardens). Adam Tihany's exuberant design integrates the kitchen and dining room around an archipelago of cooking islands: a bakery, a rotisserie/grill, and a mixed use area. The wine list—make that a wine *text,* as it runs well over 30 pages—is organized not only by varietal type, but also by point of origin. Peppered with historical Napa Valley anecdotes and proposals for wine and food couplings, it's a fascinating read.

★ Wappo Bar Bistro

1226-B Washington, Calistoga. ☎ 707/942-4712. AE, MC, V. Reservations recommended. Closed Tues and for dinner on Wed. ECLECTIC. **$$**.

A block off the main drag, this fledgling bistro is the definition of hip in the Napa Valley. The interior is an arty blend of the polished and the patinated: Gleaming copper tables are spotlighted by parchment-shaded lamps under an exposed-beam ceiling. Framed collages line the walls, lending a further touch of texture to the room. At lunch and dinner you'll find an alchemy of Mediterranean and Asian tastes—roast lavender chicken with garlic is served with new potatoes in lemon and capers and eggplant fans; duck carnitas Yucateco; and *vatapa* (a Bahian fish stew brimming with black beans, coconut, plantain, and peanuts).

Additional Sources for Picnic Eats

Oakville Grocery

7856 St. Helena Hwy., Oakville, ☎ 707/944-8802 or 800/736-6602

V. Satuui

1111 White Lane, St. Helena, ☎ 707/963-7774

Shopping in the Napa Valley

Amelia Claire

1230 Main, St. Helena. ☎ 707/963-8502.

Forward footwear for women.

The Artful Eye

1333A Lincoln, Calistoga. ☎ 707/942-4743.

The strong suit of this contemporary crafts/art gallery are the art glass and the "techno-romantic" jewelry by Thomas Mann: intricate stainless steel pieces with an industrial edge.

Calistoga Roastery

1631 Lincoln Ave., Calistoga. ☎ 707/942-5757.

A sweet, funky place to watch newly blissed-out hot springers and mud-bathers wobble in from the spas across the street and order their caffeine charge. Breakfast and sandwiches can be had indoors or out on the sundeck. Amuse yourself with the pre-Nintendo batch of games on hand: cribbage, backgammon, etc.

Calistoga Wine Stop

1458 Lincoln #2, Calistoga. ☎ 707/942-5556.

Among the thousand-odd vintages displayed in this restored rail car, the connoisseur may find some rarities—witness the '93 Ramspeck pinot noir. The vast majority of stock is Californian in origin. No need to worry about lugging bottles home; they're old hands when it comes to shipping purchases.

Calla Lily

1222 Main, St. Helena. ☎ 707/963-8188.

Bed and bath linens to die for are sentimentally arrayed here. Egyptian cottons, Irish linens, Italian and Belgian laces, and other fabulous fibers just beg to be touched.

Eccola

1309 Main, St. Helena. ☎ 707/963-1733.

Delectable lingerie and loungewear in styles from sensual to straight-laced.

Gloriosa

1215 Washington, St. Helena. ☎ 707/942-4062.

Were Lewis Carroll to collaborate with Claude Monet on a line of home accessories, the result might resemble this ebullience of floral-patterned ceramics, paintings, and pillows.

Greystone Campus Store

2555 Main St., St. Helena. ☎ 707/967-2001.

The professional cook's tools used by students at the Napa Valley branch of the prestigious Culinary Institute of America are available here, as well as their snazzy custom-designed chef's uniform: traditional hound's-tooth check pants in teal-and-white, coordinated with a jacket embroidered with the school's logo in metallic copper and teal.

The Model Bakery

1357 Main St., St. Helena. ☎ 707/963-8192.

Enter this airy, homespun space, take a seat in one of the compellingly incongruous suave Italian chairs, and ponder the best way to break your fast. Start with the Morning Buns, croissant dough filled with brown sugar and rolled in cinnamon sugar while warm. Or maybe the house biscotti, studded with currants, hazelnuts, and anise. Brick wall ovens are the secret ingredient in all the house-baked goods.

Mosswood

1239 Main St., St. Helena. ☎ 707/963-5883.

Garden accoutrements both classic and contemporary here: cast terra-cotta pavers with botanical motifs, to bird houses of broken pottery that would warm the cockles of Julian Schnabel's intellectual property lawyers.

Murray & Gordon Wine Bar and Market

6770 Washington St., Yountville. ☎ 707/944-8246.

A happy hybrid of the American general store and European wine bar, this is a convenient spot to pick up take-out foods, as well as sample some of the 200-plus Napa wines offered for sale. Or opt to eat in at the 16-seat cafe, which serves breakfast, lunch, and afternoon tea.

My Favorite Things

1289 Main St., St. Helena. ☎ 707/963-0848.

Aptly named if you have an unquenchable yen for cutesy country goose accessories and patchwork pillows.

Napa Valley Coffee Roasting Co.

1400 Oak, St. Helena. ☎ 707/963-4491.

At 4 o'clock on any given weekday, this light-filled, spacious cafe is packed with locals dishing the latest grape gossip. Newly roasted beans and coffee paraphernalia are also sold.

Noodles

1325 Main St., St. Helena. ☎ 707/963-1823.

Make this modern rustic storefront a prepicnic stop for its fresh Italian bread, pasta, and prepared sauces and soups (the squash blossom is a real treat).

On the Vine

1234 Main St., St. Helena. ☎ 707/963-2209.

Skip the hand-painted silk scarves and embroidered denim stuff and head for the baubles. You'll find a great collection of jewels with a food and wine theme, ranging from cafeteria-chunky cups-and-saucers charm bracelets to sterling wire-whisk earrings, all at surprisingly reasonable prices.

One Song

1407 Lincoln, Calistoga. ☎ 707/942-8959.

A sybaritic assemblage of toiletries (the Grotto products are particularly artfully packaged, with combos of soap, slate, and natural sponges) is complemented by the Ecosport organic cotton casual clothes for adults and kids.

Palisades Market

1506 Lincoln, Calistoga. ☎ 707/942-9549.

This sophisticated roadside stand proves a far more aesthetic alternative to the CalMart supermarket across the street when stocking up on al fresco provisions. There's an abundant deli and salad selection, marvelous produce, and a well-chosen wine and beverage stock. Sit on the bench under the green-and-white striped awning and people-watch to your heart's content.

R.S. Basso

1219 Main St., St. Helena. ☎ 707/963-0391.

"A big shipment just came in," entreated a clerk, as if to account for the exquisite chaos that reigns at this expansive home furnishings emporium. And what marvelous cargo it is: everything from quirky drawer pulls to tapestry-canopied beds to bibelots extraordinaire—all ranging in cost from pennies to other-worldly.

Reeds

1302 Main St., St. Helena. ☎ 707/963-0400.

Natural fabrics—silks, linens, fine cottons—in neutral palettes are skillfully cut and draped into elegantly casual outfits and party dresses.

St. Helena Antiques

1231 Main St., St. Helena. ☎ 707/963-5878.

All manner of time-worn items, more than a few with ties to the local industry. A fascinating collection of corkscrews, weathered bottle-drying racks, and other obscure oenophernalia make for intriguing browsing.

Stillwaters

1228 Main St., St. Helena. ☎ 707/963-1782.

Fisherfolk with an advanced addiction (dare we say hooked?) to gadgetry come here to revel in Ron

Sculatti's Innovative Fishing Systems (IFS), a super-specialized line of rod and reel storage gear.

Tántau

1400 Oak, St. Helena. ☎ 707/963-3115.

Adjoining the Napa Coffee Roastery, this is a spirited collection of adornments for the body and home. Evelin Wauder's colorful comb-finished furniture is a standout.

Tin Barn Antiques

1510 Lincoln, Calistoga. ☎ 707/942-0618.

Have fun foraging through old furnishings and odd clothing in this multidealer space.

Vanderbilt and Company

1429 Main St., St. Helena. ☎ 707/963-1010.

This stalwart tabletop source seems to have run out of steam. Their once-inventive merchandise displays seem tired, and the stock itself is neither fresh nor cutting edge. Vietri fans, though, can still take delight in the store's selection of the vivid Italian pottery.

Wexford & Woods

1347 Lincoln, Calistoga. ☎ 707/942-9729.

A collection of antique Irish pine armoires form a quaint backdrop for a myriad of imported essential oils, fragrances, soaps, and lotions.

Wilkes Sport

1219 Main St., St. Helena. ☎ 707/963-4323.

There are certain types of men who just can't do without their Wilkes fix; at this wine country branch of the San Francisco haberdasher, gentlemen vintners will find more relaxed, but no less dapper, apparel.

Sonoma County

Driving Directions

From San Francisco: Follow California Highway 101 north over the Golden Gate, turn right onto Route 37 at Novato, and continue east to its junction with Route 121. Take 121 to the Highway 12 turnoff (on the left), and follow it straight into Sonoma Plaza. Driving time is about an hour.

From the East Bay: From northbound Interstate 80, take Route 37 to Route 29. There's a prominently signed junction with Route 12/121; turn left and follow Highway 12 to town. Driving time is approximately 75 minutes.

Useful Numbers

Sonoma Valley Visitors Bureau, 453 First St. E., Sonoma, CA 95476; ☎ 707/996-1090; fax: 707/996-9212.

Sonoma County Farm Trails, P.O. Box 6032, Santa Rosa, CA 95406; ☎ 707/586-FARM. The *Sonoma County Farm Trails Map* is a great guide to fresh-from-the-source produce, plants, and livestock. Free copies are available at any Chamber of Commerce in the county; or write to the above address.

Towns in Sonoma County

On the Pacific side of the Mayacamas Mountains, the city of **Sonoma** is the hub of its namesake appellation. The atmosphere of early California is palpable around its town square, with historic buildings on every side. The area offers fewer places to stay than does the valley to the east, but the quality of those lodgings that are tucked into the unspoiled countryside of the Russian River and Valley of the Moon is on a par with Napa's best.

Heading northwest from Sonoma, set in the verdant cradle that is the Valley of the Moon, **Glen Ellen** and **Kenwood** are quiet townships where wineries outnumber other amenities.

By comparison, the county seat, **Santa Rosa,** is a mini-metropolis. With a population topping 100,000—and all the necessities needed to support it, from an airport to shopping malls to hospitals—the city continues to attract those seeking a break from the clamor of San Francisco.

Westward, the fertile farmland surrounding **Sebastopol** is planted with orchards of all types (it's famous for Gravenstein apples), various berry crops, and small livestock enterprises. While the town itself isn't of much interest, many of the farmers actively court visits by the public, offering a literal taste of the area.

Between Santa Rosa and the Pacific Ocean lies the Russian River Valley, whose twisting, redwood-shaded length is punctuated with the occasional vineyard, vacation homes, and diminutive resort communities. The most established of these is **Guerneville,** where a mix of funky riverfront cottage motels, upscale bed-and-breakfasts, and a cache of surprisingly good (but often ephemeral) restaurants appeal.

Turning north, fields of grapevines alternate with rolling, forested hills from tiny **Windsor** up to

Healdsburg and on to laid-back **Cloverdale.** Of these three, Healdsburg has the most in the way of country comforts to extend to the visitor: Beguiling shops and eateries ring a traditional town square, with a goodly selection of inviting lodgings nearby.

Sonoma County Wineries

Where Napa is contained, Sonoma sprawls. A wise visitor hoping to see all there is will allot a considerable amount of time for driving between touring and tasting stops.

Cloverdale

J. Fritz Winery

24691 Dutcher Creek Rd., Cloverdale. ☎ 707/894-3389.

The trio of tall portals at the entrance are meant to symbolize the sun, soil, and rain—the essential ingredients to good grape growing. Their arching forms reference the cyclical rhythm of nature. Incorporating these ecological values into the architecture of the winery illustrates owner Jay Fritz's and wine-maker David Hastings's shared commitment to understanding—not overwhelming—the land and its fruits. Only free-run juice is used to produce their white wines, which Hastings, in a nod to his training at Germany's Geisenheim Universität, patiently coaxes into blends that are optimal for barrel aging.

Guerneville

Korbel Champagne Cellars

13250 River Rd., Guerneville. ☎ 707/887-2294.

It's a pleasant surprise to come upon the stately red brick structures of Korbel in the midst of some of Sonoma's lushest scenery; the winery's celebrated gardens pay a kind of cultivated homage to nature. In springtime, tulips, daffodils, and other flowering bulbs brighten the grounds, while over the summer and into fall, more than 250 strains of antique roses blossom. In the tasting room, you're encouraged to lift miniature flutes of the fruit of the vine and enjoy all the *méthode champenoise* varieties: brut, extra dry, sec, natural, blanc de noirs, and rouge.

Healdsburg

Field Stone Winery and Vineyard

10075 Hwy. 128, Healdsburg. ☎ 707/433-7266.

A fieldstone facade eased into an oak-shaded hillside is home to some of California's best cabernet sauvignon

Hop Kiln Winery

and petite sirah bottlings, the latter rendered more elegant than much of the competition because of a touch of viognier in the blend.

Hop Kiln Winery

6050 Westside Rd., Healdsburg. ☎ 707/433-6491.

At the turn of the century, the odd silhouettes of hop kilns—boxy stone buildings with steep roofs capped by shed-like structures—were a common sight throughout the north coast region of California. With the decline in hop farming, most of these distinctive kilns were abandoned; this 1905 specimen was restored in 1974 thanks to the efforts of winery owner Marty Griffin. It's now on the National Register of Historic Places. After tasting the assorted reds (several fine zinfandels originate here) take a bottle to the duck pond out back and enjoy.

Jordan Vineyard & Winery

1474 Alexander Valley Rd., Healdsburg. ☎ 707/431-5250.
By appointment.

Memorable cabernet sauvignon and chardonnay emanate from this 275-acre vineyard, which is crowned by an imposing stone chateau sited on an oak-covered knoll that overlooks the Alexander Valley. The blending of traditional wine-making aesthetics with new world technologies is especially evident in their *J* sparkling wine, which utilizes the only Coquard grape press in the United States.

Piper Sonoma

11447 Old Redwood Hwy., Healdsburg. ☎ 707/433-8843.

This house is the first of the California sparkling producers to release a complete vertical selection of recently disgorged wines; the "Library Collection" bottles date from 1980 through the first 8 vintages. These offer a chance to evaluate the result of extended aging on the yeast while quite literally drinking in the winery's heritage. Pinot noir partisans might be interested in sampling "BearBoat," a still varietal that's wine-maker Rob MacNeill's pet project.

Kenwood

Kenwood Vineyards

9592 Sonoma Hwy., Kenwood. ☎ 707/833-5891.

Lemon-grass sauvignon blancs, peppery zinfandels, merlots touched with an earthy cherry, black currant-kissed cabernets: These are some of the savory varietals that Kenwood has created over the past quarter-century from their weathered redwood barn set well back from the main road. The collector's "Artists Series" of vintage cabernet sauvignons are graced with labels by such talents as Jim Dine, Sam Francis, and Charles Mingus. Weekends often see special food- and wine-pairing events on the premises.

Kunde Estate

10155 Sonoma Hwy., Kenwood. ☎ 707/833-5501.

Family-owned and operated for just shy of a century, Kunde's state-of-the-art wine-making facilities have access to some ancient growths, in a best-of-both-worlds scenario. In the far reaches of their Wildwood vineyard are a pair of particularly storied plantings. The gnarly Shaw zinfandel vines were sown in 1879 (they continue to yield an intense, spicy fruit), and the Drummond cabernet sauvignon block is the source of the first varietal cab produced in America, via cuttings from Chateaux Margaux and Lafite Rothschild. It's more than likely one of the extended Kunde clan will be on the premises to sign a bottle for you—just ask at the new visitors' center, a modern take on the old cattle barn that once stood on the site.

Jordan Vineyard & Winery

Landmark Winery

101 Adobe Canyon Rd., Kenwood. ☎ 707/833-1144; 800/452-6365.

The chardonnays from this modern mission-style winery have repeatedly brought home the gold medal from competitions around the world. For visitors who desire a thorough immersion in life in the wine country, there is a fully appointed, 1-bedroom guest cottage overlooking the vineyard, a fine base of operations for extended stays.

Santa Rosa

Matanzas Creek Winery

6097 Bennett Valley Rd., Santa Rosa. ☎ 707/528-6464.

The bucolic sight of 4,500 lavender plants in full and fragrant bloom welcomes visitors to this progressive producer of chardonnay, sauvignon blanc, and merlot. At its release, their 1990 "Journey" chardonnay (named in a reflection of owners Sandra and Bill MacIver's philosophical approach to wine-making) rocked the California wine world with its $70 price tag, still the bottles were quickly snapped up by those who found its oak-laden complexity both compelling and promising.

Sebastopol

Iron Horse Vineyards

9786 Ross Station Rd., Sebastopol. ☎ 707/887-1507.
By appointment.

The sparkling vintages issued by this family-run enterprise have been served at state occasions by 3 presidents: Reagan, Bush, and Clinton. Crisp and elegant in style, they are aged a minimum of 3 years *en triage* by wine-maker Forrest Tancer. Visitors of a literary bent will recognize the winery as the setting for Joy Sterling's book *A Cultivated Life: A Year in a California Vineyard.*

Sonoma

Bartholomew Park Winery

1000 Vineyard Lane, Sonoma. ☎ 707/935-9511.

In 1857, Hungarian nobleman Agoston Haraszthy, the acknowledged father of the California wine industry, erected a diminutive Palladian villa in the midst of his vast vineyards; today, a reconstruction of that building anchors the grounds of Bartholomew Park Winery. A museum chronicles the historic property's colorful past and present. In the hills above the winery, some 3 miles of marked hiking trails course through a cross-section

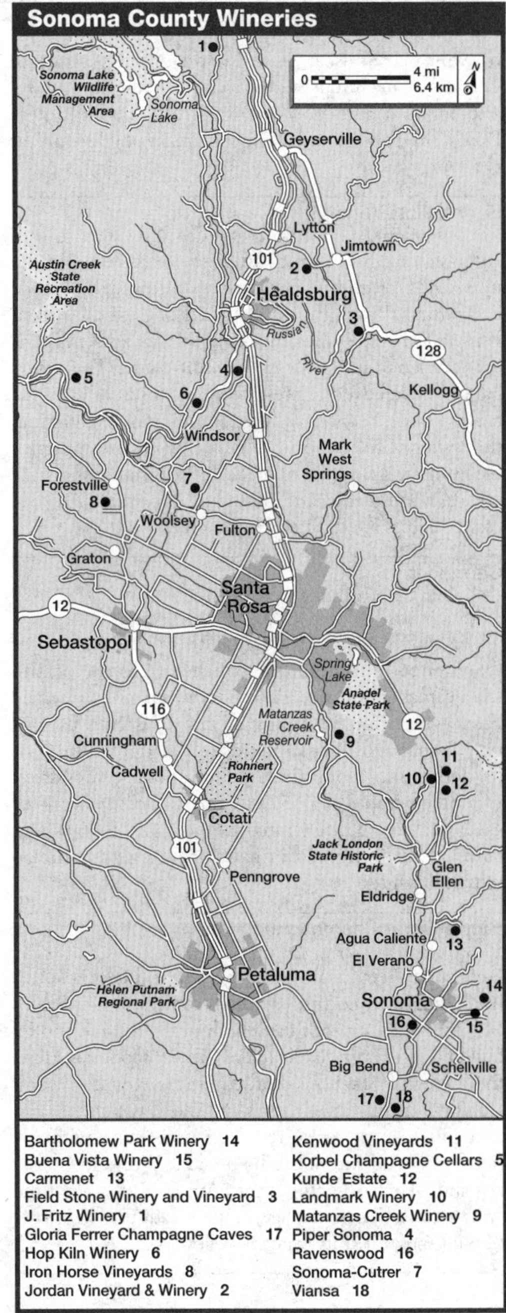
Sonoma County Wineries
0
4 mi
6.4 km
N
Sonoma Lake Wildlife Management Area
Sonoma Lake
Geyserville
Lytton
Jimtown
101
Austin Creek State Recreation Area
Healdsburg
Russian River
128
Kellogg
Windsor
Mark West Springs
Forestville
Woolsey
Fulton
Graton
Santa Rosa
12
Sebastopol
Spring Lake
Anadel State Park
116
Matanzas Creek Reservoir
Cunningham
Cadwell
Rohnert Park
Cotati
Jack London State Historic Park
Glen Ellen
Penngrove
Eldridge
Agua Caliente
El Verano
Petaluma
Helen Putnam Regional Park
Sonoma
Big Bend
Schellville
Bartholomew Park Winery 14
Buena Vista Winery 15
Carmenet 13
Field Stone Winery and Vineyard 3
J. Fritz Winery 1
Gloria Ferrer Champagne Caves 17
Hop Kiln Winery 6
Iron Horse Vineyards 8
Jordan Vineyard & Winery 2
Kenwood Vineyards 11
Korbel Champagne Cellars 5
Kunde Estate 12
Landmark Winery 10
Matanzas Creek Winery 9
Piper Sonoma 4
Ravenswood 16
Sonoma-Cutrer 7
Viansa 18

of Sonoma landscape—redwood groves, stands of gnarled manzanita, wildflower-flecked meadows—and make a fine post-picnic stroll. Bartholomew Park's single-vineyard varietals are available only at the winery.

Buena Vista Winery

18000 Old Winery Rd., Sonoma. ☎ 800/926-1266.

After staking his claim to this area of Sonoma in the mid-19thC, Agoston Haraszthy journeyed to France and returned with thousands of cuttings of the prized *vitis vinifera* grape vines, thus establishing Buena Vista as the state's first producer of premium wines. The original ivy-covered stone press house now serves as a gracious visitors' center, where in addition to sampling the winery's wares, you can create an impromptu picnic from the smorgasbord of locally made cheeses, meats, breads, condiments, and desserts. More than 70 tree-shaded tables are situated by the creek.

Carmenet

1700 Moon Mountain Dr., Sonoma. ☎ 707/996-5870.
By appointment.

Twin redwood turrets signal the pavilion that is Carmenet, hugging the southern slopes of the Mayacamas Mountains. The winery's name—an archaic French term for the family of grape varieties used in traditional Bordeaux blends—is a declaration of its dedication to producing "mountain wines from mountain grapes." A 15,000-square-foot network of caves was dynamited into the volcanic tuff, where barrel tastings are held of its assertive estate meritage reds and whites.

Gloria Ferrer Champagne Caves

23555 Hwy. 121, Sonoma. ☎ 707/996-7256.

Reflecting their Catalan heritage, José and Gloria Ferrer have erected a *cava* that's a sketch straight out of Spain: Plastered arches stretch the length of the red-tile-roofed building that sits gracefully in the Carneros foothills. Here, the owners of the black-bottled Freixenet winery put a California spin on their sparkling wares, which you can taste either in the great room, its walls hung with antique tapestries, or out on the broad terrace—in February and March, sometimes into April, this is one of the wine country's best vantage points to admire the carpet of wild mustard at its brilliant-yellow peak.

Ravenswood

18701 Gehricke Rd., Sonoma. ☎ 707/938-1960.

The conviviality that pervades this casual, knoll-top winery belies the seriousness of its wines. Brazen, rich reds—mostly zinfandels, with some notable merlots and cabernet sauvignons—have given rise to the unofficial house motto, "No Wimpy Wines Allowed." Many of the grapes come from dry-farmed, 70- to 100-year-old vineyards, from which highly concentrated fruit is harvested. Ravenswood relieves the dog days of summer by hosting weekend barbecues, well-accompanied by their wines, of course.

Viansa

25200 Arnold Dr., Sonoma. ☎ 707/935-4700; 800/995-4740.

In a tribute to their ancestry, Sam and Vicki Sebastiani concentrate on hand-crafted Italian varietals, among them nebbiolo, sangiovese, aleatico, and charbono. These all pair quite nicely with the tasty foodstuffs purveyed at the vineyard's own Tuscanesque marketplace, where you can orchestrate a snack or lunch of *tortas* and *panini* to enjoy at the picnic tables that overlook 90 acres of recently restored wetlands. The Sebastianis undertook that conservation project in partnership with Ducks Unlimited; the resulting avian oasis attracts more than 135 species of waterfowl and shorebirds per day, an achievement recognized by Viansa's receipt of the 1995 National Wetlands Award.

Windsor

Sonoma-Cutrer

4401 Slusser Rd., Windsor. ☎ 707/528-1181. *By appointment.*

This producer of premium estate-bottled chardonnay has adopted many of the Grand Cru standards and practices established by the French, including maintaining low vine yields and unfiltered bottling—the latter a delicate operation that when done successfully, allows one to enjoy the wine as if it were being tasted straight from the barrel. The Cutrer Vineyard, 1992 vintage, is the initial release of the winery's Grand Cru Program. A sporting side note: The property is the site of the U.S. Open and World Championship Croquet tournaments.

Accommodations in Sonoma County

★★ Applewood

13555 Hwy. 116, Pocket Canyon, Guerneville, CA 95446. ☎ 707/869-9093. 16 rooms. AE, D, MC, V. **$$$$**.

Devoted innkeepers Darryl Notter and Jim Caron added 6 new rooms to Applewood just last year, allowing a lucky few more visitors to experience their congeniality. The 1920s' Craftsman-style structure is poised at the crest of a hill, where it captures the cool breezes of the Russian River, which flows a few minutes' walk away. Quarters are constant in quality yet distinct in character, furnished in a handsome English eclecticism. From room 10, you're steps away from the pool and hot tub; in number 8, a redwood-shaded balcony beckons. By popular (very popular) demand, meal service has expanded beyond breakfast to include a 4-course prix fixe dinner; the menu might include Sonoma chicken followed by Tuscan strawberry and brandy cream cake. *Amenities:* Outdoor pool, restaurant, conference facilities, in-room VCRs, 1 room wheelchair accessible.

★ The Cottage on Summer Hill

P.O. Box 1540, Glen Ellen, CA 95442. ☎ 707/935-6789; 800/549-8509. 1 bedroom. No credit cards. Accepts personal checks. **$$$**.

Dotting the edge of a thousand-acre wildlife preserve, this private hideaway (with full kitchen) beguiles with its sensuous simplicity. The classic modern decor is enlivened by a tapestry of textiles in sandy neutral hues; Chinese antiques accent the rooms. The natural setting needs no such embellishment; from the deck or hot tub, you'll be treated to down-valley views that at sunset are unforgettable. *Amenities:* Spa, VCR.

★ El Dorado Hotel

405 1st St. W., Sonoma, CA 95476. ☎ 707/996-3030; 800/289-3031; fax: 707/996-3148. 26 rooms. AE, MC, V. **$$**.

If you're looking for a respite from navigating the wine country's meandering byways, it's worth noting that there are 17 vineyards within a mile of this downtown Sonoma retreat. Accommodations at the El Dorado stylishly straddle the centuries with their design: rooms feature four-poster beds, but they're streamlined, burnished steel models. Glass doors open onto balconies overlooking either the hotel's quiet courtyard or the colorful town square with its palm trees and historic buildings. On the ground floor, Piatti (see page 193) even eliminates the need to drive to dinner. Midweek and winter rates are a real bargain. *Amenities:* Outdoor pool, restaurant, conference facilities, 2 rooms wheelchair accessible.

★ Gaige House

13540 Arnold, Glen Ellen, CA 95442. ☎ 707/935-0237; fax: 707/935-6411. 8 rooms. AE, D, MC, V. **$$$**.

It's a sedate, turn-of-the-century Italianate Queen Anne on the outside; inside, the refurbished Gaige House reveals its true colors as a showplace of individuality. An admix of modern art and global artifacts, collected by Ardath Rouas (one of the forces behind the luxe Auberge du Soleil resort in neighboring Napa Valley), imparts an international air to the guest rooms; the woodsy acreage on Calabazas Creek is reassuringly rural. Breakfasts are equally urbane—perhaps a Brie omelet or oatmeal waffles with turkey sausages. *Amenities:* Outdoor pool, conference facilities, 1 room wheelchair accessible.

Glenelly Inn

5131 Warm Springs Rd., Glen Ellen, CA 95442. ☎ 707/996-6720. 8 rooms. MC, V. **$$**.

Wraparound covered verandahs on both floors of this hip-roofed, peach clapboard building mark it as an example of French colonial architecture; it was, in fact, built in 1916 by immigrants Adolphe and Anastacie Larigné as a resort. Today, fully restored, it continues the tradition of hospitality, with sturdy country furnishings and Scandinavian linens in each room, all of which have private entrances off the porches. Innkeeper Kristi Hallamore looks to the lush Glenelly gardens and orchard in preparing breakfast: Guests might enjoy glazed apple and pear rings and leek-nutmeg tarts in addition to home-baked breads and muffins. *Amenities:* Spa.

★★ Kenwood Inn & Spa

10400 Sonoma Hwy., Kenwood, CA 95452. ☎ 707/833-1293; 800/353-6966. 12 rooms. AE, MC, V. **$$$$**.

Framed by a stone archway and a fragrant copse of oleander and bay laurel, this intimate Italianate villa pampers guests with fireplaces and featherbeds in rooms colored in a sumptuous palette of golds, greens and burgundies. "Peasant fare with flair" is how resident chef Charles Holmes characterizes his cooking; extending the Italian atmosphere, breakfast might feature Tuscan white beans with rosemary baby artichokes alongside poached eggs and tomato toast. Further physical rejuvenation stems from the spa, which offers herbal wraps, therapeutic massages, and other stress-reducing services. *Amenities:* Outdoor pool, spa services available, private dining room for guests, conference facilities, 1 room wheelchair accessible.

Madrona Manor

1001 Westside Rd., Healdsburg, CA 95448. ☎ 707/433-4231; 800/258-4003; fax: 707/433-0703. 21 rooms. AE, D, MC, V. **$$$**.

Built in 1881, this mansard-roofed mansion is a commanding presence. Sited on a small knoll, its 3 ornate stories rise precipitously, a harbinger of the equally imposing interior. Richly carved antiques abound in the guest rooms, assembled with a selective eye. It's hard to imagine that the quarters in the Carriage House wouldn't suffer by comparison, but their middle-of-the-road contemporary furnishings are a particularly bland disappointment. Headed by Todd Muir, the restaurant (**$$$**) serves an inventive Californian/French menu, with produce often harvested from the inn's own gardens; it's a worthy destination in itself, with reservations a must. *Amenities:* Outdoor pool, restaurant, conference facilities, 1 room wheelchair accessible.

Sonoma Hotel

110 W. Spain, Sonoma, CA 95476. ☎ 707/996-2996; 800/468-6016. 17 rooms, 5 with private bath. AE, D, MC, V. **$**.

On the quietest corner of the plaza, the rooms in this unassuming 1880 building have seen their share of history; most recently, poet Maya Angelou wrote "Gather Together in My Name" in the cozy, slope-ceilinged garret that is number 21. Beds of mahogany, maple, oak, brass, or iron are found in a panoply of styles; those quarters that share the immaculate bath facilities have in-room washbasins. At press time, the Red Moon Saloon had just opened on the premises for weekend business

Sonoma Hotel

to promising notices. *Amenities:* Restaurant.

★ Sonoma Mission Inn and Spa

18140 Hwy. 12, Sonoma, CA 95476. ☎ 707/938-9000; 800/862-4945. 170 rooms. AE, D, MC, V. **$$$$**.

A pair of rosy Spanish bell towers signal your arrival at this historic retreat, where the rich and famous come to recharge on a regular basis. The staff adheres to a laissez-faire attitude towards the pursuit of fitness; you're free to abstain or partake of any and all of the treatments. It's easy to be content just lolling by the pools (which are filled with naturally warm artesian mineral water that gurgles up from more than a thousand feet below the Inn), but if you opt for the spa programs, you'll emerge equally relaxed. The same forgiving approach is taken by the kitchen: take your pick of low-fat, low-calorie dishes or yield to temptation. Guest rooms are tasteful, shying away from the flamboyance that afflicts many resort hotels; some feature fireplaces. Don't be deterred by the ugly commercial ventures that bookend the entrance to the property—its 8 acres of manicured lawns and stands of eucalyptus ensure a very private stay. *Amenities:* Large health club, full-service spa, 2 outdoor pools, 2 restaurants, conference facilities, 2 lighted tennis courts, 3 rooms wheelchair accessible.

Thistle Dew Inn

171 West Spain, Sonoma, CA 95476. ☎ 707/938-2909; 800/382-7895. 6 rooms. AE, MC, V. **$$**.

Arts and crafts furnishings circa 1910 by Gustav Stickley and Charles Limbert appoint these sunny guest rooms, with cheerful color supplied by antique quilts hand-stitched in Shadows and Squares, Irish Log Cabin, and Broken Star patterns. Forget the car and borrow one of the Inn's bicycles to tour the Valley of the Moon (in this area, the terrain is forgivingly flat); try to make it home in time for afternoon hors d'oeuvres and to share your experiences with the other guests. *Amenities:* 2 rooms wheelchair accessible.

Restaurants in Sonoma County

★ Babette's

464 1st St. E., Sonoma. ☎ 707/939-8921. MC, V. Wheelchair accessible. Closed Sun and Mon. FRENCH. **$$**.

A surprisingly authentic French hideaway; not of the Michelin-star mold, but in the corner bistro manner. Graze through the menu of traditional Gaullic tidbits—oysters, escargot, onion soup au gratin—or loosen your belt and order the namesake Feast, a 5-course extravaganza. More than 30 local wines are poured by the glass.

★ The Buckley Lodge

1717 Adobe Canyon Rd., Kenwood. ☎ 707/833-5562. MC, V. Reservations recommended. Wheelchair accessible. Closed Tues. AMERICAN. **$$$**.

Nestled in the forested foothills below Sugarloaf Ridge, the Buckley Lodge offers robust yet refined American food, attuned to the ways and means of the wine country. Meats, fish, and poultry are grilled or roasted, and accompanied by seasonal produce; the swordfish steak on warmfennel salad with oranges and black olives is a treat for the eyes as well as the taste buds. The agrarian ambiance reaches its peaceful pinnacle at the outdoor tables on Sonoma Creek, where you might catch a glimpse of a deer or a steelhead trout.

The Coffee Garden

415-421 1st St. W. Sonoma. ☎ 707/996-6645. MC, V. Wheelchair accessible. AMERICAN **$**.

The sidewalk tables on the square are usually claimed by the restless youth of Sonoma, while the garden patio in the rear is strictly a tourist scene, but a lovely one at that, overflowing with native flora and a 160-year-old fig tree. The adobe brick building itself is noteworthy, as well; it was constructed by Salvador Vallejo, brother of Mexican general M. J. Vallejo, in the late 1830s.

★ East Side Oyster Bar & Grill

133 East Napa St., Sonoma. ☎ 707/939-1266. AE, MC, V. Reservations recommended. Wheelchair accessible. SEAFOOD/ECLECTIC. **$$**.

It's hard to go wrong at the East Side. The big brick patio veiled by market umbrellas is an al fresco felicity and the tiny, 5-table interior captivates with its austere whitewashed walls, small carved marble fireplace, and bentwood chairs. Likewise, the menu presents its own delicious dilemmas. Do you start with oysters on the half-shell with apple cider mignonette, or go right to the thick grilled pork chop rubbed with Navajo spices with a side of tomatillo and chayote salsa? Decisions, decisions.

Piatti

405 1st St. West, Sonoma. ☎ 707/996-2351. AE, MC, V. Reservations recommended. Wheelchair accessible. ITALIAN. **$$**.

A mural of plump roma tomatoes parades across the faux-finished walls, establishing a whimsical countenance to this inviting trattoria, with its terra-cotta floors and rough-hewn pine chairs. The white pizza topped with prosciutto, mushrooms, roasted garlic, and cheese is a good choice, as are any of the pasta plates—look for the ravioli in lemon cream sauce or the farfalle with salmon and spinach.

Sonoma French Bakery

470 1st St. East, Sonoma.
☎ 707/996-2691. Wheelchair accessible. Closed Mon. BAKERY. **$**.

No nouveau nostalgia here; the French Bakery is the genuine article. Pick out a crusty *pain* or fresh brioche, then head across the street to the park and *mange.*

Steiner's Bar

487 1st St. W. Sonoma.
☎ 707/996-3812. Wheelchair accessible. **$**.

There aren't too many places where you can swagger through a set of real swinging saloon doors, order a boilermaker at the battered bar, and down it . . . in a pretty little garden out back. But Steiner's is the happily schizophrenic exception.

Sunnyside Coffee Club and Blues Bar

140 E. Napa St., Sonoma.
☎ 707/935-0366; AE, MC, V. Closed for dinner. AMERICAN. **$$**.

Street-facing French doors and simple wooden chairs stained in muted colors lend this cafe a polished country kitchen quality. Flip through the newspaper (sections are bound in those neat library sticks) over bacon and eggs and chat up the locals. The blues performances, alas, are a thing of the past: Nearby residents found the volume objectionable.

Zino's Ristorante

420 1st St. East, Sonoma.
☎ 707/996-4466. AE, D, MC, V. Wheelchair accessible. ITALIAN. **$$**.

The timeless tableau of red checkered tablecloths and straw-wrapped fiascoes of Chianti puts in an appearance here. Apropos the setting, the cooking doesn't aspire to much beyond spaghetti and meatballs, but they're decently prepared. In the dining room, the best tables look onto the plaza; beware the so-called "patio" seating—a lonely column of tables squeezed between neighboring buildings with nary a potted plant in sight.

Additional Sources for Picnic Eats

The Cherry Tree #2

1901 Fremont, Sonoma,
☎ 707/938-3480.

Jimtown Store

6706 Hwy. 128, Healdsburg,
☎ 707/433-1212.

Shopping in Sonoma County

Antiques Center of Sonoma

120 W. Napa St., Sonoma. ☎ 707/996-9947.

If you're enamored of wonderful old Parkers, Watermans, and other writing implements with soul, this small collective has an affordable cache. The rest of the wares seem unremarkable, but one man's trash is another man's treasure, as they say.

Artifax

450-C 1st St. E., Sonoma. ☎ 707/996-9494.

Indian Buddhas, African beads, and Japanese brush sets are among the international exotica that tempt at this atmospheric store, where incense and ethnic music waft through the air.

Cat & the Fiddle

153 W. Napa St., Sonoma. ☎ 707/996-5651.

Chock-a-block with the ruffles and lace that set a romantic's heart apounding, you'll discover English and French country antiques.

The Chocolate Cow

452 1st St. E., Sonoma. ☎ 707/935-3564.

The aroma alone threatens to add an inch to your waist, but don't let that stop you from sampling the fudge, ice cream, and candies made right on the premises of this old-time sweet shop.

Coyotes Best of the West

100 W. Spain St., Sonoma. ☎ 707/939-8488.

Buckaroos of all ages will appreciate the old and new cowboy collectibles here, such as original Hopalong Cassidy pocket knives and modern Roy Rogers watches packaged in mini-lunchboxes. There's also a round-up of buckskin fashions, a few pieces of Ponderosa-style furniture, and vintage Western artworks.

The Flag Store

520 Broadway, Sonoma. ☎ 707/996-8140.

From historic pennants to emblems of emerging countries, the Flag Store has it in stock. Pick up a reproduction of the "Bear Flag Revolt" banner that flew for 25 short days when Sonoma was the self-proclaimed capital of the Republic of California.

Gallery Gae Shulman

115 E. Napa St., Sonoma. ☎ 707/939-9600.

Call them mixed-media crafts or recycled artworks, the interesting wares here merit a look-see.

Good Day Sunshine

29 E. Napa St., Sonoma. ☎ 707/938-4001.

Outstanding among the wealth of California crafts here are Catherine Krause's woven chenille vests and tunics and Viki Aniko's cotton quilted jackets. A sign near the more delicate displays politely warns "Little hands must be held."

J. Sumner Gallery

111B E. Napa St., Sonoma. ☎ 707/939-8272.

Four walls (and the floor and ceiling, too) of wild kitty-themed constructions—paintings, tableware, and other decorative incarnations in neon hues—that'll blow Woody Jackson's docile graphic Guernseys off the map.

Jeanine's Coffee & Tea

464 1st St. E., Sonoma. ☎ 707/996-7573.

In addition to the house-roasted and blended brews, there are cups and mugs for every liking, whether it's the hollow head of Daffy Duck or a bone china model perfect for the crooked-pinkie set.

Kaboodle

453 1st St. W., Sonoma. ☎ 707/996-9500.

Here's a glut of garden accessories. A pair of galvanized sheet-metal side tables have a bit of an edge to their design, but the rest of the merchandise is mostly mainstream.

Margaret Douglas Gallery

124 W. Napa St., Sonoma. ☎ 707/935-6254.

There are some real bargains to be found at this first-rate art glass gallery. "Goofy Cups" by Bill Akers go for $110; in a more urban location, that price would easily increase by half. Bowls by Michele Savelle and James Mongrain's Greco-European goblets and pitchers are similarly terrific values.

Milagros

414 1st St. E., Sonoma. ☎ 707/939-0834.

Vivid Oaxacan wood carvings of fantastic creatures, pierced tin starburst lamps from Guanajuato, and Talavera bowls will please the discerning collector of Mexican crafts. On the kitschy side, there are Virgin Mary gearshift knobs and rosaries with peep holes that contain miniature Biblical scenes.

Plaza Books

40 W. Spain St., Sonoma. ☎ 707/996-8474.

Everything an antiquarian book shop should be: logically organized, neat, and brimming with tantalizing titles bound in leather and linen. The stock on California history and authors can provide hours of satisfying browsing.

Readers' Books

127 E. Napa St., Sonoma. ☎ 707/939-1779.

Independent bookstores still flourish in these parts, unbowed by the invasion of the megachains and untainted by loud-mouth spoken word *artistes.* Wander through the rooms of this literary lair, and add a line to the community haiku book as you depart.

Robin's Nest

116 E. Napa St., Sonoma. ☎ 707/996-4169.

A den of off-price kitchen and cooking stuff, there are some pleasantly stylish surprises to be had here: Matte graphite ceramic bowls were a recent steal at a mere $6 apiece.

Sign of the Bear

435 1st St. W., Sonoma. ☎ 707/996-3722.

If you're in need of a 4-foot willow cheese tray or a 24-inch springform pan, you'll find it in this commodious cookware store. There's plenty of other specialized gizmos to enrapture the serious home chef.

Sonoma Cheese Factory

2 Spain St., Sonoma. ☎ 707/996-1931.

The total cheese experience all under one roof: Watch it being made (the wheels are hand-rolled), sample a few of the hundreds of varieties, then send a pound home or pack some off on a picnic. The Viviani family has been producing Sonoma Jack flavored with such ingredients as pesto, caraway, and garlic on these premises since 1931.

The Wine Exchange of Sonoma

452 1st St. E., Sonoma. ☎ 800/938-1794.

The authoritative staff can steer you to wines (and beers, too) that only a local industry insider would know about, and they take great pleasure in scooping the established wine press on new releases. Among their latest recommendations: the 1993 Crane Canyon Mourvèdre, of which a scant 70 cases were made. As you might expect, the tasting bar is imaginatively and insightfully stocked. Their seasonal newsletter, full of best buys and hot tips, is a must for connoisseurs of the grape. Worldwide shipping is available.

Works

148 E. Napa St., Sonoma. ☎ 707/935-3132.

A promising sensibility has taken root at this small gallery, which features emerging as well as established artists and artisans on its roster. Recent exhibits include a full-scale chair made of rose thorns, that poses a prickly dilemma to the viewer; and on a more functional note, brushed sterling silver tea balls fashioned into complex fishlike forms.

Zambezi Trading Co.

107 W. Napa St., Sonoma. ☎ 707/939-1333; 800/939-1333.

The massive polished wood desks, tables, chairs, and sideboards here have an involved history. More than 150 years ago, Australian traders loaded their

Africa-bound ships with tons of native red jarrah wood for ballast. After reaching their destination, the wood was discarded; eventually it was used by the British in the building of the African railroad. With the modernization of the rail system, the wooden ties were replaced by concrete foundations, and the jarrah slabs were once again cast off. Zimbabwe craftsmen have now turned the 400-year-old wood into a distinctive line of furniture.

Diversions in Sonoma County

The Great Outdoors

You might want to visit **Jack London State Historic Park** (2400 London Ranch Rd., Glen Ellen, ☎ 707/938-5216). Fans of the prolific author won't want to miss seeing the poetic ruins of his Wolf House, still standing on the 800 acres that were his Beauty Ranch. Hike the 3 miles to the summit of Sonoma Mountain, and you'll be rewarded with a fabulous view of the Valley of the Moon—one London himself surely enjoyed.

San Pablo Bay National Wildlife Refuge (Hwy. 37, just west of Hwy. 121, ☎ 510/792-0222) is a marshy 332-acre plot that attracts upwards of 250 species of birds; bring your coat, binoculars, and camera and revel in its salty-aired solitude.

Aerial Amusements

Open cockpit rides in a 1940 Boeing "Stearman" biplane or a World War II Navy SNJ-4 war plane are available through **Aeroschellville** (23982 Arnold Dr., Sonoma Valley, ☎ 707/938-2444). Those with nerves of steel and stomachs of iron can request an aerobatic flight featuring loops, rolls, and other maneuvers.

Horseback Riding and Wagon Rides

Sonoma Cattle Company (2400 London Ranch Rd., Glen Ellen, ☎ 707/996-8566) is an option for horseback enthusiasts in Sonoma County. Group trail rides wind through Jack London State Historic Park, providing a glimpse of the beautiful land the writer knew and loved.

A different kind of experience is provided by **Wine Country Wagons** (P.O. Box 1069, Kenwood, ☎ 707/833-2724). Pulled by Belgian draft horses, wagons of 10 or more people tour several local vineyards, then sit down to a 5-course catered buffet on a shady creek bank.

THE BASICS

Before You Go

Tourist Offices and Information

The **San Francisco Convention and Visitors Bureau** (201 3rd St., Suite 900, San Francisco, CA 94103-3185; ☎ 415/974-6900) can provide a wealth of maps, discount coupons, and brochures to help you plan your visit. Pretrip questions or post-trip complaints about local merchants can be resolved through the **Better Business Bureau of San Francisco** (☎ 415/243-9999).

For information on **Oakland,** contact the Visitors and Convention Bureau, 550 10th St., Suite 214, Oakland, CA 94607 (☎ 510/839-9000). **Berkeley**-bound travelers can reach the city's Convention and Visitors Bureau at 1834 University Ave., Berkeley, CA 94703 (☎ 510/549-7040).

For those mouse potatoes who'd rather interface on-line than in-person, there are several informative World Wide Web sites worth browsing. Among them:

ArtDirect's Guide to San Francisco Listings detail visual and performing arts, as well as parks and gardens.

URL: http://www.artdirect.com/california/san.francisco/homepage

Raves Dates, times, places, and prices for these extemporaneous cultural confabs.

URL: http://hyperreal.com/raves/sf/calendar/sfrcal.html

Restaurant Guide More than 12,000 eateries categorized by name, cuisine, and location. Add your own comments to the reviews.

URL:http:/hamilton.netmedia.com/ims/rest ba_rest_guide.html

The Sunday Chronicle Datebook Updated weekly, these feature the famous Little Man's movie ratings and the latest on theater, music, art, and events for kids.

URL:http://sfgate.com/new/schron/datebook/index.html

Money

ATMs are abundant. Cardholders linked to the **Cirrus** system can call 800/424-7787 to locate the nearest cash machine.

Large amounts of money can be procured using the American Express Moneygram.You needn't be a member to use this wire transfer service, which is available from any American Express travel office.

When to Go

It bears remembering that more than 400 miles separate the desert of Los Angeles from the delta of the Bay Area; Mark Twain wasn't joking when he quipped the coldest winter he ever experienced was a summer in San Francisco.The chills the author experienced were, and are, a trick of the fogs that are produced by cold ocean fronts butting up against the warm inland air masses.These summer soups cover a very narrow band—just a few miles wide where there is a coastal shelf, and perhaps only a few hundred yards wide where cliffs rise

rapidly from the surf. In a typical late summer, you can set your watch by the inland march of the tule; at 4 o'clock it looks like a roll of cotton has unwound straight through the Golden Gate. After the marine haze dispels in August, San Francisco enjoys its sunnier days, its approximation of summer cooled by balmy ocean breezes. An imitation of winter strikes between November and February, with weather that is damp and rainy rather than really cold.

Broadly speaking, San Francisco has a temperate marine climate: November through February are wet, June through October are dry. Spring and fall are the most pleasant seasons in which to visit; at the height of summer the mercury seldom climbs much above 70° F (21° C) and in winter it rarely falls below 40° F (5° C). **Bay Area forecasts** can be accessed ☎ 415/936-1212. For conditions around the globe ☎ 1-900WEATHER; this call costs 95¢ per minute.

Calendar of Events

Californians can be serendipitous about anything, so if you're going to plan a trip around one of these happenings, it's best to double check and call ahead of time. (Note that some of the events are not held at the same time each year.)

January

Second Week: *San Francisco Sports and Boat Show* (☎ 415/469-6065).

Second Sunday: *Shrine East-West All-Star Football Classic* (☎ 415/661-0291).

February

Early February: *San Francisco Ballet* season opens (☎ 415/865-2000).

Early February: *Chinese Lunar New Year celebration.* The exact date changes yearly, but is in late January or early February (☎ 415/982-3000).

First Weekend: *Golden Gate Kennel Club All-Breed Dog Show* (☎ 415/530-1466).

March

Sunday Closest to St. Patrick's Day: *St. Patrick's Day Parade* (☎ 415/467-8218).

Mid-March: *Bay Area Music Awards (Bammies)* (☎ 415/974-4000).

Usually the Last Week: *Grand National Junior Rodeo and Horse Show* (☎ 415/469-6000).

Easter Sunday: *Easter Sunrise Service,* Mt. Davidson (☎ 415/974-6900).

April

Sometime in April: *San Francisco International Film Festival.* Has also been in March (☎ 415/567-4641).

Two Weekends in Mid- to Late April: *Cherry Blossom Festival* (☎ 415/922-6776).

Through October: *Oakland A's baseball season.* Oakland Coliseum (☎ 510/638-0500).

Through October: *San Francisco Giants baseball season.* 3Com/Candlestick Park (☎ 800/SF-GIANT).

Last Week: *San Francisco Landscape Garden Show.* Fort Mason (☎ 415/750-5108).

May

Sunday Nearest May 5: *Cinco de Mayo celebration* (☎ 415/826-1401).

Week Before Memorial Day: *Carnaval* (☎ 415/826-1401).

A Sunday in Mid-May: *San Francisco Examiner Bay to Breakers Run* (☎ 415/777-7770).

Week After Mother's Day: *Festival of Greece,* Oakland (☎ 510/531-3400).

June

First Sunday: *Union Street Festival of Arts and Crafts* (☎ 415/346-4446).

Last Week: *San Francisco International Lesbian and Gay Film Festival* (☎ 415/703-8650).

Third or Last Weekend: *Lesbian and Gay Freedom Day Parade* (☎ 415/864-3733).

Mid-June: *Beethoven and Mozart Festival* (☎ 415/864-6000).

Mid- to Late June: *North Beach Festival* (☎ 415/403-0666).

Mid-June Through August: *Stern Grove Midsummer Music Festival* (☎ 415/398-6551).

July

July 4: *Chronicle Fourth of July Celebration and Fireworks,* Fisherman's Wharf. (☎ 415/556-0560).

All Month: *Summer Pops Concerts,* San Francisco Symphony (☎ 415/431-5400).

A Sunday in Mid-July: *San Francisco Marathon* (☎ 415/296-7111).

Mid-July: *Cable Car Bell-Ringing Championship,* Union Square (☎ 415/923-6202).

August

A Weekend in Early August: *Escape from Alcatraz Triathlon* (☎ 415/924-7500).

Through December: *Oakland Raiders* football season opens, Oakland Coliseum (☎ 510/638-0500).

Through December: *San Francisco 49ers* football season opens, 3Com/Candlestick Park (☎ 408/562-4949).

A Weekend in Early August: *Japantown Nihonmachi Street Fair* (☎ 415/771-9861).

Last Weekend: *San Francisco County Fair* (☎ 415/703-2729).

September

Through June: *San Francisco Symphony* season (☎ 415/864-6000).

Last Weekend: *San Francisco Blues Festival* (☎ 415/979-5588).

Through February: *San Francisco Opera* season (☎ 415/565-3227).

All Month: *Shakespeare in the Park* (☎ 415/666-2221).

October

First Sunday: *Castro Street Fair* (☎ 415/467-3354).

Weekend Closest to Columbus Day: *Columbus Day Celebrations and Blessing of the Fleet* (☎ 415/434-1492).

Last Week: *Grand National Livestock Exposition, Rodeo, and Horse Show* (☎ 415/469-6065).

Through April: *Golden State Warriors* basketball season, Oakland Coliseum (☎ 510/638-6300).

Mid-October: *Pacific Fine Art Festival* (☎ 209/296-1195).

Through June: *American Conservatory Theater* season (☎ 415/749-2ACT).

Two Weeks in Mid-October: *San Francisco Jazz Festival* (☎ 415/864-5449).

Late October: *Halloween and Pumpkin Festival* (☎ 415/346-4561).

Late October: *Accordion Festival* (☎ 415/775-6000).

November

First Weekend: *Bay Area Book Festival* (☎ 415/861-2665).

Last Week: *San Francisco International Auto Show* (☎ 415/673-2016).

Late November: *Christmas tree lighting ceremony,* Pier 39 (☎ 415/981-8030).

Through early January: *Victorian Celebration of the Seasons* (☎ 415/964-9320).

December

Near Christmas: *Santa Parade* (☎ 415/826-1401).

December 31: *First Run* (☎ 415/668-2243).

What to Pack

San Francisco is an intensely fashion-conscious city and visitors will feel less conspicuous dressing up—conservatively or artistically—rather than down. To illustrate this point: For men, jackets and ties are widely worn, but rarely required. Choose your traveling wardrobe with flexibility in mind; to remain comfortable during days when temperatures fluctuate as much as 20°, pack mid-weight clothing that can be layered. The proliferation of souvenir sweatshirt stores along the waterfront isn't happenstance—I promise, that the leather jacket you shed at lunchtime will be your best friend come sunset. Good walking shoes are critical, as are an umbrella and raincoat during winter months.

That said, if you're going to be spending some time in the wine country—especially during the summer—be aware that Napa and Sonoma valley temperatures can and regularly do soar into the 90s F/30s C.

Some common sense reminders: Don't forget to bring a backup pair of eyeglasses and extra prescription medications. A plastic bag slipped into a carry-on or purse can keep a drippy umbrella or swimsuit from soaking your belongings. And of course, irreplaceable items such as jewelry or photos should be left at home, unless you've confirmed that your hotel has a safe in which they can be stored.

Traveling with Laptops, Cameras, Camcorders and Videotapes

Test and make sure that your laptop computer, camera, or camcorder is in fine working order before you leave. Also be sure that it is loaded with batteries and, if necessary, that you have spares.

Though airport security X-ray machines are said not to damage the hard disks or floppy disks of **laptop**

computers, you may want to have your computer hand-checked, especially if the X-ray machinery is dated. Do not let your computer or disks go through metal detectors as the magnetic field can harm the disks. Once in flight, most airlines let passengers use their computers—though not at takeoff or landing, since they can interfere with the plane's electronics.

Film should be stored in a dry, cool space; never keep it in a car's glove compartment or in the sun. Most airports claim that their security X-ray machines at the airport gates will not damage film less than ISO 400. However, there is a cumulative effect; if you pass through several airports, you will be wise to ask the security personnel to hand search your camera and film. In the United States, they will do so. Never put your film in baggage that is checked into the hold of the aircraft; the X ray intensity is great, and lead bags for film are unlikely to help—the security personnel may boost the strength of the X ray to see what's in the lead bag.

If you prefer to have your **camcorder** hand-checked going through airport security, be sure that it has fully charged batteries since security will need to test it.

Videotape is not harmed by X-ray scanners, but can be damaged by magnetic fields, such as those of metal detectors that you walk through at airport security.

General Tours

Escorted Tours

Two well-established tour operators that run deluxe tours in the United States are **Tauck Tours,** 11 Wilton Rd., Westport, CT 06881 (☎ 203/226-6911 or 800/468-2825), and **Maupintour,** Box 807, Lawrence, KS 66044 (☎ 913/843-1211 or 800/255-4266). In the first-class category, tour operators include **Collette Tours,** 162 Middle St., Pawtucket, RI 02860 (☎ 401/728-3805 or 800/717-9191); **Domenico Tours,** 751 Broadway, Bayonne, NJ 07002 (☎ 800/554-8687); and **Globus,** 5301 South Federal Circle, Littleton, CO 80123 (☎ 303/797-2800 or 800/221-0090). Globus also operates a budget tour company called **Cosmos,** which can be reached at the same address and phone number.

Independent Packages

Many airlines and tour operators offer packages that can be less expensive than making individual bookings. Airlines usually offer a package of airfare and accommodations with or without car rental. Check with **American Airlines FlyAway Vacations** (☎ 800/321-2121), and **United Airlines Vacation Center** (☎ 800/328-6877). Before you make your choice, find out if any airlines are offering a special sale on fares (you might save more money by booking a discounted flight and arranging your own lodging). If you plan on renting a car at your destination, check whether an airline has a tie-in package with a car rental agency that will save you money.

A tour operator that specializes in independent packages (that are not escorted) is **Globetrotters SuperCities,** 139 Main St., Cambridge, MA 02142 (☎ 617/621-0099 or 800/333-1234). It sells package trips to the Kentucky Derby and Rose Bowl, as well as major cities in the United States.

In all package deals, find out what is or is not included in the price, such as airport transfers and taxes.

Reservations

If you want to secure tickets to entertainment or sporting events in advance of your visit, contact **BASS Tickets** (☎ 800/225-2277), **Just Tix** (☎ 800-FOR-TIXX), or **Telesis Ticket Services** (☎ 800/585-8499).

For Travelers with Disabilities

General

Organizations that dispense advice and assistance to the disabled (for free or a small donation) are: **MossRehab,** 1200 W. Tabor Rd., Philadelphia, PA 19141 (☎ 215/456-9603; TDD 215/456-9602—phone inquiries only); **The Society for the Advancement of Travel for the Handicapped** (SATH), 347 5th Ave., Suite 610, New York, NY 10016 (☎ 212/447-7284; fax 212/725-8253); and **Information Center for Individuals with Disabilities,** Fort Point Place, 27-43 Wormwood St., Boston, MA 02210 (☎ 617/727-5540 or 800/462-5015; TDD 617/345-9743).

The *Directory of Travel Agencies for the Disabled,* published by Twin Peaks Press, Box 129, Vancouver, WA 98666 (☎ 360/694-2462 or 800/637-2256), is $19.95 plus $3 shipping and lists close to 400 agencies worldwide. One such agency that specializes in cruises, tours, and independent travel for the disabled is **Flying Wheels Travel,** 143 W. Bridge St., Box 382, Owatonna, MN 55060 (☎ 507/451-5005 or 800/535-6790).

In the Bay Area

Current information on accessibility—including the new Talking Signs program recently installed in portions of the city—may be obtained from the **Mayor's Office of Community Development, Disability Coordinator,** 10 United Nations Plaza, Suite 600, San Francisco, CA 94102 (☎ 415/554-8925; TDD 415/554-8749). The **Easter Seal Society** (☎ 415/752-4888) is another source for material. In Oakland, Bonnie Lewkowicz at **Escape Artists Travel** (☎ 510/652-1700) is well-versed in the needs of traveling disabled persons.

For travelers planning to use public transportation, the **Muni Access Guide** can be obtained by writing Muni Accessible Service Program, 949 Presidio Ave., San Francisco, CA 94115; for assistance ☎ 415/923-6142 weekdays or 415/673-MUNI anytime. Muni operates more than 30 accessible bus lines in addition to accessible metro service.

A **Paratransit Taxi Service** provides discount cabs to qualified disabled persons unable to use public fixed-route transportation; request a certification form from the **San Francisco Paratransport Broker** (☎ 415/202-9903).

California law requires new hotels, restaurants, and other public buildings to be accessible to persons in wheelchairs and to have wheelchair-accommodating rest rooms. Older establishments may or may not have facilities that are so adapted—they are exempt from the requirement by virtue of their age. At theaters, a call ahead to arrange for signers or headsets can make performances more enjoyable.

Other referrals:

Environmental Traveling Companions (☎ 415/474-7662) coordinates white-water rafting, sea kayaking, and cross-country skiing trips for persons with a wide range of disabilities.

Jose Can You See (☎ 415/552-JOSE) organizes escorted tours for the sight-impaired.

A Different View (☎ 415/479-6958) is a local source for braille maps.

At the new **Main Library** (☎ 415/557-4400), there's a state-of-the-art information center featuring "talking" computers and signs that guide visually impaired readers through the stacks. Deaf and hearing-impaired patrons can find books and closed-caption videos (☎ 415/557-4434).

The California Relay Service facilitates telephone communications. TDD to voice ☎ 800/735-2929. Voice to TDD ☎ 800/735-2922.

Crisis Line for the Handicapped (☎ 800/426-4263) is a 24-hour emergency line.

For Travelers with Children

The Buddy System (2269 Chestnut St., Suite 181, ☎ 415/648-3330) gives parents a break by hosting personalized tours for kids to such popular attractions as Pier 39, Fisherman's Wharf, and the Exploratorium.

Child care services are available on an hourly or daily basis. Among local providers:

American Childcare Service (353 Sacramento St., Suite 600; ☎ 415/285-2300)

Nannycare USA (5337 College Ave., Suite 339, Oakland; ☎ 510/848-1232 or 800/448-2915)

Starr Belly Child Care Services (404 Bryant; ☎ 415/642-1950)

Temporary Tot Tending (2217 Delvin Way, South San Francisco; ☎ 415/355-7377; after 6pm ☎ 415/871-5790)

For child-friendly activities and sights around the bay, see the chapter "Frisco for Kids."

Car Rentals

Most major companies have outlets in San Francisco and you can make advance reservations through the following toll-free numbers:

Alamo (☎ 800/327-9633)

Avis (☎ 800/331-1212)

Budget (☎ 800/601-5385)

Dollar (☎ 800/800-4000)

Enterprise (☎ 800/325-8007)

Hertz (☎ 800/654-3131)

National (☎ 800/CAR-RENT)

Thrifty (☎ 800/367-2277)

Motorcycle Rentals

If you're more the wind-in-your-face type, **Dubbelju Motorcycle Rentals** (271 Clara, San Francisco; ☎ 415/495-2774) can put qualified riders on a BMW or Harley-Davidson. California law requires both driver and passenger to wear helmets; Dubbelju has a few on hand, but recommends you bring your own proper-fitting headgear. Rates start at $74 per day, with weekly terms available. Open Monday through Saturday 9am–1pm, and by appointment. MC,V.

Arriving

By Plane

San Francisco International Airport (SFO; South San Francisco; ☎ 415/761-0800) is the 5th-busiest airport in the United States and the 7th-busiest in the world, handling 1,260 flights a day and served by 50 major scheduled carriers. Domestic airlines fly into the North and South terminals; the Central Terminal handles overseas flights. Arrivals are on the lower level; departures, the upper floor. Ground transportation connections are found on the lower level. A free shuttle service is provided between terminals and to the very remote long-term airport parking lots. There is protected short-term parking for some 7,000 vehicles, but this garage is often full (☎ 415/877-0227 for current status).

Savvy visitors often arrange to fly into the smaller, closer, and less-congested **Oakland International Airport** (OAK; Doolittle and Airport Way, Oakland; ☎ 510/839-7488). A typical day sees 130 flights take off from its 2 terminals. Hourly and economy parking lots are on-site, and the airport is served by BART.

Airline Toll-Free Telephone Numbers

San Francisco International Airport

Alaska Airlines (☎ 800/426-0333)

America West Airlines (☎ 800/235-9292)

American Airlines (reservations ☎ 800/433-7300; flight information ☎ 800/223-5436)

Continental Airlines (☎ 800/525-0280)

Delta Airlines (reservations ☎ 800/221-1212; flight information ☎ 800/325-1999)

Northwest Airlines (reservations ☎ 800/225-2525; flight information ☎ 800/441-1818)

Southwest Airlines (☎ 800/435-9792)

Trans World Airlines (☎ 800/892-1976)

USAir (reservations ☎ 800/842-5374; flight information ☎ 800/943-5436)

United Airlines (☎ 800/241-6522)

Oakland International Airport

Alaska Airlines (☎ 800/426-0333)

America West Airlines (☎ 800/235-9292)

American Airlines (reservations ☎ 800/433-7300; flight information ☎ 800/223-5436)

Delta Airlines (reservations ☎ 800/221-1212; flight information ☎ 800/325-1999)

Horizon Air (☎ 800/547-9308)

Southwest Airlines (☎ 800/435-9792)

United Airlines (☎ 800/241-6522)

By Train

Amtrak rail services (☎ 800/872-7245) to the Bay Area terminate either in Oakland, at the C. L. Dellums station, 245 2nd St., or in neighboring Emeryville, at 5885 Landregan St. San Francisco–bound passengers are carried on the final leg of their journey by bus to the city's **Transbay Terminal** at First and Mission streets.

Staying in San Francisco

Getting Around

Between the Airports and the City

Budget travelers and those already familiar with the city often take the SFO Airporter bus—it's economical and stops at central locations where it's easy to connect with other forms of local transit. For first-time and leisure visitors, shuttle services combine cost-efficiency with convenience.

BY BART TRAIN Maybe by the year 2020, the safe, clean, and generally reliable BART trains will run to SFO; as usual, the evergreen issue has been stymied by bureaucrats and politicos. However, Oakland's airport is linked to the BART system: an AirBART shuttle bus delivers travelers to the Coliseum BART train stop; from there it's a 10-minute ride to downtown Oakland, 30 minutes to downtown San Francisco. The AirBART ticket is $2 (train fare additional).

BY BUS **SFO Airporter** (☎ 415/495-8404 or 800/532-8405). The fare is $9 one way; $15 round-trip. Service linking downtown and SFO every 10 to 20 minutes, 5am–11pm.

Marin Airporter (☎ 415/461-4222) The fare each way is $10. Serves Sausalito and other Marin County locations, 4:30am–midnight.

BY DOOR-TO-DOOR SHUTTLE Reservations are necessary for travel to the airports; incoming travelers at SFO won't have any trouble hitching a ride to downtown on the spot, as vans bearing destination signs circulate constantly. Visitors arriving at OAK should arrange ahead of time for pick-up.

American Airporter Shuttle (☎ 415/546-6689) The one-way fare is $12; round-trip is $17.

Bayporter Express (☎ 415/467 1800 or 800/ 287-6783) One way to Oakland is $12; to San Francisco, $15. Service to and from Oakland International Airport.

Supershuttle (From SFO ☎ 415/871-7800, to SFO ☎ 415/558-8500) The one-way fare is $11.

Lorrie's Airport Service (☎ 415/334-9000) The fare is $10 each way.

BY TAXI The approximate fare from SFO to downtown San Francisco is $24. Voluntary ride-sharing for 2 or more persons to a maximum of 3 destinations is permitted—the flat $24 fare should be divided among the travelers.

BY CAR **From SFO,** it's a straight shot on U.S. Route 101 north to San Francisco.

At off-peak times, the trip can be made in 30 minutes; during rush hours, leave upwards of an hour ahead to get to or from the airport.

From OAK, take Interstate 880 north to 980, then follow 80 west over the Bay Bridge ($1 toll) into San Francisco. If the roads are clear—a rare occurrence—you'll spend about 40 minutes in transit. The Bay Bridge sits near a freeway junction that isn't called "the Maze" for nothing; traffic delays here are very unpredictable.

A caveat: Several of the major freeways around the Bay Area are still undergoing repairs to the damage resulting from the 1989 Loma Prieta earthquake; drivers are well-advised to carry a detailed map should detours be encountered. For advisories on road conditions, ☎ 415/557-3755.

Within the City

Just for its scenic properties, San Francisco is a walker's town: The variety of architecture, the character of the neighborhoods and people, and its cartographically challenging terrain all combine to make the city a promenader's paradise. But when practical matters such as inclement weather and pressing schedules are factored into the equation, it often makes sense to hail a cab or hop on a cable car.

BY TAXI If you chose to forgo a car of your own, the comparatively small size of San Francisco makes for cab rides that remain affordable. The 1st mile is charged at $1.90, with each additional mile adding $1.50 to the fare. Taxis queue up at most downtown hotels, but it can be difficult to flag one down from elsewhere on the street; in these cases, it's best to telephone for a radio-dispatched car.

City (☎ 415/468-7200)

De Soto (☎ 415/673-1414)

Luxor (☎ 415/282-4141)

Pacific (☎ 415/776-6688)

Sunshine (☎ 415/776-7755)

Veteran's (☎ 415/552-1300)

Yellow Cab (☎ 415/626-2345)

BY LIMOUSINE Small groups traveling together may find a limousine service worthwhile. Cars are available for sightseeing tours or as general transportation. Some companies to try:

Carey/Nob Hill Limousine (☎ 415/468-7550)

Chauffeured Limousine (☎ 415/344-4400 or 800/338-8200)

Gateway Limousine (☎ 800/486-7007)

RLM Executive Limousine (☎ 415/431-1993 or 800/431-1993)

Squire Limousine (☎ 415/761-3000 or 800/872-3090)

BY PUBLIC TRANSIT San Francisco's Municipal Railway—universally referred to as **Muni,** and selectively referred to as the "Muni-serable Railway"—comprises 3 methods of transport: cable cars, buses, and streetcars. In total, they make every corner of the city accessible (for route information, ☎ 415/673-MUNI, or purchase a detailed map at the Visitor Center).

One-way fare for buses and streetcars is $1 (exact change is required; dollar bills are acceptable); for cable

Cable Car

cars, it's $2 (cable-car conductors will make change). If you plan on using public transportation frequently, definitely take advantage of the 1-, 3- or 7-day **Muni Passport:** Holders are entitled to unlimited rides throughout the system, you don't have to worry about exact change for the fare, and the savings can be considerable. The passport, available at the Visitor Information Center at Hallidie Plaza (Powell and Market streets), also brings discounted admission to more than 2 dozen visitor attractions.

Bay Area Rapid Transit or BART (☎ 415/992-2278 for info) is a light rail system with lines running south from San Francisco to Daly City and east to Oakland, Berkeley, and other East Bay cities. BART is used more for travel to and from the suburbs than within the city proper. Trains operate Monday through Friday 4am–midnight, Saturday 6am–midnight, and Sunday 8am–midnight. Fares are dependent on the distance traveled, with tickets available at each station.

OTHER LOCAL BUSES **Alameda County Transit** (☎ 510/839-2882) serves East Bay cities such as Berkeley and Oakland.

Golden Gate Transit (☎ 415/332-6600) runs from the Transbay Terminal at First and Mission streets to Marin and Sonoma counties.

BY CAR Once in the city, a motorist's greatest travail is parking. A most unwanted souvenir of San Francisco is a ticket for not curbing one's wheels—turn the tires toward the street when facing uphill, or towards the curb when facing downhill. Free street parking is often restricted to resident permit holders; meters typically accept only quarters. Violations are a major source of income for the city and thus are rabidly pursued, so pay attention to the color-coded curbing. A red swath means stopping or parking is forbidden at all times, yellow indicates a maximum half-hour loading time for vehicles with commercial plates, blue spaces are reserved for vehicles with disabled-passenger permits, green allows for 10 minutes' parking, and white spots give a 5-minute limit during business hours. Never park at bus stops or fire hydrants, or—despite local custom, it is illegal—in crosswalks.

Public garages are often the best bet for stays of several hours; here's a listing of them by location:

Chinatown: 433 Kearny St., ☎ 415/956-8106; 733 Kearny St., ☎ 415/982-6353

Civic Center: 355 McAllister, ☎ 415/863-3187; 370 Grove, ☎ 415/626-4484

Convention Center/Yerba Buena Gardens: 255 3rd St., ☎ 415/777-2782; Museum Parc, 3rd and Folsom streets, ☎ 415/543-4533

Downtown: Sutter–Stockton, the largest and least expensive in the Union Square area, ☎ 415/982-8370; 833 Mission St., ☎ 415/982-8522; Mason and Ellis streets, ☎ 415/771-1400—ask for the garage; Ellis–O'Farrell, 123 O'Farrell St., ☎ 415/986-4800; 333 Post St., ☎ 415/397-0631

Embarcadero Center: Validated parking for shoppers and diners, ☎ 415/398-1878; 250 Clay St., ☎ 415/433-4722

Fisherman's Wharf: 665 Beach at Hyde St., ☎ 415/673-5197

Mission District: 90 Bartlett near 21st St., ☎ 415/567-7357

North Beach: Along with Chinatown, this dense neighborhood has the worst street parking in the city. (766Vallejo St., ☎ 415/558-9147)

Union Street: 1910 Laguna St., ☎ 415/563-9820; 2055 Lombard St., ☎ 415/495-3772

Visitor Information

SHOPPING AND BUSINESS HOURS Weekdays and Saturdays, retailers generally open between 9 and 10am and close at 5:30 or 6pm. On Thursdays, many shops stay open until 9pm; Sunday hours are from noon to 5pm. Museums and galleries are customarily closed on Mondays. Standard working hours are kept by offices: Monday through Friday 9am–5pm.

PUBLIC HOLIDAYS January 1; Martin Luther King Jr. Day, 3rd Monday in January; President's Day, 3rd Monday in February; Memorial Day, last Monday in May; Independence Day, July 4 (but businesses close on nearest Monday or Friday); Labor Day, 1st Monday in September; Columbus Day, 2nd Monday in October; Veterans Day, November 11; Thanksgiving, 4th Thursday in November; Christmas, December 25.

Banks and almost all businesses are closed on these days, although department stores often stay open for sales. Good Friday is a half-day holiday; many offices close on Easter Monday.

BANKS AND FOREIGN EXCHANGE Normal business hours for banks are Monday through Friday 10am–5pm. An increasing number of banks are open on Saturday.

Unless you have an account, you may be assessed a hefty service charge for cashing travelers checks or exchanging foreign currency at banks. But there are alternatives. In addition to the **American Express Travel Service Offices** listed under "Useful Addresses and Phone Numbers," try: **Bank of America Foreign Exchange Office** (Central Terminal, San Francisco International Airport; ☎ 415/742-8079; daily 7am–11pm), **Thomas Cook Foreign Exchange** (75 Geary St.; ☎ 800/CURRENCY; Mon–Fri 9am–5pm, Sat 10am–4pm), **Foreign Exchange Ltd.** (415 Stockton St.; ☎ 415/397-4700; Mon–Fri 8am–5:30pm, Sat Apr–Sept 10am–2pm).

LOCAL MEDIA As befits a highly literate city with a long newspaper tradition, there is plenty to read in San Francisco. The major newspapers are the morning ***Chronicle*** and the afternoon ***Herald Examiner;*** these 2 dailies join forces to produce the Sunday edition. Many San Franciscans consider *Chronicle* writer Herb Caen's column—a mix of society and political gossip, dorky humor, and personal musings—as essential to starting the day as a low-fat extra-foam decaf cappuccino. For international news, the ***San Jose Mercury News*** provides better reportage than either of the 2 San Francisco papers, and is widely available.

Also worthwhile are the free ***SF Weekly*** and ***San Francisco Bay Guardian*** for weekly local news, arts, and entertainment listings. ***San Francisco Focus*** is a monthly glossy magazine with stories of local interest.

On television, the Public Broadcasting Service affiliate is KQED (channel 9), which also maintains the city's National Public Radio station **(88.5 FM).**

PUBLIC REST ROOMS After years of mind-numbing debate, the city of San Francisco has begun to install public toilets around town. Mayor Frank Jordan cut the, er, ribbon, to the premiere public potty at Market and Powell streets in June of 1995, pointing out to his concerned constituency that since the booths' doors are on a 20-minute timer, they needn't worry about someone squatting in the residential sense of the word. The dark green privies are in the process of being located at popular spots throughout the city; keep a quarter handy.

Department stores and large hotels usually have clean public facilities, too. That's not the case with train or bus station bathrooms, which you'd be wise to avoid.

RUSH HOURS Morning freeway rush hour begins at 6am, peaks between 7 and 8:30, then ebbs by 9:30am; the evening crush begins by 4pm and thins out after 7pm. If it's rainy, these hours can multiply exponentially.

SAFETY For police, fire, and medical emergencies, dial **911** from any phone.

As in any metropolitan area, some fundamental precautions merit taking. Walk on well-lighted, well-traveled streets, facing traffic. Be particularly alert if you're venturing into the Tenderloin, the Mission, or Golden Gate Park at night; go with a companion, stride confidently and purposefully, and keep a firm grip on your wallet or purse.

When driving, keep the car doors locked. Don't leave your auto with cameras or packages visible on the seats—that's an invitation no petty thief would turn down. After dark, park in attended lots or amply lit areas, and be mindful of your surroundings before getting back into your car.

SMOKING Smoking is prohibited in elevators, buses, theaters, and cinemas. In restaurants, it's usually restricted to the bar area. Many hotels now have nonsmoking floors, and you can request a smoke-free rental car from most agencies.

TAXES A nonrefundable sales tax of 8.5% is levied in San Francisco; it is waived if you have your purchases shipped out of state. Hotel room tax is 14%.

TIPPING Waiters expect a tip of 15% of the bill before tax, but you may want to tip more if service has been especially good, less if it has been poor. Taxi drivers, barkeeps, and hairdressers should also receive 15%. Doormen and valet parking attendants will expect $2, airport porters and hotel bellhops $1 per bag, and rest room attendants $1. When there is no fixed charge for leaving coats and parcels, $1 per item is courteous.

Useful Addresses and Phone Numbers

Visitor Information

San Francisco Visitor Information Center (Hallidie Plaza, 900 Market St. at Powell; ☎ 415/391-2000). Walk-in service Monday through Friday 9am–5pm, Saturday 9am–3pm, Sunday 10am–2pm, with longer hours in summer. Multilingual staff.

Twenty-four hour recorded events info: ☎415/391-2001 (English), 415/391-2003 (en Français), 415/391-2004 (auf Deutsch), 415/391-2122 (En Español), 415/391-2101 (Japanese), 415/392-0328 (TDD/TTY).

Hot Lines

AIDS Shanti Project (☎ 415/864-2273)
Alcoholics Anonymous (☎ 415/621-1326)
Poison Control Center (☎ 800/523-2222)
San Francisco Health Department Psychiatric Emergency Services (☎ 415/206-8125)
San Francisco Women Against Rape (☎ 415/647-7273)
Suicide Prevention (☎ 415/781-0500)
Travelers Aid Society (☎ 415/781-6738)

Transit Information

AC Transit (☎ 800/559-4636)
BART (☎ 415/992-2278)
Golden Gate Transit (☎ 415/332-6600)
Muni (☎ 415/673-6864)

American Express Travel Service Offices

Downtown: 237 Post St., ☎ 415/981-5533
Financial District: 295 California St., ☎ 415/788-4367; 455 Market, ☎ 415/512-8250
Fisherman's Wharf: 2500 Mason St., ☎ 415/788-3025

Medical and Dental Care

Davies Medical Center (Castro and Dubose streets, ☎ 415/565-6000). Full-scale general and acute care hospital offering urgent care (☎ 415/565-6600), 24-hour emergency care (☎ 415/565-6060), and physician referral (☎ 415/565-6333).

San Francisco Dental Office (132 Embarcadero, ☎ 415/777-5115). Comprehensive dental care by appointment and 24-hour emergency treatment.

Travel Medical Group (490 Post St., Suite 225, ☎ 415/981-1102). "House calls" 24 hours daily.

Emergencies

Police, Fire, Ambulance (☎ 911)

Late-Night Pharmacy

Walgreen Drug Store (135 Powell St., ☎ 415/391-4433). Monday through Saturday 8am–midnight, Sunday 9am–9pm. AE, D, MC, V accepted.

Lost Passports

Contact your consulate for assistance.

Portraits

The Natural Setting

The prosperity of California and its principal cities has always been derived from the land: gold in the north, oil in the south, and the fruitful topsoil in between. This has always been matched by a parallel richness in beauty.

San Francisco Bay, 496 square miles of water behind the Golden Gate, is among the world's finest and most visually pleasing natural harbors. The city itself, draped over tumbling hillsides and surrounded by water on three sides, offers an almost inexhaustible range of vistas. The flora of the Bay Area is equally compelling. In 1,017-acre Golden Gate Park, replete with lakes and waterfalls, meadows, forests, and gardens, San Francisco has an inner-city recreation area second to none.

It was not always so well manicured. Before the settlers tamed it, the San Francisco peninsula was an inhospitable, barren expanse of rocky hills and sand dunes, swamps, tidal marshes, and lagoons. Nowadays, the best local taste of this former ruggedness is to be found along the cliffs and beaches fronting the Pacific.

Californians in general, and San Franciscans in particular, are acutely concerned with the health of their fertile-but-fragile natural environment. In fact, the Bay Area is a center of global ecological activism: Greenpeace, Friends of the Earth, and the Sierra Club all have their headquarters here. Complementing these international watchdog groups are local grassroots organizations, such as the Greenbelt Alliance and the Bay Institute, which work to ensure that the immediate region's conservation interests are wisely and progressively served.

A Brief History

The earliest known inhabitants of the San Francisco area were semi-nomadic Native Americans of the Modoc and Ohlone tribes. They numbered perhaps 150,000 in their prime, speaking a score of distinct languages and hundreds of regional dialects. The clans fared badly after the arrival of European settlers: Their communities were ravaged by alien diseases, displaced by land-grabbing homesteaders, and virtually obliterated by armed conflicts. By the advent of the 20thC, the state's entire Native American population had diminished to 16,000.

The European expeditions gathered pace in the 16thC, when Spanish explorers sought to expand their king's Mexican dominion ever farther to the north and west. The first white man known to have seen California was Juan Rodriguez Cabrillo, a Portuguese navigator in the service of Spain. In 1542 he sighted San Pedro harbor (near what is now Long Beach) and named it "Bay of Smokes" after the Native American campfires he saw there.

The Spanish interest flagged for almost 40 years until it was revived by the news that Sir Francis Drake had anchored his *Golden Hinde* near what is now San Francisco and claimed the new land for England. So the Spanish began to explore again. In 1602 Sebastian Vizcaino reasserted his monarch's claim over California, but only in 1697 did Jesuit missionaries receive royal warrants to enter the territory, and it was another 70 years before the first permanent Spanish colony was established at San Diego. With the Jesuits out of favor by then, it was left to Franciscan friars and the Spanish army to extend the northward penetration. By 1823 the forces of the cross and the sword had established a chain of 21 missions along 600 miles of the Camino Real (King's Highway). Among these was a 1776 military post and mission, San Francisco de Asis.

Earnest development began in the 19thC. In 1821, Mexico won its independence from Spain, retaining California as a colony. Relations between the Californios and their Mexican governors were strained, sometimes violent. But the watershed came in the early 1840s with the quickening influx of American settlers. The Californios welcomed them; Mexico banned their further immigration. Finally, in 1846, a small group of *yanquis* staged what became known as the Bear Flag Revolt in Sonoma, declaring the California Republic a sovereign state. Twenty-three days later, Commodore John D. Sloat raised the American flag over Monterey and claimed California for the United States.

Another surge of immigration followed almost immediately. News of John Marshall's discovery of gold in January 1848, near what is now Sacramento, prompted what has been described as the greatest mass movement of people since the Crusades. In 1847, the territory's population was 15,000. By 1850, when California became the 31st state, it was nudging 100,000. A decade later, it had quadrupled. The '49ers, as the gold rushers were called, accounted for the majority of these new arrivals. Much of the growth was in and around San Francisco, which fast emerged as the hub of the West Coast.

Ten years after the gold rush, the discovery of the Comstock Lode in neighboring Nevada precipitated a "silver stampede" that further established San Francisco's pre-eminence. The completion of the Southern Pacific Railroad in 1876—linking San Francisco to the East—put a lock on the city's prosperity and the personal fortunes of the first residents of Nob Hill, the mining and rail magnates.

An enclave of wealth, style, and cosmopolitan sophistication, San Francisco was riding high when the Great Earthquake struck on April 18, 1906. In the conflagration that followed, 2,500 people died or were missing, and 5 square miles—including the grand mansions of the barons of commerce—were destroyed. Legions of the newly-homeless encamped in Golden Gate Park.

Reconstruction plans were drawn even as the ruins smoked, and within 3 years 20,000 new buildings were erected. A more sober but no less spirited San Francisco emerged from the trauma and heralded both its recovery and the opening of the Panama Canal in 1914 with the Panama-Pacific International Exposition, an extravaganza of trade and manufacturing exhibits housed in a remarkable series of architectural fantasies.

The public relations campaign worked. Newcomers continued the western pilgrimage well into the new century: The 1930s brought farmers from the parched heartland; the 1940s brought Europeans fleeing war and tyranny as well as tens of thousands of servicemen who demobilized on the West Coast at the end of World War II. Since the 1950s, people from around the world searching for a better life have added to San Francisco's greatest resource: the ambitious, enterprising minds of its people.

The decades since have seen more social than statistical growth. In the 1960s and early 1970s, the social and sexual upheaval that changed the very shape of American life had its locus in San Francisco. The tumult continued into the 1970s, with the birth of the modern gay rights movement. It has been said that what happened in California yesterday happens everywhere else tomorrow, a maxim any San Franciscan will tell you is still true today.

Landmarks in San Francisco History

1579: Sir Francis Drake lands near San Francisco, christens the land "New Albion," and claims it for England.

1769: Father Junipero Serra establishes Spain's first California colony at San Diego. Gaspar de Portola's expedition reaches San Francisco Bay.

1776: As the American colonies declare independence from Great Britain, a Spanish mission and *presidio* (fortress) are founded at San Francisco.

1777: Felipe de Neve makes Monterey capital of California.

1781: The pueblo of Los Angeles is founded.

1796: First American ship, Ebenezer Dorr's *Otter,* anchors in a California port.

1812: As the United States fights the War of 1812, Russian fur traders establish a colony at Fort Ross on the Sonoma coast.

1821: Mexico wins independence from Spain, retaining California as a colony.

1828: Jedediah Smith is the first white man to cross the Sierra Nevada.

1845: Mexico ineffectually bans immigration of U.S. settlers into California.

1846: American insurgents against the Mexican government of General Mariano Vallejo, in the Bear Flag Revolt at Sonoma, are overthrown as the United States declares war on Mexico and seizes control of California. The settlement of Yerba Buena changes its name to San Francisco.

1848: John Marshall discovers gold in the American River near Coloma, setting off the gold rush of 1849.

1850: California joins the Union, becoming the 31st American state.

1854: Sacramento is named the Golden State's permanent capital.

1861: As the United States is torn by the Civil War, California remains a bystander, its sympathies divided between Union and Confederacy. The state's first vineyards are planted with 1,400 varieties of vines imported from Europe.

1868: The University of California is established at Berkeley.

1869: The first transcontinental railroad is completed at Promontory Point, Utah, linking California with the east and ending the era of the Pony Express and clipper ships around Cape Horn.

1872: End of the Modoc War, the last major confrontation with the Native Americans of California.

1873: The first San Francisco cable car begins operation.

1876: Electricity comes to San Francisco.

1904: A.P. Giannini founds the Bank of Italy in San Francisco. Eventually, it becomes the Bank of America.

1906: The Great Earthquake (estimated to be 8.6 on the Richter scale) and fire level much of San Francisco. Rebuilding began almost immediately.

1915: The Panama-Pacific International Exhibition is held in San Francisco. First transcontinental telephone call is made.

1927: San Francisco International Airport opens.

1932: San Francisco opens its Opera House.

1934: Bloody confrontation between the Industrial Association scabs, the International Longshoreman's Union, and the San Francisco police occurs.

1935: Donald Douglas's great airplane, the DC3, ushers in the age of air travel and launches California as the center of aerospace technology. Construction of the Central Valley aqueduct begins.

1936: Construction of the Bay Bridge completed.

1937: The Golden Gate Bridge is opened.

1945: As World War II draws to a close, the United Nations founding assembly is held in San Francisco.

1958: Planar technique of producing transistors is devised by Fairchild Semiconductor, an electronics company in Santa Clara Valley, southeast of San Francisco, paving the way for the silicon chip.

1960: Candlestick Park opens.

1963: Alcatraz prison closes.

1964: California surpasses New York as the most populous state in the nation. John Steinbeck wins the Nobel Prize for literature.

1967: Ronald Reagan is elected Governor of California. The Summer of Love reaches a climax in Haight-Ashbury; the Free Speech movement begins in Berkeley.

1974: Bay Area Rapid Transit (BART) trains connect the East Bay with San Francisco.

1978: San Francisco Mayor George Moscone and city supervisor Harvey Milk are assassinated; Dianne Feinstein is appointed mayor.

1986: Downtown construction is limited by the city of San Francisco.

1989: The second worst earthquake in U.S. history (7.1 on the Richter scale) rocks the Bay Area, causing more than $2 billion in damage.

1991: California imposes water rationing after 5 years of drought.

1992: Fire sweeps through the Oakland hills, causing $1.5 billion in damage.

1993: First buildings in Yerba Buena Gardens development open.

1994: The Presidio army base is turned over to the National Park Service.

1995: New San Francisco Museum of Modern Art opens; City Hall closes for repairs.

Historical Who's Who

Adams, Ansel Easton (1902–84). Photographer. His breathtaking, black-and-white photographs of Yosemite and the Sierra helped establish photography as an art form. He cofounded the New York Museum of Modern Art's photography department in 1940 and helped establish the California School of Fine Arts in 1946. A native of San Francisco and an active conservationist, he served as a director of the Sierra Club for almost 40 years.

Brubeck, Dave (b. 1920). Pianist and jazz composer. Born in Concord, California, Brubeck led experimental jazz groups in San Francisco in the 1940s. In 1951, he organized a quartet with Paul Desmond and Gerry Mulligan, achieving international fame in the 1950s and 1960s. His signature composition is "Take Five."

Caen, Herb (b. 1916). Author; newspaper columnist. He was born in Sacramento and moved to San Francisco in 1936. His behind-the-city-scene column for the *San Francisco Chronicle* is an institution, which he has written for more than half a century. His books include *Don't Call it Frisco, Baghdad By the Bay,* and *Only in San Francisco.*

Coolbrith, Ina (1841–1928). Poet. Coolbrith became the state's first poet laureate in 1915. Born Josephine Smith (her father was the brother of Joseph Smith, founder of the Mormon Church), her early poems were published in the *Los Angeles Star.* She came to San Francisco in 1860 and began working in the Oakland Library, where she encouraged a young Jack London to write. With Bret Harte, she edited the *Overland Monthly.*

Coppola, Francis Ford (b. 1939). Filmmaker. Coppola is best known for his movies *Apocalypse Now* and *The Godfather* trilogy. *The Conversation* was filmed in San Francisco. Coppola owns and works in offices in Columbus Tower, in North Beach.

Columbus Tower

Crocker, Charles (1822–88). Financier and railroad magnate. Born in Troy, New York, Crocker came west during the gold rush and made his fortune selling supplies to the miners. One of the "Big Four" partners in the transcontinental railroad, he oversaw construction of the Central Pacific Railroad and served as president of the Southern Pacific Railroad.

DiMaggio, Joe (b. 1914). Baseball player. He began his career with the San Francisco Seals, before becoming the New York Yankees' star center fielder. In the 1950s he married Marilyn Monroe at San Francisco City Hall. They rushed to Saints Peter and Paul Church in North Beach for the publicity photos, however.

Duncan, Isadora (1878–1928). Modern dancer. Born in a house at the corner of Geary and Taylor streets, Duncan went on to win international fame by creating interpretive dances that scandalized American audiences, but found acceptance in Europe. She was killed in an automobile mishap.

Feinstein, Dianne (b. 1933). Politician. A native San Franciscan, she attended Stanford University. Feinstein was appointed mayor upon the assassination of George Moscone. After running unsuccessfully for governor, she was elected U.S. senator. A Democrat, Feinstein is considered a political centrist—a supporter of both reproductive rights and capital punishment.

Ferlinghetti, Lawrence (b. 1919). Poet and bookseller. A prominent figure in the Beat era, in 1953, he founded—and still operates—City Lights Bookstore, the first paperback bookshop in America. In 1956, Ferlinghetti published Allen Ginsberg's *Howl*.

Garcia, Jerry (1942–95). Musician. Lead guitarist and vocalist of the psychedelic rock band the Grateful Dead. More than any other band, the Dead epitomized the turbulent 1960s. They had consistently remained one of the top touring acts until shortly before Garcia died of complications from long bouts of drug addiction.

Hammett, Dashiell (1894–1961). Writer. Drawing on his experience with the Pinkerton Detective Agency, Hammett penned hard-boiled detective novels, including *The Maltese Falcon* and *The Thin Man*. He had a long involvement with playwright Lillian Hellman. In the 1950s, Hammett was imprisoned for refusing to testify before the House Un-American Activities Committee.

Hearst, William Randolph (1863–1951). Newspaper publisher and congressman. Hearst's career began at the *San Francisco Examiner*, which was owned by his father. He built a tremendous media empire in newspapers, magazines, and films. His sumptuous residence in San Simeon, California, is a very popular tourist attraction.

Hopkins, Mark (1813–78). Railroad magnate. Born in Henderson, New York, he went to California at age 36 and became a partner in Collis Huntington's mining supply business. Later, he served as treasurer of the Central Pacific Railroad Company and was one of its "Big Four" founders.

Huntington, Collis P. (1821–1900). Railroad magnate. A Connecticut Yankee by birth, Huntington went west during the gold rush, where he became the state's richest hardware merchant with Mark Hopkins. Another one of the "Big Four" partners in the Central Pacific Railroad Company, he later became a lobbyist for railroad concerns. His nephew, Henry, founded the Huntington Library in San Marino, California.

Joplin, Janis (1943–70). Musician. One of the most charismatic rock-and-roll voices of the 1960s, Joplin moved from Texas at the age of 18 and began her career in San Francisco with Big Brother and the Holding Company. She died from an overdose of heroin.

Kerouac, Jack (1922–69). Writer. Raised in Lowell, Massachusetts, Kerouac came to San Francisco in the 1950s. Known for his personal, free-flowing narrative style, he was a prominent voice of the Beats. His most famous work—perhaps the epitomizing moment of the Beat era—was *On the Road* (1957). Other novels include *The Subterraneans* and *Doctor Sax*.

Kingston, Maxine Hong (b. 1940). Writer. Kingston burst onto the literary scene with *The Woman Warrior* in 1976, and followed it with *China Men*, which won the National Book Award. *Tripmaster Monkey* (1989) won the PEN fiction award. A graduate of the University of California at Berkeley, she returned there to teach in 1991.

London, Jack (1876–1916). Writer. Born in San Francisco, London grew up across the bay in Oakland, helping support his family by working on the waterfront. Ina Coolbrith, then a librarian at the Oakland Library, encouraged his literary leanings. A legendary figure, he was a hobo, factory worker, sailor, and prospector. In 1897, London went to the Klondike during the Alaskan gold rush. His most famous work, *The Call of the*

Wild, grew out of his experiences there. Among his 50-plus books are *The Sea Wolf*, *White Fang*, and *The People of the Abyss*.

Milk, Harvey (1931–78). Politician. Originally from Brooklyn, Milk moved to San Francisco where he owned a camera store at 575 Castro St. that sported a sign reading "Yes, we are very open." He became a member of the San Francisco Board of Supervisors in 1977, the first openly gay person to hold a major public office. He was assassinated in 1978 in City Hall, along with Mayor George Moscone, by Dan White. A candlelight parade is held every year in November to mark their deaths.

Shilts, Randy (1951–94). Journalist. Shilts wrote for both the *San Francisco Examiner* and the *San Francisco Chronicle* as well as gay publications *The Advocate* and *Christopher Street*. His first major book, *The Mayor of Castro Street*, was about Harvey Milk. The author of *Conduct Unbecoming* (about gays in the military), Shilts died of AIDS, the subject of his other important book, *And the Band Played On*.

Stanford, Leland (1824-93). Railroad magnate; politician. Another of the "Big Four" founders of the Central Pacific Railroad. He was Governor of California from 1861–3 and founded Stanford University in Palo Alto.

Tan, Amy (b. 1952). Writer. Born of Chinese immigrant parents in Oakland, her first book, the best-selling *Joy Luck Club*, paints a moving portrait of four Chinese women and their daughters in San Francisco. She is also the author of *The Kitchen God's Wife*.

Thompson, Hunter S. (b. 1939). Journalist. A long-time political columnist for the *San Francisco Examiner*, Thompson is the author of several gonzo-genre books, including *Fear and Loathing in Las Vegas* and *Fear and Loathing on the Campaign Trail*.

The Cultural Condition

One hundred years ago, San Francisco already had a population that was more cultured and literate than the people of any other city in the West. They might have been educated elsewhere, but they brought their learning and sophistication with them. The city also had the wealth and the inclination to sustain the arts. Local historians like to boast that even in 1850, amid the bordellos of the Barbary Coast, the city was home to at least 15 legitimate theater companies.

An outspoken, convention-busting style has distinguished creative life of this part of California since the gold rush days. It's to be found in the words of Ambrose Bierce and Hunter S. Thompson, in the imagery of Imogen Cunningham and Robert Arneson, in the music of Tony Bennett and the Kronos Quartet. Social criticism, articulating the views of the underdog, and poking fun at the greedy, the pompous, and the corrupt is the norm to which the area's artists "traditionally" aspire. In keeping with the city's sometimes wild and woolly past, San Francisco's arts-and-letters community feels perfectly at home in a metaphorical silk top hat, but frequently insists on wearing it at a decidedly rakish angle.

There is hardly a shortage of significant historical literature to bolster this claim. Mark Twain's *Roughing It* is only one (and likely the best) example of his brilliant, biting reporting on the Gold Country and early San Francisco. Robert Louis Stevenson's essays, collected in *From Scotland to Silverado,* bring to life the experiences of crossing the Atlantic in steerage and early life in the Napa Valley wine country.

Among the first California-born writers to command more than local attention was Jack London. His early works, *Tales of the Fish Patrol* and *John Barleycorn,* set in his native Oakland and San Francisco, vividly contradict Stevenson's idyllic scenarios. John Steinbeck's *The Grapes of Wrath* and *East of Eden* are among the grimmest and most honest views of emigrant life in California.

An apogee of a different sort was reached by a writer who perfected a homegrown genre: the detective novel. Dashiell Hammett's *The Maltese Falcon* is unequaled in the way it captures the moods of the city through the eyes of street-wise gumshoe Sam Spade.

In more recent times, Armistead Maupin's *Tales of the City* and Tom Wolfe's *Electric Kool-Aid Acid Test* and *The Pump House Gang* chronicled the Flower Power era in much the same kind of personal journalism style that Twain practiced on an earlier California society in upheaval. The essays gathered in Joan Didion's *Slouching Towards Bethlehem* offer penetrating insights into the psyche of California. Two more recent bestsellers, *The Joy Luck Club* by Amy Tan and *Tripmaster Monkey* by Maxine Hong Kingston, shed light on the modern Asian experience in San Francisco. And Alexander Besher's *Rim* is a cyber-tale of the future set in Berkeley.

Art and Architecture

The Visual Arts

The photographs of Ansel Adams, from the 1930s onward, have given the world images of the California landscape (most notably of Yosemite National Park and Death Valley) that are as indelible as those of his contemporary (and fellow member of the influential Group f/64, which was founded in San Francisco), Dorothea Lange, whose gritty portrayals of the tragic faces of the Dustbowl changed the path of modern photojournalism. Now, the color pictures of Richard Misrach combine art and documentary as he examines the legacy of military arms testing in the California desert.

In decades past, painters as diverse as pastoral landscapist Albert Bierstadt, Social Realist Diego Rivera, and abstract expressionists Mark Rothko and Clyfford Still left their mark while studying or teaching at the San Francisco Art Institute. Works by today's practitioners continue to intrigue: the perspectival streetscapes of Richard Diebenkorn; Wayne Thiebaud's painterly, bright, still-life studies; the large-scale explorations of line and curve by Nathan Oliveira; the towering ceramic figures of Viola Frey; Raymond Saunders's explosively colorful canvases; the cryptic symbolism of Deborah Oropallo; and the thought-provoking, activist installations of Nayland Blake.

Cinematically speaking, San Francisco is trying to transcend its typecasting as a picture-perfect location setting by making the city more appealing to filmmakers on a business level. Already home to such famed production facilities as George Lucas's Skywalker Ranch and Industrial Light and Magic, the Bay Area is making another overture to the film industry by proposing that the complex of military buildings on Treasure Island be converted into full-fledged sound stages. The San Francisco Film Festival (the oldest competition of its kind in the country) continues to ascend in importance, serving as the world premiere venue for such acclaimed independent pictures as *Mi Familia* and *Crumb.* The warehouse district centered around South Park has earned the moniker "Multimedia Gulch" as the computer wunderkind tenants remain at the vanguard of this new medium, melding the latest Silicon Valley technics with pioneering visual creativity.

Architecture

The streets of San Francisco have not been directed solely by their capricious topography; harbor infill and the cataclysmic events of 1906 have literally changed the shape and appearance of the city.

In the early 1840s, Montgomery Street bounded the town's eastern seaport. With the coming of the gold rush, these waters of "Jackson Slough" were filled in with granite blocks carried around Cape Horn from China, the hulks of ships abandoned by their crews who went AWOL for *oro,* and the redwood pilings from the former Montgomery piers. The new buildings—an assortment of assayers' offices and banks—that arose on these rutted streets were mostly 3-story brick structures with deep walls, sturdy doors, and hand-wrought iron shutters, some 16 feet tall.

Much of the city's single-family homes were built between 1850 and 1900, when Victorian architecture was in flower. San Francisco's versions of these historicist confections were much more flamboyant in plan and form than their European inspirations, owing to a flexible system of timber construction known as balloon framing. The striking terrace of Matthew Kavanaugh's 6 identical houses on the eastern side of Alamo Square—nicknamed the "Painted Ladies"—is the most photographed jewel of the 14,000 redwood residences that survived the fires of 1906.

Queen Anne House

Italiante House

The gingerbread houses can be broken into 3 distinct styles, each representative of a distinct point in time. Italianate structures were in vogue between 1850 and 1875, and are characterized by bays whose side windows slant inward, pipe-stem columns flanking the front door, and flat crowns. Queen Anne houses, patterned after a style popular in England in the 1860s, are marked by rounded corners, hooded domes, sinister-looking windows, and the use of shingles as siding. Only the sharp-eyed will be able to distinguish the Stick—or Eastlake—buildings from the Italianate. These 1880-era residences can be detected by such clues as beveled corners on pillars, incised ornamentation, and horseshoe-shaped arches.

Imagine San Francisco without North Beach, Chinatown, the Financial District, Nob Hill, and Russian Hill. These are the areas which were incinerated in the aftermath of the earthquake. Rebuilding took place in both stylistic and chronological spurts, increasingly utilizing the new technology of steel-reinforced construction. The stately formality of neoclassic and Beaux Arts designs graced both temples of government and commerce through the 1920s, at which point the curvaceous Art Deco and Moderne styles embodied the progressive mood of the times.

The most notable building of the subsequent decades was Frank Lloyd Wright's 1948 brick construction on Maiden Lane, the Circle Gallery nee Morris Gift Shop. With its circular motifs and spiraling ramp leading to the upper floor, it was a laboratory of ideas for his Guggenheim Museum in New York.

From the 1960s through the 1980s, dozens of granite-clad office towers of little distinction, save for their monumental scale, sprang up throughout the Financial District, many of them originating from the hometown branch of corporate architecture firm Skidmore, Owings, and Merrill. An exception to the trend was the 1972 Transamerica Pyramid, designed by Los Angeleno William Pereira. Others tried to put their mark on the skyline with varying degrees of success: Anthony Lumsden's 1989 Marriott Hotel, with bunches of fan-shaped reflective windows crowning its 40 stories, was immediately tagged "the Jukebox" by local wags.

Although drawing boards have been stacked with designs for new commercial buildings since the boom of the mid-1980s, most of these plans have been relegated to the back burner, owing to the precarious state of the economy. Several significant postmodern projects have gone forward, though; at the Civic Center, the new Main Library by Pei Cobb Freed & Partners bridges time and place with its mix of contemporary and Beaux Arts facades. And South of Market at Yerba Buena Gardens, an international roster of architects is creating a municipal arts park, with Fumihiko Maki's Center for the Arts galleries, Swiss designer Mario Botta's Museum of Modern Art, and James Stewart Polshek's theater facility all recently completed. Still to come is the Mexican Museum, from the office of Ricardo Legorreta based in Mexico City.

San Francisco Museum
of Modern Art

Index

SAN FRANCISCO

1–2 San Francisco Bay Area
3–4 San Francisco Peninsula
5–14 San Francisco Street Atlas

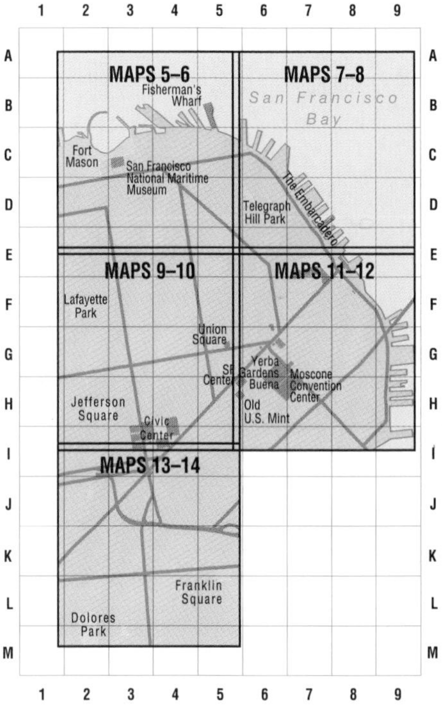

1 2 3 4 5 6 7 8 9

A B C D E F G H I J K L M

MAPS 5–6
Fisherman's Wharf
Fort Mason
San Francisco National Maritime Museum

MAPS 7–8
San Francisco Bay
The Embarcadero
Telegraph Hill Park

MAPS 9–10
Lafayette Park
Union Square
SF Center
Jefferson Square
Civic Center

MAPS 11–12
Yerba Gardens Buena
Moscone Convention Center
Old U.S. Mint

MAPS 13–14
Franklin Square
Dolores Park

KEY TO MAP SYMBOLS

City Maps

Area Maps

ROADS

- Freeway
- Tollway
- Road under construction
- Other divided highway
- Primary road
- Secondary road
- Other road

CITIES

- State Capital

BY POPULATION

Over 500,000	**San Francisco**
100,000 - 499,999	**Oakland**
25,000 - 99,999	**Alameda**
5,000 - 24,999	Piedmont
0 - 4,999	Brisbane

- Point of Interest
- Park Point

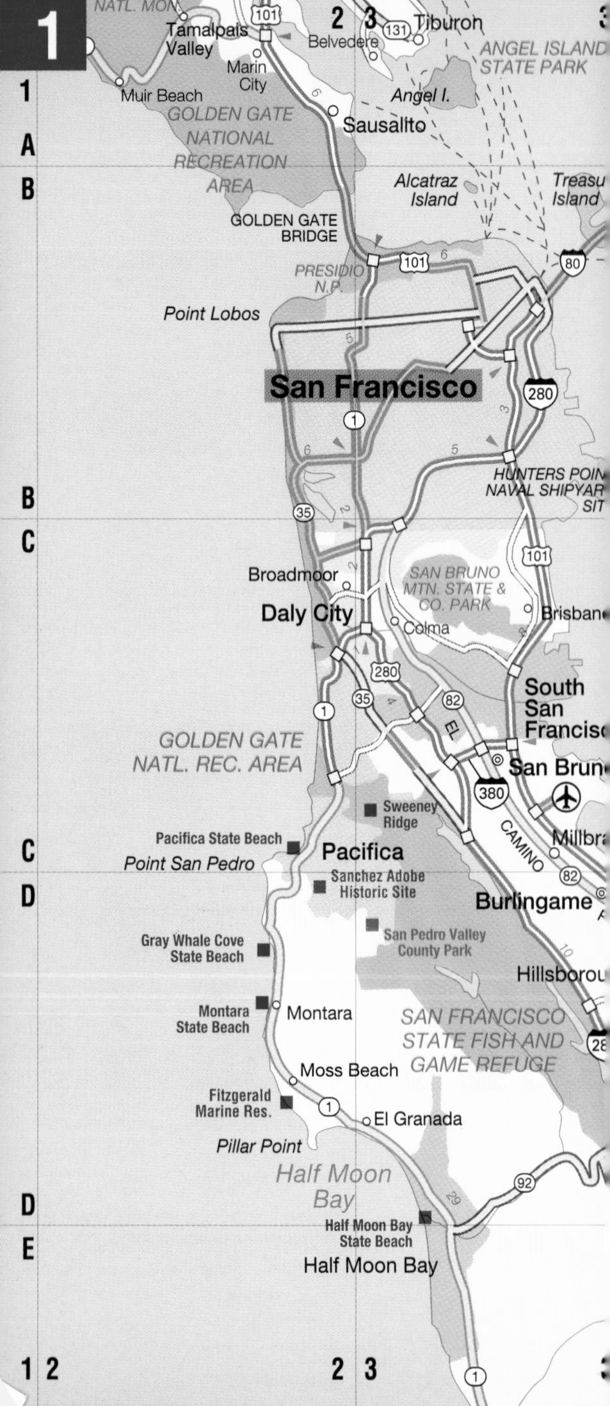

1
MUIR WOODS NATL. MON.
Tamalpais Valley
Marin City
Muir Beach
GOLDEN GATE NATIONAL RECREATION AREA
Belvedere
Tiburon
ANGEL ISLAND STATE PARK
Angel I.
Sausalito
Alcatraz Island
Treasu Island
GOLDEN GATE BRIDGE
PRESIDIO N.P.
Point Lobos
San Francisco
HUNTERS POIN NAVAL SHIPYAR SIT
Broadmoor
SAN BRUNO MTN. STATE & CO. PARK
Daly City
Colma
Brisbane
South San Francisc
EL CAMINO
San Brun
GOLDEN GATE NATL. REC. AREA
Sweeney Ridge
Pacifica State Beach
Pacifica
Millbra
Point San Pedro
Sanchez Adobe Historic Site
Burlingame
San Pedro Valley County Park
Gray Whale Cove State Beach
Hillsborou
Montara State Beach
Montara
SAN FRANCISCO STATE FISH AND GAME REFUGE
Moss Beach
Fitzgerald Marine Res.
El Granada
Pillar Point
Half Moon Bay
Half Moon Bay State Beach
Half Moon Bay
101
131
80
280
35
82
380
92
A
B
C
D
E

2
Albany
TILDEN REG. PARK
Berkeley
Orinda
Sibley Volcanic Reg. Preserve
Emeryville
Canyon
Moraga
NAVAL SUPPLY CENTER
Piedmont
REDWOOD REG. PARK
Oakland Museum
Oakland
Upper San Leandro Reservoir
ALAMEDA NAVAL AIR STATION
Alameda
Oakland – Alameda Co. Coliseum
Crown Mem. State Beach
ANTHONY CHABOT REG. PARK
San Leandro Bay Reg. Shoreline
Lake Chabot
METROPOLITAN OAKLAND INT'L AIRPORT
San Leandro
Ashland
Castro Valley
San Lorenzo
HESPERIAN BL
Cal. State Univ. – Hayward
Hayward
NIMITZ
Hayward Reg. Shoreline
San Francisco Bay
SAN FRANCISCO INT'L AIRPORT
SAN MATEO BRIDGE
San Mateo
Foster City
Coyote Hills Reg. Park
SAN FRANCISCO BAY N.W.R.
Redwood City
Belmont
DUMBARTON BRIDGE
San Carlos
Menlo Park
Upper Crystal Springs Res.
North Fair Oaks
East Palo Alto
Atherton
Filoli House and Gardens
Palo Alto
Huddart Co. Park
Stanford
Woodside

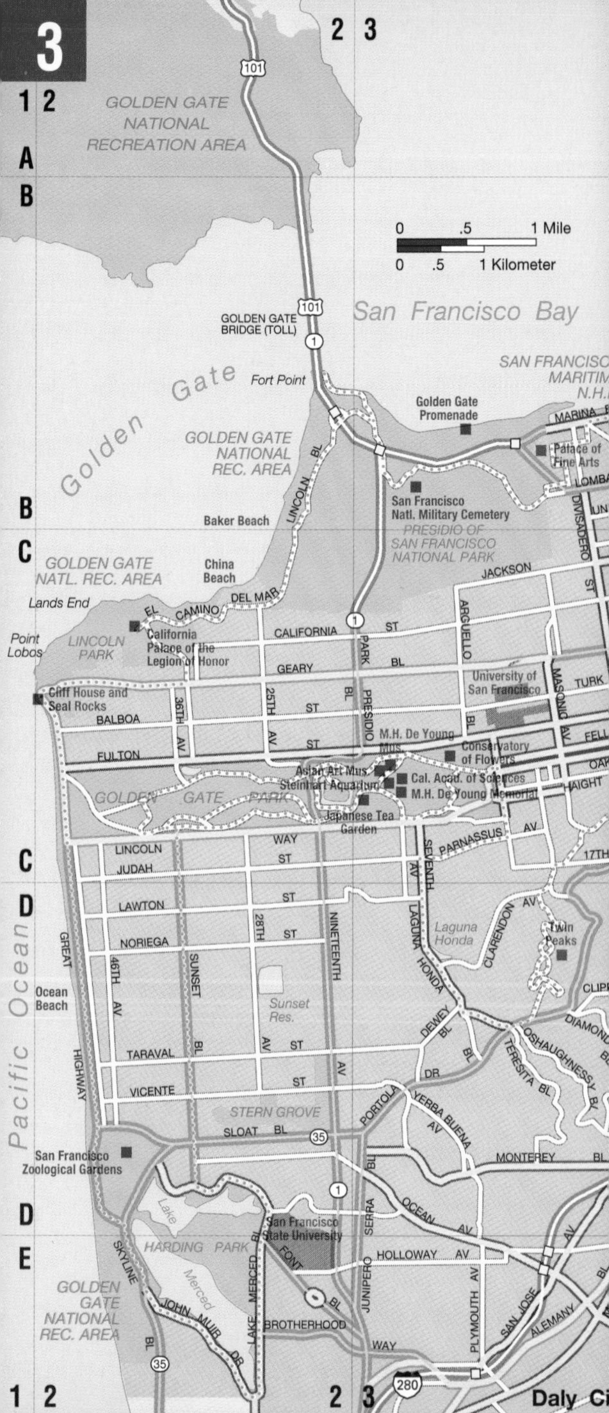
3
GOLDEN GATE NATIONAL RECREATION AREA
0 .5 1 Mile
0 .5 1 Kilometer
San Francisco Bay
GOLDEN GATE BRIDGE (TOLL)
SAN FRANCISCO MARITIME N.H.
Fort Point
Golden Gate
Golden Gate Promenade
GOLDEN GATE NATIONAL REC. AREA
Palace of Fine Arts
San Francisco Natl. Military Cemetery
Baker Beach
PRESIDIO OF SAN FRANCISCO NATIONAL PARK
GOLDEN GATE NATL. REC. AREA
China Beach
Lands End
Point Lobos
LINCOLN PARK
California Palace of the Legion of Honor
Cliff House and Seal Rocks
University of San Francisco
M.H. De Young Mus.
Conservatory of Flowers
Asian Art Mus.
Steinhart Aquarium
Cal. Acad. of Sciences
M.H. De Young Memorial
GOLDEN GATE PARK
Japanese Tea Garden
Laguna Honda
Twin Peaks
Ocean Beach
Pacific Ocean
Sunset Res.
STERN GROVE
San Francisco Zoological Gardens
Lake Merced
San Francisco State University
HARDING PARK
GOLDEN GATE NATIONAL REC. AREA
Daly Ci

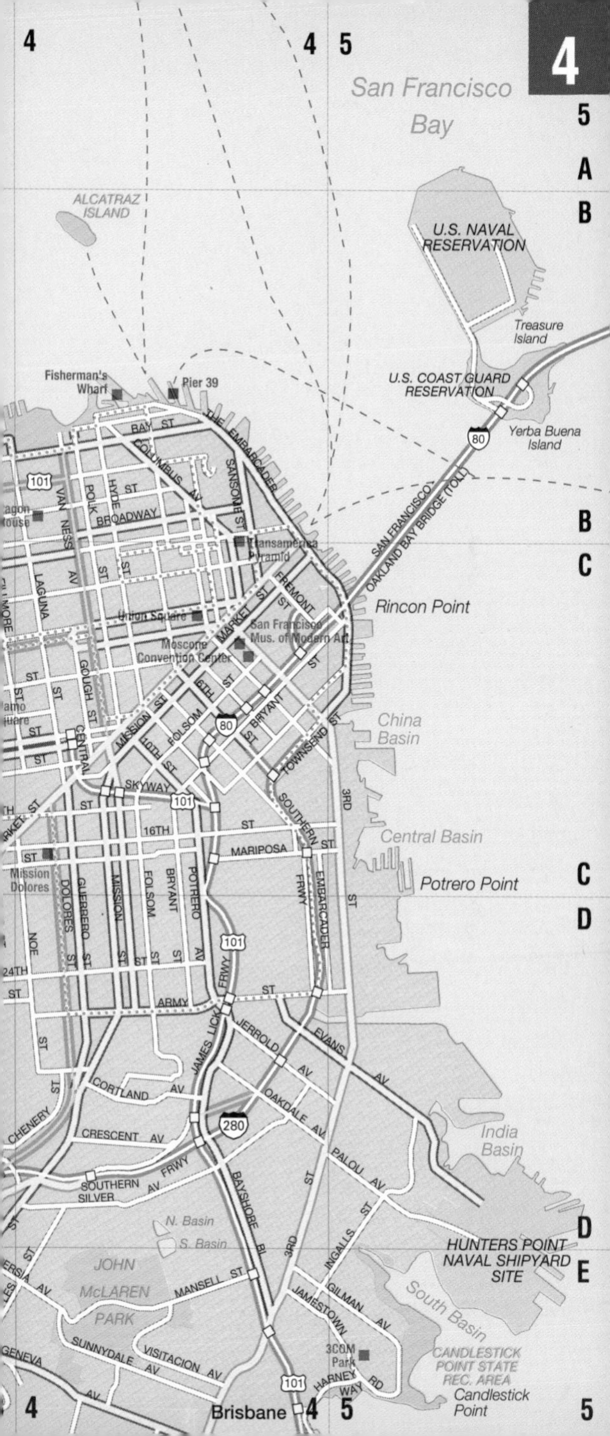

4
4
5
5
A
B
B
C
C
D
D
E
4
4
5
5
San Francisco Bay
ALCATRAZ ISLAND
U.S. NAVAL RESERVATION
Treasure Island
U.S. COAST GUARD RESERVATION
Yerba Buena Island
Fisherman's Wharf
Pier 39
THE EMBARCADERO
SAN FRANCISCO OAKLAND BAY BRIDGE (TOLL)
Transamerica Pyramid
Rincon Point
Union Square
San Francisco Mus. of Modern Art
Moscone Convention Center
China Basin
Central Basin
Potrero Point
Mission Dolores
India Basin
HUNTERS POINT NAVAL SHIPYARD SITE
South Basin
CANDLESTICK POINT STATE REC. AREA
Candlestick Point
3COM Park
JOHN McLAREN PARK
N. Basin
S. Basin
Brisbane
101
80
280

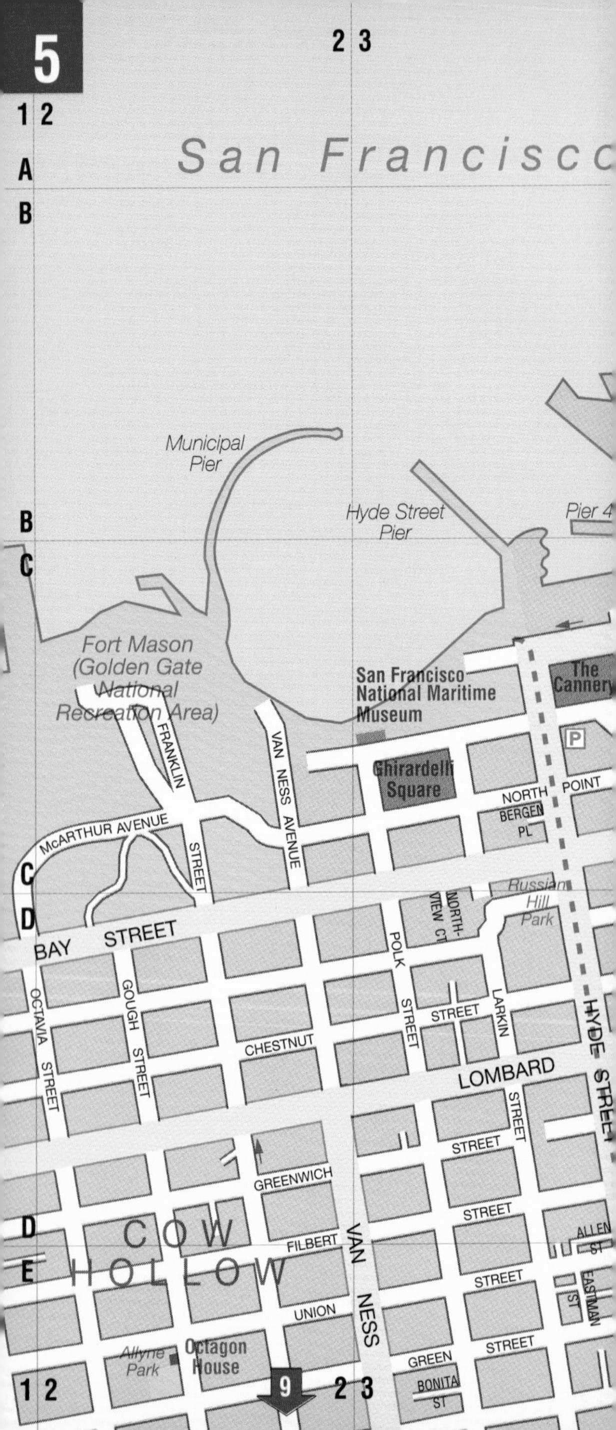
5
San Francisco
Municipal Pier
Hyde Street Pier
Pier 4
Fort Mason (Golden Gate National Recreation Area)
San Francisco National Maritime Museum
The Cannery
Ghirardelli Square
FRANKLIN
VAN NESS AVENUE
McARTHUR AVENUE
STREET
NORTH POINT
BERGEN PL
Russian Hill Park
NORTH-VIEW CT
BAY STREET
POLK STREET
LARKIN STREET
HYDE STREET
OCTAVIA STREET
GOUGH STREET
CHESTNUT
LOMBARD
GREENWICH
FILBERT
VAN NESS
UNION
GREEN
BONITA ST
ALLEN ST
EASTMAN ST
COW HOLLOW
Allyne Park
Octagon House
9

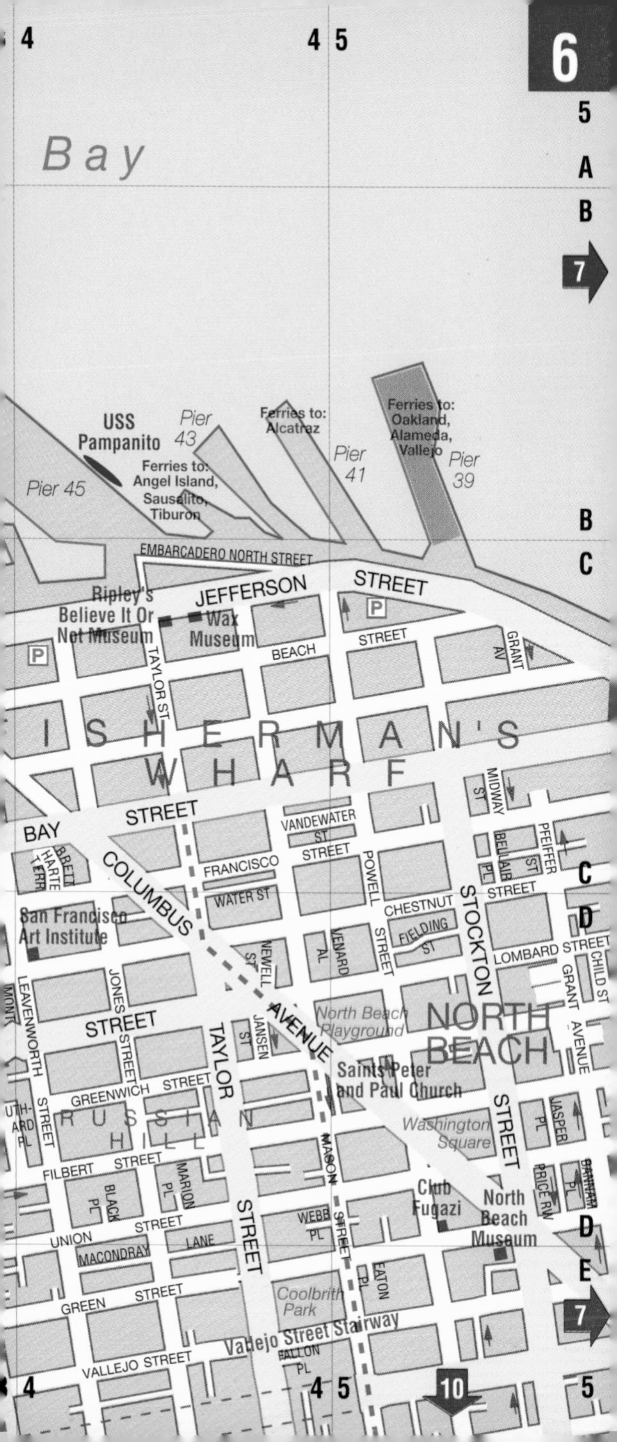

6
Bay
USS Pampanito
Pier 45
Pier 43
Ferries to: Angel Island, Sausalito, Tiburon
Ferries to: Alcatraz
Pier 41
Ferries to: Oakland, Alameda, Vallejo
Pier 39
EMBARCADERO NORTH STREET
JEFFERSON STREET
Ripley's Believe It Or Not Museum
Wax Museum
BEACH STREET
TAYLOR ST
GRANT AV
FISHERMAN'S WHARF
BAY STREET
VANDEWATER ST
FRANCISCO STREET
WATER ST
COLUMBUS AVENUE
San Francisco Art Institute
POWELL STREET
CHESTNUT STREET
FIELDING ST
STOCKTON STREET
LOMBARD STREET
MIDWAY ST
BELLAIR PL
PFEIFFER ST
CHILD ST
GRANT AVENUE
NEWELL ST
VENARD AL
LEAVENWORTH STREET
JONES STREET
TAYLOR STREET
JANSEN ST
North Beach Playground
NORTH BEACH
Saints Peter and Paul Church
GREENWICH STREET
RUSSIAN HILL
Washington Square
JASPER PL
MASON STREET
FILBERT STREET
MARION PL
BLACK PL
Club Fugazi
North Beach Museum
PRICE RW
UNION STREET
MACONDRAY LANE
WEBB PL
EATON PL
GREEN STREET
Coolbrith Park
Vallejo Street Stairway
FALLON PL
VALLEJO STREET
7
10

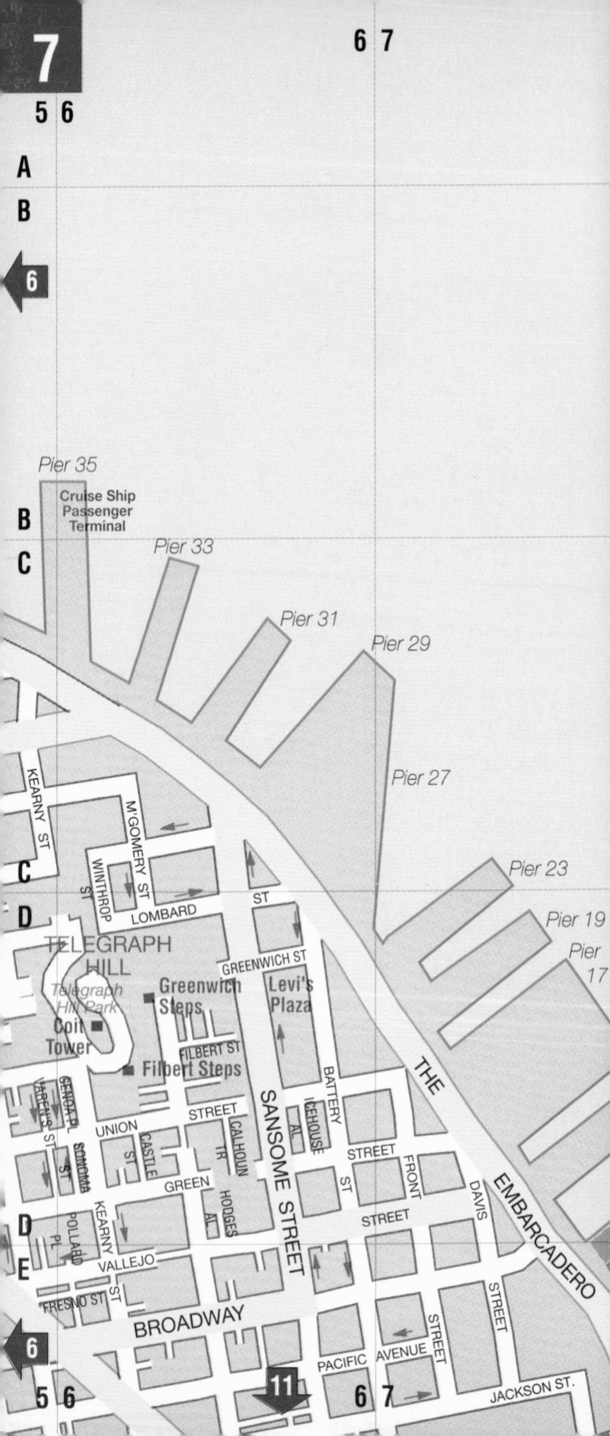
7
5 6
6 7
A
B
6
Pier 35
Cruise Ship Passenger Terminal
B
C
Pier 33
Pier 31
Pier 29
Pier 27
KEARNY ST
M'GOMERY ST
WINTHROP ST
LOMBARD ST
C
D
Pier 23
Pier 19
Pier 17
TELEGRAPH HILL
Telegraph Hill Park
Coit Tower
Greenwich Steps
GREENWICH ST
Levi's Plaza
FILBERT ST
Filbert Steps
BATTERY ST
THE EMBARCADERO
VARENNES ST
GENOA PL
UNION STREET
CASTLE ST
CALHOUN TR
SANSOME STREET
ICEHOUSE AL
SONOMA ST
GREEN STREET
FRONT ST
DAVIS STREET
HODGES AL
KEARNY
POLLARD PL
VALLEJO ST
D
E
FRESNO ST
BROADWAY
6
PACIFIC AVENUE
JACKSON ST.
11
5 6
6 7

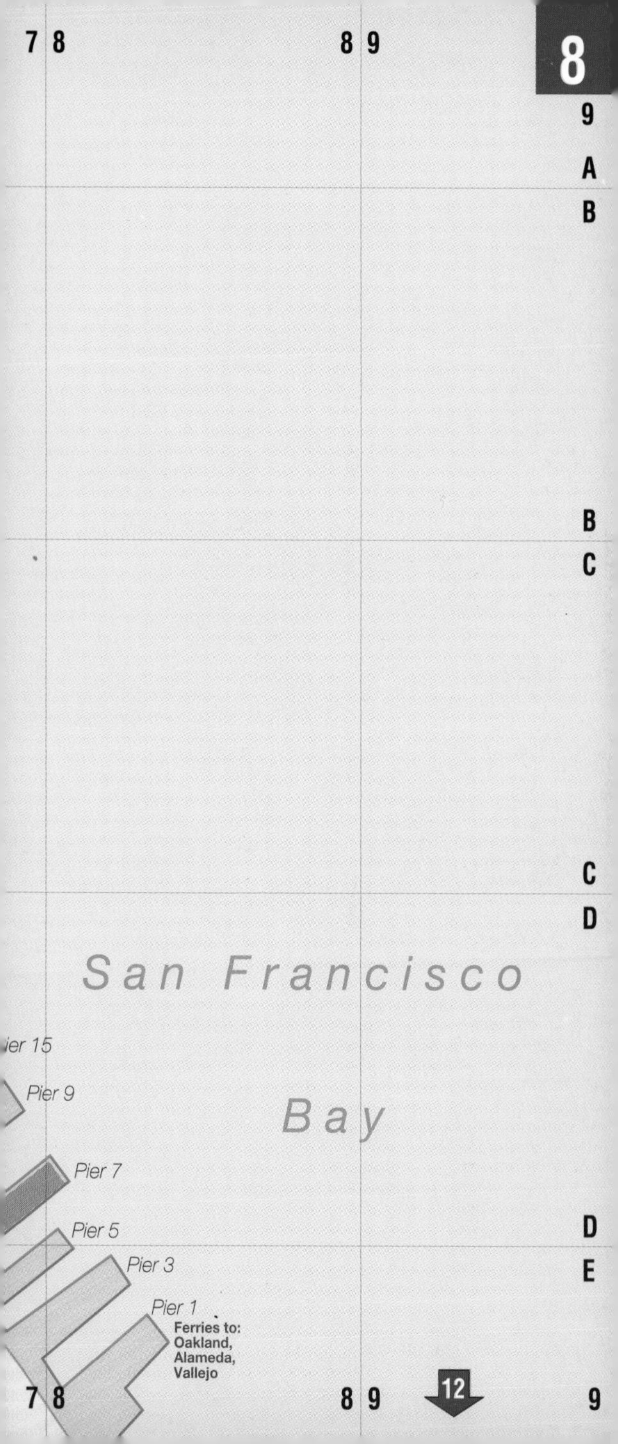

7 8
8 9
9
A
B
B
C
C
D
San Francisco
Bay
ier 15
Pier 9
Pier 7
Pier 5
D
E
Pier 3
Pier 1
Ferries to:
Oakland,
Alameda,
Vallejo
7 8
8 9
12
9

GREEN STREET
2 3 5
VALLEJO STREET
1 2
BROADWAY
AVENUE
PACIFIC
E
F
PACIFIC HEIGHTS
STREET
JACKSON
STREET
Haas-Lilienthal House
Spreckels Mansion
WASHINGTON
STREET
CLAY
Lafayette Park
STREET
SACRAMENTO
STREET
CALIFORNIA
F
G
STREET
NORRIS ST
PINE
OCTAVIA
VAN NESS AVENUE
FRANKLIN
STREET
STREET
POLK
AUSTIN
GOUGH
BUSH
LAGUNA
STREET
STREET
FERN
STREET
STREET
SUTTER
STREET
HEMLOCK
STREET
STREET
POST
CEDAR STREET
PETER YORK ST
STREET
GEARY
STREET
Japan Center
P
MYRTLE
STARR KING WAY
G
H
STREET
OLIVE
CLEARY CT
STREET
St Mary's Cathedral
ELLIS
STREET
WILLOW
STREET
EDDY
LARCH ST
Jefferson Sq
STREET
ELM ST
TURK
AVENUE
Hayward Plgd
GATE
REDWOOD
GOLDEN
H
I
Veteran's Building
City Hall
McALLISTER
War Memorial Opera House
STREET
P
STREET
1 2
FULTON
2 3 13
GROVE
BIRCH ST

10
BROADWAY TUNNEL
BERNARD STREET
LYNCH ST
PACIFIC STREET
AUBURN ST
JOHN ST
JACKSON STREET
Cable Car Barn
WASHINGTON STREET
REED ST
PRIEST ST
NOB HILL
WETMORE ST
CODMAN PL
JOICE ST
CLAY STREET
PLEASANT ST
TROY AL
SACRAMENTO STREET
Huntington Park
Fairmont Hotel
Pacific-Union Club
Grace Cathedral
Mark Hopkins Inter-Continental Hotel
PINE STREET
LEAVENWORTH STREET
MASON STREET
POWELL STREET
EUREKA PL
LARKIN STREET
HYDE STREET
BUSH STREET
JONES STREET
TAYLOR STREET
Saks
Westin St Francis Hotel
SUTTER STREET
COSMO PL
POST STREET
UNION SQUARE
Macy
GEARY STREET
HARLEM AL
Powell St Cable Car Turntable
Sgt John McAuley Park
O FARRELL STREET
ANTONIO ST
STEVELOE PL
Great American Music Hall
ELLIS STREET
COHEN PL
SF Visitors Information Center
EDDY STREET
TURK STREET
MARKET STREET
GOLDEN GATE AVENUE
DALE PL
6TH STREET
BREEN PL
STEVENSON STREET
JESSIE STREET
7TH STREET
MINNA STREET
NATOMA STREET
FULTON ST
SF Public Library
BART/MUNI Civic Center Station
CIVIC CENTER
Bill Graham Civic Auditorium
MISSION STREET
HOWARD STREET
3 4 5 6 11 14
E F G H I

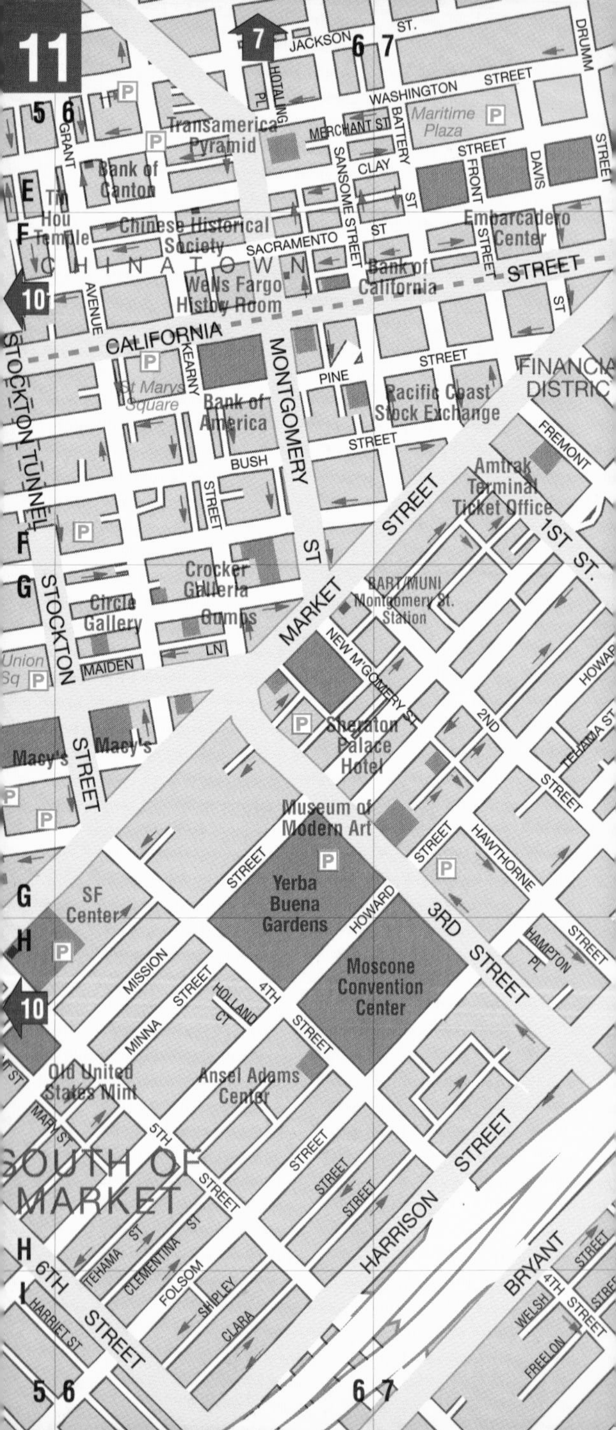
11
7
JACKSON ST.
DRUMM
WASHINGTON STREET
Maritime Plaza
Transamerica Pyramid
MERCHANT ST
BATTERY
SANSOME STREET
CLAY STREET
FRONT STREET
DAVIS STREET
GRANT
Bank of Canton
Tin Hou Temple
Chinese Historical Society
SACRAMENTO ST
Embarcadero Center
CHINATOWN
Bank of California
STREET
Wells Fargo History Room
10
AVENUE
CALIFORNIA
KEARNY
MONTGOMERY
PINE STREET
FINANCIAL DISTRICT
St Marys Square
Bank of America
Pacific Coast Stock Exchange
STOCKTON TUNNEL
BUSH STREET
STREET
FREMONT
Amtrak Terminal Ticket Office
1ST ST.
ST
MARKET STREET
STOCKTON
Crocker Galleria
Gumps
Circle Gallery
BART/MUNI Montgomery St. Station
LN
NEW M'GOMERY ST
Union Sq
MAIDEN
HOWARD
Sheraton Palace Hotel
2ND
TEHAMA ST
Macy's
Macy's
STREET
STREET
Museum of Modern Art
STREET
HAWTHORNE
Yerba Buena Gardens
SF Center
HOWARD
3RD STREET
HAMPTON PL
STREET
MISSION STREET
HOLLAND CT
4TH STREET
Moscone Convention Center
MINNA
10
Old United States Mint
Ansel Adams Center
MARY ST
5TH STREET
STREET
STREET
STREET
SOUTH OF MARKET
HARRISON
TEHAMA ST
CLEMENTINA ST
FOLSOM
SHIPLEY
CLARA
6TH STREET
HARRIET ST
BRYANT
WELSH
4TH STREET
FREELON
STREET
E
F
G
H
I
5 6
6 7

World Trade Center
Pier 2
Golden Gate Transit Ferries: Sausalito & Larkspur
Ferry Building
Hyatt Regency Hotel
No.1 Market Street
BART/MUNI Embarcadero Station
Rincon Center
Transbay Terminal
STEUART
MISSION STREET
SPEAR STREET
MAIN STREET
BEALE STREET
FOLSOM STREET
ZENO PL
GROTE PL
GUY PL
HARRISON STREET
SAN FRANCISCO OAKLAND BAY BRIDGE
80
Pier 24
Pier 28
Pier 30
Pier 32
Pier 34
Pier 36
Pier 38
Pier 40
THE EMBARCADERO
RINCON ST
1ST STREET
STILLMAN ST
PLACE
South Park
CENTRAL PL
TABER
VARNEY PL
BRANNAN STREET
OLIN P KELLY JR ST
STANFORD ST
TOWNSEND
KING STREET
RITCH
STREET
CLYDE ST
LUSK ST
7 8 8 9 9
E F F G G H H I

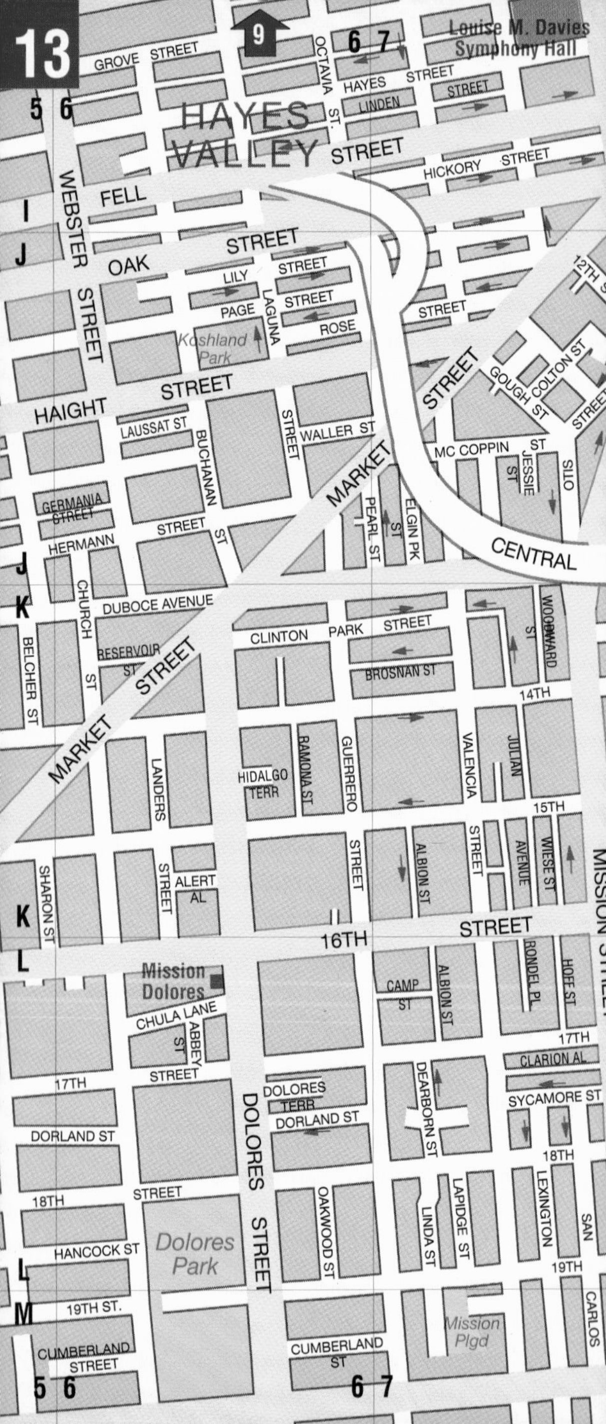

9
5 6
6 7
Louise M. Davies Symphony Hall
GROVE STREET
OCTAVIA ST.
HAYES STREET
LINDEN STREET
HAYES VALLEY
STREET
HICKORY STREET
WEBSTER STREET
FELL
OAK STREET
LILY STREET
PAGE STREET
LAGUNA
ROSE
STREET
Koshland Park
HAIGHT STREET
LAUSSAT ST
BUCHANAN ST
WALLER ST
STREET
MARKET STREET
12TH ST
GOUGH ST
COLTON ST
STREET
MC COPPIN ST
JESSIE ST
OTIS
GERMANIA STREET
HERMANN STREET
PEARL ST
ELGIN PK
CENTRAL
CHURCH ST
DUBOCE AVENUE
CLINTON PARK STREET
BROSNAN ST
WOODWARD ST
BELCHER ST
RESERVOIR ST
MARKET STREET
14TH
LANDERS STREET
HIDALGO TERR
RAMONA ST
GUERRERO STREET
VALENCIA STREET
JULIAN AVENUE
15TH
ALBION ST
WIESE ST
MISSION STREET
SHARON ST
ALERT AL
16TH STREET
Mission Dolores
CAMP ST
ALBION ST
RONDEL PL
HOFF ST
CHULA LANE
ABBEY ST
17TH STREET
17TH
CLARION AL
DOLORES TERR
DEARBORN ST
SYCAMORE ST
DORLAND ST
DORLAND ST
DOLORES STREET
18TH STREET
18TH
OAKWOOD ST
LINDA ST
LAPIDGE ST
LEXINGTON
SAN CARLOS
Dolores Park
HANCOCK ST
19TH
19TH ST.
Mission Plgd
CUMBERLAND STREET
CUMBERLAND ST
I
J
J
K
K
L
L
M

7 8
8 9
10
9
I
J
J
K
K
L
L
M
7 8
8 9
9
Muni
an Ness
Station
LASKIE ST
STEVENSON ST
JESSIE ST
HOWARD
BAUSCH ST
SUMNER ST
8TH
STREET
HALLAM ST
9TH
WASHBURN ST
GRACE ST
10TH STREET
TEHAMA ST
CLEMENTINA ST
RODGERS ST
11TH STREET
STREET
STREET
STREET
DORE ST
FOLSOM
RINGOLD ST
MISSION
MINNA
NATOMA
LAFAYETTE ST
HOWARD
KISSLING ST
SHERIDAN ST
HARRISON
STREET
SOUTH VAN NESS AVENUE
12TH
STREET
JUNIPER ST
DORE ST
BRYANT
STREET
NORFOLK ST
PLUM ST
ISIS ST
BERNICE ST
FREEWAY
101
CENTRAL FREEWAY
ERIE ST
TRAINOR ST
STREET
SHOTWELL STREET
FOLSOM STREET
HARRISON STREET
FLORIDA STREET
BRYANT STREET
HAMPSHIRE ST
POTRERO STREET
STREET
ADAIR ST
16TH STREET
Franklin Square
17TH STREET
TREAT AVENUE
STREET
MARIPOSA STREET
STREET
18TH STREET
MISSION
STREET
19TH STREET
MISTRAL ST
20TH STREET
20TH STREET

7
8
8
9
10
9
Muni
Van Ness
Station
LASKIE ST
STEVENSON ST
JESSIE ST
8TH
HOWARD
RAUSCH ST
SUMNER ST
9TH
WASHBURN ST
GRACE ST
10TH
STREET
TEHAMA ST
CLEMENTINA ST
STREET
HALLAM ST
RODGERS ST
11TH
STREET
MISSION
STREET
STREET
STREET
MINNA
NATOMA
STREET
DORE ST
FOLSOM
RINGOLD ST
HARRISON
STREET
SOUTH VAN NESS AVENUE
LAFAYETTE ST
HOWARD
KISSLING ST
SHERIDAN ST
JUNIPER ST
12TH
STREET
NORFOLK ST
DORE ST
BRYANT
STREET
PLUM ST
ISIS ST
BERNICE ST
FREEWAY
101
CENTRAL FREEWAY
ERIE ST
TRAINOR ST
STREET
SHOTWELL
FOLSOM
HARRISON
FLORIDA
BRYANT
HAMPSHIRE ST
POTRERO STREET
STREET
STREET
STREET
STREET
STREET
STREET
ADAIR ST
16TH STREET
Franklin Square
17TH
STREET
AVENUE
STREET
SOUTH VAN NESS AVENUE
TREAT
MARIPOSA
STREET
STREET
18TH
STREET
MISSION
STREET
19TH
STREET
MISTRAL ST
20TH STREET
20TH STREET
I
J
J
K
K
L
L
M
9
7
8
8
9
9